Modernization and the Working Class

The Dan Danciger Publication Series

Modernization and the Working Class

The Politics of Legitimacy

by Carlos H. Waisman

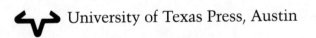 University of Texas Press, Austin

First edition, 1982

Requests for permission to reproduce material from this work
should be sent to: Permissions, University of Texas Press, Box 7819,
Austin, Texas 78712.

Library of Congress Cataloging in Publication Data

Waisman, Carlos H. (Carlos Horacio), 1943–
    Modernization and the working class.

    (The Dan Danciger publication series)
    Includes index.
    1. Labor and laboring classes—Political
activity.   2. Legitimacy of governments.   3. Political sociology.   I. Title.
HD8031.W34   306'.2   81-10397
ISBN 0-292-75065-X   AACR2

To Anna

Contents

Tables

Preface

The aim of this book is two-fold. First, it explores some aspects of the relationship between modernization and the legitimacy of the social order of capitalism. More specifically, it is an inquiry into some of the factors that contribute to the legitimation of capitalism by the industrial working class. Second, it proposes a theoretical framework for the study of the crisis brought about by the irruption of the working class into the political system. This framework is used for the conceptualization of historical materials and survey data. On the basis of the discussion of that evidence, I will speculate on some of the linkages between modernization and legitimacy.

This framework links a typology of outcomes of the crisis of incorporation and a set of concepts for the analysis of collective political action. In this analysis, I use historical materials to examine the sources of the different outcomes in the political action of elites and working classes and in structural characteristics of the society. I also discuss hypotheses about the consequences of the position of the working class in the polity. And I utilize the survey data as a basis for speculation on the effects on legitimacy of different aspects of the position of the working class in the economy.

In the following pages, concepts such as "forms of political action," "environmental factors," and "structural properties" are introduced. Whenever possible, I specify the sense in which I am using existing terms—for instance, *dissent*, *radicalism*, and *co-optation*. In other cases, however, I preferred to coin new terms to avoid misinterpretation or the constant repetition of my meaning for potentially ambiguous expressions.

Earlier versions of Chapters 2, 3, and 5 were presented at meetings, and a previous draft of Chapter 5 was published as an article. These papers are cited in the notes. I do not discuss two works which were published after the manuscript of this book was completed and which are relevant to the issues dealt with in Chapters 3 and 5. The first of these is Alfred Stepan, *The State and Society: Peru in Comparative Perspective* (Princeton: Princeton University Press, 1978). Stepan conducts a critical analysis of the literature on corporatism, emphasizes the distinction between its inclusionary and exclusionary forms (I call "corporatist" only the first of these types), and presents a series of hypotheses about the determinants of the emergence of these regimes. His treatment of the problem has some resemblances with my discussion in Chapters 3 and 5. Differences between the two approaches will be clear to the reader. The second book is David Collier (ed.), *The New Authoritarianism in Latin America* (Princeton: Princeton University Press, 1979). This work contains several excellent analyses of bureaucratic authoritarian rule. In particular, a contribution by James R. Kurth, "Industrial Change and Political Change: A European Perspective," is pertinent for the treatment in Chapter 5 of the relationship between timing of industrialization and outcomes of the incorporation of the working class. His hypotheses about the consequences of the predominance of different leading sectors during the European industrialization process are intriguing and worth pursuing.

The first chapter states the general problem of the relationship between modernization and the legitimacy of capitalism as far as the working class is concerned. Part I presents the theoretical framework and discusses the consequences of elite and working-class political action and of structural characteristics of the society for the generation and maintenance of the different formulae with which the crisis of incorporation can be solved. The typology of outcomes is introduced in Chapter 2. Chapter 3 discusses concepts for the analysis of the political action of elites and working classes. Chapter 4 is a brief examination of three cases illustrating different solutions to the crisis: Disraelian Britain, Bismarckian Germany, and Peronist Argentina. Finally, Chapter 5 discusses some of the structural correlates of the different outcomes.

Part II explores the consequences of various aspects of the position of the working class in the economy for the legitimacy of capitalism. In Chapter 6, position in the economy is broken down into analytically distinguishable aspects, which I call structural properties. These are centrality, deprivation, integration, and marginalization, and have been associated in social and political thought with different types of working-class political action. Models of strain in a social system, such as the ones that I call the status disequilibrium and the Roman Empire paradigms, are grounded on assumptions about the causal efficacy of different sets of these determinants. Chapter 7 discusses the anarchist and Marxist theories of revolution in terms of structural properties. I attempt to show that each of these theories is based on a different pair of properties. In most of the remainder of the book, I examine the relationship between structural properties and working-class political action on the basis of survey data. These originated in two studies of the Argentine working class, the established workers and the new workers studies, which are described in Chapter 8 and in the Appendix. Chapter 9 presents some general relationships between structural properties and forms of political action, and Chapters 10 and 11 carry out a more complete analysis. Finally, Chapter 12 advances some general conclusions.

The surveys analyzed in Chapters 8–11 were conducted in the late sixties. I participated in the two projects, which were interconnected. The samples and questions used in the analysis presented here are discussed in the Appendix and in Chapters 8 and 9. The survey that I call the established workers study was carried out for a government planning agency by Miguel Murmis, Silvia Sigal, and myself. Murmis was the director of the project, Sigal designed the questionnaire, she and I prepared the codebook, and I investigated the context—the sugar industry—and conducted some preliminary analyses of the data. Other publications arising from this project, one by Murmis and myself and two by Sigal, are cited in the notes. I was initially the junior member of the team and ended up inheriting the bulk of the unanalyzed data. The second survey, which here is called the new workers study, was one of several administered by the Marginality Project, directed by José Nun at the Di Tella Institute in Buenos Aires. In the established workers study, I was involved from the planning stages, but in the second project my participation was more limited. Nun allowed me to analyze the portions of this survey that deal with what I call structural properties and forms of political action, and made available to me the punched cards and the codebook. The analysis presented here is, of course, my responsibility.

I wish to thank the several people who read the whole manuscript or part of it and made valuable critical comments: S. N. Eisenstadt, Tim McDaniel, James Petras, Phillippe C. Schmitter, Charles Tilly, and anonymous readers. I have not always agreed with their evaluations and suggestions, perhaps to the detriment of the work. I wish to express my gratitude to Miguel Murmis, whose strong influence I was fortunate to receive as a student and as a friend, for his support and for creating a scholarly enclave in an environment hostile to social research. I also thank Silvia Sigal, whose sharp mind and enthusiasm set an example hard to emulate. This book began as a doctoral dissertation, and I am indebted to Seymour Martin Lipset, who supervised my graduate work, for his continuous encouragement and support, and also for his patience. I wish to convey my appreciation for the late Gino Germani, who introduced me to sociology as an undergraduate, and in graduate school contributed to focus my interest in comparative political analysis. Graciela Jacob and Beba Ballvé helped me with the new workers survey. Gail Hegebarth was a very efficient typist of the manuscript. Finally, I wish to acknowledge the financial support I received from the Ford Foundation and from the Latin American Studies Program, Harvard University, during the period in which the research reported here was carried out. A grant from the Academic Senate of the University of California assisted me in the preparation of the manuscript for publication.

INTRODUCTION

1. The Problem

The correlation between modernization and working-class acceptance of capitalist organization is curvilinear, with legitimacy lower
at middle levels of development. Exceptions abound, however, and
low levels of legitimacy still exist in some relatively advanced societies. Taking as a point of departure the conceptual framework for
the study of the incorporation of the working class to be presented in
this work, I will speculate on some of the factors that produce this
pattern.

THE LEGITIMACY OF CAPITALISM

Contemporary analyses of political modernization tend to focus
on models built around a series of "crises" or "problems" to be
"solved" by political systems at different points of development. Selecting alternative solutions at these critical junctures helps determine future choices, for political modernization is a process with
multiple starting points, patterns of evolution, and outcomes.[1]

One critical issue involved here is the political integration of
classes generated or mobilized by the process of industrialization.
The industrial bourgeoisie and the working class have been the pro-
tagonists of the most important crises of incorporation. The outcomes of these crises are a central aspect of the political development
of modern societies. Thus, Germani has analyzed modernization as a
process of mobilization and integration,[2] and Huntington has viewed
the development of institutional channels to absorb the explosion of
participation as the crucial element in political modernization.[3] The
incorporation of the working class, in particular, has been considered critical. Thus, Lipset has listed the three major political problems that have emerged in Western nations in modern times as follows: the place of the church, the admission of the lower strata to

full political and economic citizenship, and the struggle over distribution of income.[4]

Incorporation has generally been discussed in the context of the extension of rights or of citizenship. To this tradition belong the classical studies by Bendix,[5] Marshall,[6] and Rokkan.[7] On the other hand, qualitative differences in the integration process, as well as the related issue of elite strategies toward the emerging strata, have received less attention. Exceptions are Huntington's discussion of strategies of reform,[8] Lipset's distinction between "incorporative" and "insulative" patterns,[9] and Moore's analysis of conservative modernization.[10] As we will see, the question of incorporation entails both political and ideological aspects—or, in Parsons's terms, inclusion and value generalization[11]—and it can be solved at either of these two levels or at both. For this reason, it is important to keep in mind the diversity of possible outcomes. This diversity will be the focus of my discussion.

Three hypotheses (not mutually exclusive) have been formulated in order to explain the relationship between the degree of modernization and working-class acceptance or rejection of capitalist institutions. The first one locates the source of opposition to or support for the social order in the working class's position in the political system; the other two attribute a causal role to their position in the economic system, either from the point of view of production or from the point of view of consumption.

The political determinant has been emphasized by Marshall, Lipset, Bendix, and other contemporary social scientists. The underlying hypothesis is that working-class opposition to the social order results from its exclusion from political participation. Once incorporation into the political system takes place, consensus would gradually emerge.[12] The other two theories locate the source of strain outside the political system and specifically in the economy. These explanations appeared for the first time in the nonacademic literature: the anarchists set forth the objective deprivation thesis, whereas the importance of the position in the productive process was stated, of course, by Marx. The second proposition would be that working-class opposition to the social order arises from deprivation and marginality to the industrial world. Once capitalism develops—bringing a rise in standards of living and integration of the working class into modern society—dissent will wane. Finally, the third perspective asserts that working-class discontent is caused by its position in the productive process. The essence of the argument is that discontent is caused by the centrality of the working class in capitalist society. Further, opposition to the social order will peak at specific points within the dynamics of capitalism and when marginalization processes are at work.

All the participants in this century-old debate would agree that each of these determinants is, to varying degrees, in operation. They would disagree, however, about the relative weight of each one and about the direction of the relationships. These different perspectives are, in the last instance, variants of the two models of strain in a social system that have been developed in social and political thought and in the contemporary academic literature. The first is a "status disequilibrium" model. In it, revolutionary potential is expected among dissatisfied insiders, typically in a social stratum whose political power and power of disposition of economic resources are lower than its actual control of these resources. This paradigm suits not only its most obvious referent, an argument based on status inconsistency, but also the Marxist theory of revolution, both in relation to the bourgeoisie in feudal society and to the working class in advanced capitalist society. The second model can be labeled the "Roman Empire" paradigm: opposition to the social order is expected to arise among outsiders, especially among deprived outsiders. Much of contemporary social science subscribes to this hypothesis, as well as political theorists ranging from Bakunin to Marcuse.[13] My analysis will allow me to reach some conclusions about the contexts in which these three determinants are effective and about the direction of the relationships. At this point, it will be useful to take a look at the processes leading to the constitution of the working class and to the alternatives the powerholders face when this new class appears in the political arena.

THE FORMATION OF THE WORKING CLASS

The industrial working class forms when precapitalist social relations dissolve and individuals are released by the precapitalist sector into industrial capitalism. At the level of the social structure, modernization can be considered as the dual process of the dissolution of precapitalist or "traditional" social relations and the generation of capitalist or "modern" ones. At the microsocial level, modernization can be viewed as a process of release and absorption of individuals. Both aspects are relatively independent, so that when the rate of release is higher than the rate of absorption, a marginal sector appears.

The use of the concepts "precapitalist" and "capitalist" social relations here follows Marx's treatment, especially in the *Grund-*

risse.[14] Precapitalist social relations are those relations of production which presuppose the existence of "extraeconomic coercion,"[15] i.e., the fact that individuals are tied to specific economic positions by force, law, or custom rather than by economic forces (as is the case in capitalist social relations), and/or the control, by the "direct producers," of means of production or consumption.

Extraeconomic coercion implies the existence of either vertical ties of subordination—as in slavery or serfdom—or of horizontal ties to a community—as in the cases of "primitive communism" and the "Asiatic mode of production." The existence of vertical ties presupposes a surplus, but there is the case of surplus-producing agents not involved in vertical ties, i.e., who appropriate their own surplus (the artisan or the independent peasant in market agriculture).

The access by the "direct producers" to the control of means of production or consumption may be a second distinctive characteristic of precapitalist social relations. Marx distinguishes between actual control of the means of production, i.e., the ability to decide on their use, and property, i.e., a legal claim to possession, a consequence of which is the right to control the surplus. In most types of precapitalist social relations, there was a dissociation between control and property—serfdom is the paradigmatic example—and this is why extraeconomic coercion was a prerequisite for transferring surplus to the superordinate class.

Finally, most types of precapitalist social relations involved the access by "direct producers" to a consumption fund, i.e., to means of subsistence whose supply was relatively independent of the economic rewards that producers obtained through the relations of production. This was the case where land was controlled individually by the peasant, e.g., serfdom, as well as in situations of collective control, such as primitive communism and the Asiatic mode of production.

The formation of the working class presupposes the dissolution of all these ties—to a superordinate class or to a community of producers, and to the control of means of production and consumption—and thus the formation of a free labor market. The development of capitalism consists of the formation of this free labor market, which is the counterpart of the centralization of the control of means of production. The existence of capitalism presupposes, therefore, the generation of a class which is free both positively—because its members are personally free and not tied to specific positions in the economy—and negatively—because they are also "free" from sources of support other than their wages. This is why capitalist social relations can be defined as relations of production that are based on wage labor, and why social positions in modern society in which individuals control means of production but do not hire wage laborers—e.g., artisans, family farmers—or in which there is subsistence production should be considered precapitalist.

MOBILIZATION AND PREEMPTIVE MODERNIZATION

Once the working class has been formed, and regardless of its degree of mobilization, the issue of political integration presents itself. Basically there are two models of solution, depending on whether the process is initiated by the working class or by the established elites. (By this latter term, I mean the superordinate classes in the economy and the state bureaucracy. The utilization of the term "elite" does not imply the assumption that these sectors are internally cohesive and/or that their relationship is an alliance. As we will see in Chapters 4 and 5, the degree of unification of the established elite is variable.) The first of these two models is the mobilization case: nonparticipants demand participation—or a higher level, or a more modern form—and ruling elites must respond to the challenge. The second model is the conservative or preemptive modernization case: social groups which are functionally relevant but heteronomous—the situation that Germani has called "availability"[16]—can be incorporated by elites seeking to strengthen the social order. As Rokkan and Bendix have pointed out, "extension of citizenship" has many times resulted from the initiative taken by conservative elites rather than from pressures by excluded strata.[17]

To analyze the participation of excluded classes and strata in these two "solutions," it is useful to think of mobilization as a three-stage process. The stages—passive nonparticipation, heteronomy, and independence—can be formulated on the basis of two dimensions: location in the political system and degree of autonomy. The first dimension refers to whether a group is located at the center or in the periphery of the system. The center/periphery distinction denotes the group's degree of functional relevance to the polity, i.e., to what extent the group's behavior has significant consequences for the social order. A group is located in the political periphery when its relevance as a contender for power or as a power base is very low. Examples are slaves in ancient societies, serfs in the middle ages, and isolated peasants in contemporary traditional societies. On the other hand, a group is located at the center when it "counts," regardless of its level of activity or independence. As for the second dimension, autonomy, it refers to the ability to carry out independent political action. By definition, the degree of autonomy is relevant only for groups in the center.

These two dimensions yield a typology of stages of mobilization (Table 1). Groups in the first stage are outside the political system. Subordinate classes and strata in precapitalist societies have seldom superseded it. On the other hand, the two main classes generated by industrialization—the bourgeoisie and the working class—are likely to omit stage I altogether, because their ability to convert their control of economic resources into political power—or, at least, into a power base—places them at the center.

The second stage corresponds to Germani's situation of availability, and it is here that excluded groups count as power bases, assuming that there are elites capable of and interested in strengthening their power by controlling previously excluded strata. The problem is, of course, that heteronomous groups are "available" as members in alternative coalitions, for in most societies the autonomous contenders for power are several. Their number includes not only the established elite or fractions thereof, but also anti–status quo intelligentsia fractions in search of a power base.

The third stage occurs when the mobilized group has developed "class consciousness" and is capable of independent action, i.e., of political action not controlled by established elites or other outside groups. In many instances, the transition from stage I to stage II is associated with the physical movement of individuals from peripheral to central regions of a society. The transition from stage II to stage III typically occurs during the generation of a new social class. The formation of the working class involves these two types of transition.

At any stage of mobilization, a social group's political action can be analyzed from the point of view of its objective consequences for the social order. This issue will be discussed further within a conceptual framework for the study of collective political action.

In studying a complex social process such as the incorporation of the working class into the political system, two deterministic approaches should be avoided. The first one is the "pure interest" type, which sees social processes as the interaction between rational actors—in this case, working classes and ruling elites—in pursuit of their interests. The second approach, a "pure structuralist" one, considers the legitimation of capitalism as a more or less automatic consequence of parts of the social structure, be they relations of production or the value system. An adequate approach should combine both perspectives and view social life as a series of results of the interaction between social structure and social action. To understand

Table 1. *Stages of Mobilization*

| | | Location in the Political System | |
		Periphery	Center
	Low	I. Passive nonparticipation	II. Heteronomy
Degree of Autonomy	High		III. Independent political force

the process of legitimation, one should be aware that outcomes are shaped by both the political action of the contenders for power—whose awareness of "objective" interests and unification in the pursuit of them vary—and by the economic, political, and cultural processes of the social structure—whose effects must be ascertained with reference to political action. This study will attempt to analyze the working class's incorporation into the political system on the basis of the different structural factors as well as the political action of the power contenders.

PART I. OUTCOMES, COLLECTIVE ACTION, AND STRUCTURAL CORRELATES

2. Outcomes of the Process of Incorporation

The different outcomes of the process of incorporation of the working class into the political system can be organized into a typology which is obtained from the combination of two dimensions, both of which refer to the resulting political system: the degree of centralization of power and the degree of legitimacy. If these dimensions are dichotomized, four ideal types of outcome of the crisis of incorporation emerge. These types will be called accommodation, exclusion, co-optation, and polarization. It is my impression that the empirical variability of results is encompassed reasonably well by these four alternatives.[1]

The types indicate the success or failure of the institutionalization of a "political formula" for consensus in an industrial, capitalist, high-participation society. For this reason, there is a close correspondence between the outcomes of the process of incorporation and the political regimes which are eventually established in the society—except, of course, in societies in which ethnic or religious cleavages are very salient. Accommodation generates tendencies toward—or better, is a central aspect of the process of development of—stable liberal democracy, and analogous relationships can be predicated between polarization and unstable democracy, exclusion and authoritarianism, and co-optation and corporatism.

CENTRALIZATION OF POWER, LEGITIMACY, AND OUTCOMES

The two dimensions, centralization of power and legitimacy, are, of course, continua, but it makes sense to think of them as dichotomies. Degree of centralization of power will be treated here as an attribute whose values are monism and pluralism. Because we are interested in this dimension with specific reference to the working class, the relevant indicator is whether this class participates in the polity as an independent political actor, i.e., whether the labor movement and the working class–based political parties, if they exist, are autonomous. Alternatives to independent participation are two: suppression or restriction of participation, and participation under the control of the ruling elites or of the state. Liberal democracies, both stable and unstable, are, of course, examples of independent participation, and authoritarian, fascist, and corporatist regimes are cases of either exclusion or controlled participation. The dichotomization of this variable into monism and pluralism is an extreme simplification, not only because intermediate stages are very frequent, but also because of the imperfect correlation that exists between the granting of trade-union rights and the extension of citizenship at the specifically political level. Differences between France and Germany have been pointed out in this connection.[2] However, for our present purpose, the dichotomization of centralization of power will suffice.

In the second dimension, the degree of legitimacy, two levels can also be distinguished: "high" and "low." What I mean by legitimacy here is the generalized acceptance of the social order of capitalism rather than the acceptance of political institutions, incumbents, or policies. Legitimacy in this sense denotes an acceptance, "natural, without questioning,"[3] of the basic social relations that prevail in the society and of the class system erected upon them. This generalized social consensus is not incompatible with dissent with respect to specific institutions—political institutions included— and policies. An example of high legitimacy in this sense is American society, where the acceptance of capitalism is not an issue as far as the working class is concerned. The indicator of low legitimacy would be the existence of widespread working-class support for anticapitalist movements and parties—support that is either manifest, as in European unstable democracies, or latent, as in most authoritarian regimes that exist in relatively industrialized societies.

Some remarks about legitimacy are pertinent. First, acceptance of capitalism does not necessarily imply conscious or active support. It simply refers to a situation in which the nature of economic institutions is not questioned. Second, it should be stressed again that the assessment of the legitimacy of capitalism is made here exclusively with respect to the working class. Third, we are referring to the acceptance of the central principles of the social organization of capitalism—basically, the centralization of the control of the means of production—rather than to the legitimacy of economic policies or practices that, to a greater or lesser extent, benefit business inter-

Table 2. *Outcomes of the Crisis of Incorporation*

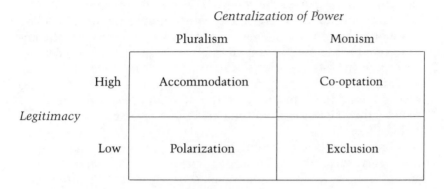

Centralization of Power

		Pluralism	Monism
Legitimacy	High	Accommodation	Co-optation
	Low	Polarization	Exclusion

ests. Hence, support for government regulation of the economy, progressive taxation, and so on, is not inconsistent with the acceptance of the central characteristics of capitalism. Finally, dissent is defined simply as lack of acceptance, i.e., as generalized anti−status quo beliefs which do not necessarily imply the advocacy of an elaborate ideology, such as socialism, which would provide a complex argument against capitalism as well as a blueprint for an alternative form of economic organization.

Table 2 shows the typology of outcomes of the crisis of incorporation obtained as a result of the combination of degree of centralization of power with degree of legitimacy.

ACCOMMODATION

The first pattern, accommodation, refers to the situation in which both political and ideological incorporation, or inclusion and value generalization, have taken place. On the one hand, independent—i.e., not elite- or government-controlled—trade unions and working class−based parties are admitted by the established elites. On the other hand, the working class legitimates the social order, and a relatively consensual society emerges as the outcome of the process. This description fits the cases of Britain, the United States, other British offshoots, and the Scandinavian nations. Britain provides the classic example of this type of incorporation: before pressures for participation could generate stable polarization, the extension of the franchise, as well as other incorporative policies, gradually produced accommodation. West Germany also belongs to this type: the removal of the Junkers and the policies applied by occupying powers created the conditions for accommodation.

The solution of the crisis of incorporation of the working class through accommodation seems to be a necessary but not a sufficient condition for the establishment and maintenance of liberal democracy in an industrial society. Moreover, the accommodation of the working class is generally associated with the presence of such other preconditions for democracy as the accommodation of the bourgeoisie, the existence of cultural traditions favorable to pluralism, and the like.

Once established, accommodation generates a pragmatic, non-ideological style of resolution of industrial conflict, and this is a powerful incentive for the maintenance and spread of a political culture focused on bargaining rather than on confrontation. This is why accommodation tends to be a relatively stable outcome: not only is this type of solution to the crisis compatible with conflict—unlike corporatist legitimacy, as will be shown later—but its mechanisms of conflict management tend to preserve and enhance consensus. This does not mean, of course, that accommodation is immune to pressures for shifts toward other patterns such as polarization. These pressures, however, are likely to arise from exogenous, i.e., extrapolitical, processes rather than from the accommodation agreement itself. Both established elites and the working class may conceivably be radicalized by economic and social factors, such as a depression or a conflict over values in the noneconomic sphere. In order for pluralist legitimacy to decay, however, pressures for discontent with the social order should be both intense and long-lasting. This is so because legitimacy in general, and pluralist legitimacy in particular, resembles a capital—Blondel's expression "capital of trust" is very adequate[4]—in that it takes time to be built and time to be spent. And the threshold for breakdown is high in a polity that has been organized on the basis of the principle of exchange of pluralism for legitimacy: a polity of this type should be able to "borrow" from the capital accumulated through past performance and thereby to manage conflict longer and more effectively than any other type of system.

POLARIZATION

The second type of outcome, polarization, occurs when the working class has been granted independent participation but when no value generalization follows. In these cases, trade unions and working-class parties become the institutionalized centers of social dissent. Examples of this pattern are those industrial democracies that have large communist and other anticapitalist parties, such as France and Italy, and industrializing nations such as Chile (up to the overthrow of Allende) and Uruguay (until the early seventies). Weimar Germany, prefascist Italy, and the Spanish republic also fit this type. France is perhaps the ideal example, for this type of outcome has prevailed in that country since industrialization began, except for the brief interlude of Vichy and the occupation.

This combination of participation and illegitimacy is intrinsically unstable. The unified political community that exists in stable liberal democracies is absent in societies of this type, in which equilibrium is maintained more by the sheer relation of forces than by affective constraints. This does not mean, of course, that unstable democracies resemble a Hobbesian world. In most of them there is a partial consensus, so that stability is not dependent only upon instrumental considerations taken by the contenders for power. However, when compared to the pluralist legitimacy case examined above, this type of polity appears both more conflict-prone and more vulnerable to the consequences of conflict. It is more prone to conflict because the distinction between society and polity is blurred in a system of this type. This is due to the transformation of organizations of all types into direct contenders for power. Huntington's description of what he calls a "praetorian society" fits this outcome: "In a praetorian system social forces confront each other nakedly . . . each group employs means which reflect its peculiar nature and capabilities. The wealthy bribe; students riot; workers strike; mobs demonstrate; and the military coup. In the absence of accepted procedures, all these forms of direct action are found on the political scene."[5]

On the other hand, liberal democracies with low levels of legitimacy are less capable of withstanding conflict. The confrontation among social forces tends to be guided by global ideologies, so that parties tend to strive for the maximization of their interests rather than for stable compromises. And whenever compromises are reached, they are likely to be tactical, i.e., dictated by the relation of forces. Conflict is likely to become cumulative rather than crosscutting, and the deepening of polarization into two radical coalitions, one authoritarian and the other revolutionary, is an ever-present possibility. In fact, all the countries mentioned above have experienced nondemocratic regimes. With the exception of Uruguay, all of them underwent periods of very intense mass mobilization, upheaval, takeover, or constitutional access to power by the radical left; and all of them experienced radical right-wing regimes, either authoritarian or fascist.

EXCLUSION

The third outcome, exclusion, involves simply the absence of incorporation. It is typified by two features. On the one hand, established elites refuse to accept independent trade unions, and working class–based political parties are outlawed. On the other hand, the capitalist social order is rejected by the working class. Exclusion and dissent can be causally related in any direction, and they can also be generated relatively independently of each other. However, dissent is the immediate trigger of exclusion. This is in agreement with Goode's hypothesis about the correlation between the value discrepancy separating rulers and the ruled and the likelihood of the use of force as a means of social control.[6] The outcome is an exclusionary dictatorship. Examples of this pattern are all the authoritarian regimes, in Linz's sense,[7] that existed in societies in which the working class was a significant political actor, these ranging from Imperial Germany and czarist Russia to the Franco and Salazar regimes and the contemporary military governments in Argentina, Brazil, Chile, and Uruguay, which O'Donnell has called "bureaucratic authoritarian."[8] Fascist regimes should also be included since their exclusionary character vis-à-vis the working class is obvious. Fascism is, however, an instance of unsuccessful co-optation: these regimes established a corporatist apparatus for the purpose of integrating the working class into a monistic high-participation system. This attempt failed, for the working class remained, both in Italy and in Germany, the sector least incorporated into the totalitarian community.

It is important to distinguish two types of exclusionary regimes. The first of these corresponds to the case in which a preindustrial authoritarian political system fails to incorporate the working class or, in a more extreme case, both the bourgeoisie and the working class. Power continues to be monopolized by the agrarian elite and/or the bureaucracy, and mobilization is answered with coercion. At its limits, no political activity—not even the articulation of immediate interests—is permitted, especially as far as the working class is concerned. This is the type of setting in which the preconditions for revolution are maximized, in spite of typical last-minute attempts by the powerholders to institute partial reforms, the classic instances of "too little, too late." Czarist Russia is the typical example of this type of situation.[9]

The second type of exclusionary regime corresponds to the case of an unstable democracy in which the level of polarization is such that a revolutionary takeover takes place, or becomes a possibility, or is at least perceived as possible by significant segments of the elite. Three classical instances include the formation of working class–based radical governments (as in France and Spain in the thirties and Chile in the seventies), intense mobilization of the working class (as in Italy after World War I or Brazil in the early sixties), and a deep economic crisis in a country in which a well-organized mass left exists (as in Germany in the early thirties). Under these circumstances, sectors of the elite and of the middle classes are likely to radicalize toward the right, and an anti–working class coalition, made up of significant fractions of all social classes except the working class, is likely to emerge. The outcome is an authoritarian or fascist regime whose central aim is the coercive demobilization of the working class.

How stable is exclusion as an outcome of the crisis of incorporation? In principle, it would seem that imposition is self-defeating in the long run, for coercion is bound to trigger resistance. However, there are grounds for supposing that under certain circumstances force may provide in the long run an affective basis for rule, thus generating a political community. Experimental evidence suggests that the relationship between coercion and resistance is curvilinear: even though, in a first phase, the greater the intensity of force, the higher the level of resistance, in a second stage the relationship between both variables is negative.[10] The examination of the evidence about high-coercion regimes, such as Nazi Germany, suggests that the disappearance of resistance was not only due to the physical destruction and emigration of actual and potential opponents. The continued application of coercion is likely to produce a "cultural revolution": subjects eventually change their beliefs, and compliance is "authentic" rather than hypocritical. Bettleheim's description of the conversion of inmates in a concentration camp provides an example in an extreme situation.[11] Cognitive dissonance theory offers a simple behavioral interpretation of this phenomenon: given that noncompliance becomes impossible and that it would be unbearable for individuals to behave at variance with their beliefs for a protracted period, beliefs are likely to change. Fear and love are not necessarily incompatible, as Machiavelli thought.[12] This is why imposition can engender legitimacy.

In order for exclusion to be stable, therefore, two conditions should be met. First, rulers should be in a position to employ very high levels of coercion for an extended period of time, and second, they must possess the capability to resocialize the coercively demo-bilized population. The first condition presupposes the total control of the means of coercion by the ruling elite, as well as the absence of any constraints with respect to the utilization of force. The second condition implies a very high level of control of social interaction outside of the family, and of socialization mechanisms. This implies, in turn, the existence c. a mass party and the generation of a total-itarian society. Among regimes in capitalist societies which have been exclusionary vis-à-vis the working class, only fascist regimes have been close to meeting these conditions, and even they have failed to resocialize the working class. It can be concluded, there-fore, that even though there exists the theoretical possibility that ex-clusion could become a basis for consent under certain conditions, there are no examples of this goal having been achieved vis-à-vis the working class. Continued coercion can, all the same, generate a sta-ble regime, but power rests entirely on sheer force.

CO-OPTATION

The fourth type of outcome, co-optation, refers to a situation in which the working class is included in the polity as a heteronomous participant under the control of the established elite. Co-optation is, therefore, a combination of accommodation and exclusion. As in the case of accommodation, there is both political and ideological incor-poration of the working class. As in the case of exclusion, on the other hand, the elite does not acknowledge the legitimacy of inde-pendent trade unions and working class–based political parties. The implementation of co-optation supposes a precondition: the "will-ingness" of the working class to be co-opted. Unlike the case of ex-clusion, finally, the capitalist social order is not opposed by the working class: dissent would render co-optation impossible.

The political mechanism through which co-optation is imple-mented is corporatism, i.e., a system of representation of interests, in the context of a capitalist society, in which the representative or-ganizations are, in Schmitter's terms, "recognized or licensed (if not created) by the state and granted a deliberate representational mo-nopoly . . . in exchange for observing certain controls on their selec-tion of leaders and articulation of demands and supports."[13] This definition of corporatism is broader than the one found in classical corporatist doctrines, for it does not imply that functional criteria of representation are prevalent or exclusive. The reason for this is that, while doctrinaire corporatism has nowhere been institutionalized, the broader mechanism defined above has been, i.e., the control of functional and political representation by the state, and it in fact flourishes throughout the so-called Third World.[14] Corporatism in this sense is not, therefore, a museum piece, but a central feature in the political organization of contemporary societies. It is the institutional infrastructure of most of the regimes conventionally called "populist." The reference to the control of representative organizations by the state also distinguishes my use of the term from that of Schmitter, whose definition applies not only to "state" corporatism but also to what he calls "societal" corporatism, i.e., those pluralist polities in which interest groups play an institutionalized role in decision-making, as is the case in Scandinavian and other European countries. And, finally, since I am applying the label to high-participation regimes only, this definition of corporatism is narrower than that of O'Donnell, Collier, Malloy, and other authors, who include also those instances, such as in the "bureaucratic authoritarian" regimes in Latin America, in which a nonparticipant labor movement is controlled by the state.[15]

The earliest attempt to incorporate the working class into the political system under state control probably took place in czarist Russia at the beginning of the century when the Moscow head of the Okhrana formed unions under police control—with Moscow University professors drafting the statutes—for purposes which included the organization of demonstrations in favor of the czar and functions such as the communal singing of patriotic songs.[16] I mentioned above that the fascist regimes in Italy and Germany are cases of unsuccessful co-optation, and the same can be said about the Franco and Salazar authoritarian regimes. These are four examples of a corporatist facade which concealed a reality of exclusion. On the other hand, substantive corporatism—sometimes under a liberal-democratic guise—has been successfully implemented in several Latin American nations: the Vargas regime in Brazil, Perón's government in Argentina, and the political structure that evolved in Mexico after the revolution are cases of co-optation of the working class. In all of these examples, workers belonged to an elite-controlled party—which, in the case of Mexico, is even organized along functional lines—and trade unions which were strongly influenced or controlled by the state. The fact that corporatism, in its different forms, is also pervasively found in other areas of the Third World suggests the very clear possibility that, as Schmitter has suggested, this is a distinct path of political modernization.[17] This issue will be discussed at greater length when the structural correlates of outcomes are examined.

Table 3. *Dimensions of Centralization of Power*

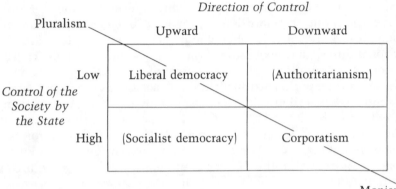

Pluralism

Control of the Society by the State	*Direction of Control*: Upward	Downward
Low	Liberal democracy	(Authoritarianism)
High	(Socialist democracy)	Corporatism

Monism

We may turn now to the issue of the stability of co-optation as an outcome of the crisis of incorporation. As was the case with accommodation, co-optation is a high-legitimacy outcome. The two patterns differ, however, with respect to the degree of centralization of power, and this fact has significant consequences with respect to stability.

In order to grasp the difference between accommodation and co-optation, it becomes necessary to break down centralization of power, which is a complex dimension, into two axes of autonomy-subordination. The first axis is vertical and corresponds to the direction of control of political inputs. The second axis is horizontal and refers to the consequences of political outputs. In more classic terms, the two axes are the direction of the flow of participation and the degree of control of the society by the state. Table 3 shows the bidimensional difference between the two high-legitimacy outcomes.

In an ideal case of liberal democracy, control flows from the bottom, the control of the society by the state being minimal. In an ideal case of corporatism, on the other hand, participation is controlled from the top, and the society is "coordinated" by the state. Both the *Führerprinzip* and *Gleichschaltung* are the logical consequence of the thorough penetration of a society by corporatism. This arrangement, in order to persist, requires not only the effective control of representative organizations by the state, but also the consent of the ruled. And here resides precisely the weakness of corporatism: a decrease in the level of consent would automatically lead to a state of polarization. In such a case, representative organizations would cease to be "transmission belts" in a Leninist sense, and they would become, rather, organizational weapons. Unlike ruling elites in authoritarian regimes, which aim at demobilizing and thus disorganizing the working class, the elites in corporatist regimes use the working class as a mass base, and mobilize and organize the labor movement in order to enhance elite power. This is why co-optation is vulnerable to pressures toward either polarization or exclusion: its stability rests on the absence of discontent among the working class, and this means, in the last instance, that some form of continuous redistribution is needed. The threshold for institutional breakdown is, for this reason, lower in co-optation than in accommodation.

CONCLUDING REMARKS

To conclude this presentation of the four types of outcome, two observations are necessary. In the first place, it should be stressed again that these patterns are ideal types. In real political life, there are no "pure" outcomes: even though one type prevails at any point in time, secondary traits belonging to other patterns can usually be found. Thus, the history of electoral laws in many accommodation societies shows that exclusionary aspects persisted for a long time, and tendencies toward co-optation in otherwise exclusionary regimes were already noted. The case of Bismarck's carrot-and-stick policies toward the working class, to be examined later, illustrates the complexity of concrete regimes. However, a dominant type can always be discerned.

In the second place, patterns vary over time. After a generalized first stage in which exclusion was the dominant form, different polities experienced different types of evolution. As was noted above, the stability of types is variable. In those countries where accommodation was institutionalized, this type has generally been very stable. There are, however, instances in which the other outcomes have lasted for very long periods: polarization in France, exclusion in Spain, co-optation in Mexico. Other countries, such as Germany or Argentina, have had frequent shifts. In principle, it would seem that both in the case of the two low-legitimacy outcomes as well as in the case of the two high-centralization ones, one form tends to veer toward the other: polarization is prone to a shift toward exclusion and vice versa; the same tension exists between corporatism and exclusion. Propositions about typical sequences could be developed on the basis of comparative analysis.

3. A Conceptual Framework for the Analysis of Collective Political Action

In this chapter, a conceptual framework for the analysis of processes leading to the different outcomes will be presented. This framework consists of a model of collective political action.[1]

It can be expected that a process as complex as the incorporation of the working class into the political system will be the result of multiple causes and that the weight of the different contributing factors will vary empirically. In the previous chapter, references were made to some of the causal mechanisms or preconditions that seem to be associated with the emergence or the maintenance of outcomes. Thus, the examination of accommodation suggested that the willingness of both the elite and the working class to undertake the accommodation agreement, i.e., to exchange legitimacy for pluralism, was a crucial precondition for the institutionalization of this outcome. In the discussion of polarization, on the other hand, it was stressed that the high level of politicization of social forces is one of the factors that contributes toward making this outcome unstable. When speculating on the conditions that should be present for exclusion to generate a political formula for legitimacy, I asserted that the total centralization of the means of coercion by an elite not bound by constraints in relation to the use of force, and the control of secondary interaction and socialization mechanisms by the state, are prerequisites for the achievement of that goal. Finally, in the discussion of co-optation, it was stated that the institutionalization of this outcome presupposes the "willingness" of the working class to be co-opted.

The simplest possible conceptual framework for the study of determinants of outcomes could be based on the analysis of the interaction between the two main contenders, i.e., established elites, who hold economic and political power, and the outsiders whose incorporation is at issue, i.e., the working class. Second, there seem to be many relevant factors that are neither elite nor working-class

traits and that might enhance or inhibit the power of the two contenders: these background characteristics can be subsumed under
the inclusive heading of environmental factors.

It could be argued that a two-contender model, "elite vs. working class," is too simple to account for the complexity of political
life for two reasons. First, in each concrete case there are other social
forces, such as the middle classes or the peasantry, whose role might
be central. Second, neither of the two main contenders is a homoge-
neous political actor. Both "elite" and "working class" are labels for
heterogeneous aggregates made up of individuals whose background
characteristics are similar, but whose degree of political unification
is problematic: the unity of a social class as a political force cannot
be assumed by definition.

These two objections are valid. The conceptual framework to be
proposed here can be applied, however, in such a way that these
shortcomings are attenuated. In the first place, classes and strata
other than the elite and the working class can be considered to belong to the relevant "environmental factors." Second, the concepts
to be discussed here seem to be adequate for the analysis of social
groups at different levels of political unification. And, as we will see,
the typology of forms of political action, to be used in relation to the
working class, is especially useful in order to account for political
diversity within large aggregates.

In relation to the two main contenders, I am primarily interested in concepts useful for the analysis of their political action
rather than in the description of background characteristics that are
mobilized as resources in political action. A problem in this connection is that the same concepts would not be equally adequate for the
study of the political action of an organized minority, such as an
elite, or of a large collectivity, such as the industrial working class.
The way in which these two types of social force utilize their power
in the context of social interaction is likely to be very different. For
this reason, different levels of complexity of collective political action will be distinguished. The simplest classification consists of
two extreme levels and an intermediate one. The highest level of
complexity—which is likely to correspond to the political action of
organized minorities, such as established elites—will be called a
strategy, and the lowest one—which is probably an adequate description of the action of an emergent collectivity, such as a "new" working class—will be labeled "forms of political action." The intermediate level of complexity, finally, can be termed "ideologically oriented
action."

In what follows, these concepts—elite strategies, forms of political action of the working class, and environmental factors—will be examined. As the latter category serves as background, it will be useful to begin the discussion with a brief reference to these factors.

ENVIRONMENTAL FACTORS

Environmental factors were defined above in a residual manner—as those contributing factors which are neither traits of the elite nor traits of the working class, but which affect the political action of these two main contenders and thus exert influence on the outcome of the process of incorporation. A positive definition would be as follows: environmental factors are a set of resources and constraints, actual or potential, which enhance or decrease the probability of occurrence of the different outcomes. These resources and constraints admit many possible classifications and many possible levels of specification. In this chapter, a very simple classification will be presented. As for the level of detail, an enumeration of potentially relevant environmental factors would not only be endless but also of very limited value, for only a few of them are likely to be relevant in any specific case.

Two types of environmental factors will be distinguished: characteristics of other classes and strata, and aspects of the social structure. The latter will be called systemic resources.

Let us begin with the first category. As was noted above, groups other than the elite and the working class contribute to the determination of the outcome. These other social classes and strata are available as partners for political coalitions. The two most significant of these have been the peasantry and the urban middle classes, but other groups, such as urban marginals and agrarian middle classes, have played important roles in many societies. Further, urban middle classes are seldom a unified social force: in different contexts, these strata can be divided into two or more significant segments, and it can also happen that only specific fractions of the urban middle classes, such as the intelligentsia, are actors whose action affects the outcome of the process of incorporation. The point here is that groups other than elites and working classes can become allies of the main contenders, can be their hegemonizers, or can be under their hegemony.

The aspects of the social structure called systemic resources can be broken down into three types: economic, referring to the economic surplus that exists in the society; political, corresponding to the apparatus of coercion; and cultural, the political culture and ideologies that exist in the society. My interest lies in the amount of each resource that is available and in the distribution of its control among contenders for power. Resources could be classified further as internal vs. external. This distinction is particularly important, for the endowment of resources that is internally available is partially determined by exogenous processes: economic aid, military aid or intervention, ideological influences, and so on are net additions to or subtractions from the amount of surplus, the coercive resources, and the political beliefs and practices that are "available" in a society at a given moment. All these factors can be associated with the outcome of the process of incorporation, and some of the possible relationships between environment factors and outcomes will be examined later.

THE LEVELS OF COMPLEXITY
OF COLLECTIVE POLITICAL ACTION

In principle, it is important to note that the variability of collective action cannot be adequately encompassed by a single model of individual action, such as the conceptual scheme of purposive behavior. The conspiracy and the jacquerie stand out as extreme examples of situations in which a model of this type would be most appropriate and totally inadequate. However, it is fruitful to look at collective political action as a continuum between two polar models of individual action: reactiveness and purposiveness. The underlying dimensions in that continuum are two Parsonian pattern variables: diffuseness-specificity and affectivity-neutrality. (It should be recalled that this latter term refers to the control of affectivity rather than to its absence.)

Most classifications in the literature can be fitted into this continuum. Thus, Gusfield has distinguished three types of social movement on the basis of the nature of their goals and of the character of their constituencies: expressive, which is goalless or pursues goals not related to the sources of group dissatisfaction; status, which seeks to maintain or increase the prestige of a group; and class, which aims at protecting specific group interests.[2] Tilly and his colleagues have analyzed lower-class collective action on the basis of a typology of relationships between groups in relation to resources—personnel, property, premises, symbols. They classify collective action into three types: competitive, when different groups contend for the same resources; reactive, when a group resists claims by outsiders on resources that it controls ("reactive" here denotes a collective response rather than the "lower" pole of the purposiveness continuum); and proactive, when a group lays claim on resources it did not control previously.[3] Even though these types can be found at any level of purposiveness, they are likely to rank relatively "high" on the continuum, for they seem to imply some significant degree of specificity—even in the "reactive" case, in the specific sense this term has for Tilly and his coworkers.

I will distinguish different levels of complexity, i.e., of interrelationship among the elements of action—actor, goals, means, and consequences—according to the degree of fit of the purposive model. As noted above, three levels seem relevant for the analysis of collective political action: a high level of specificity and neutrality (a strategy), a low level (forms of political action), and an intermediate level (ideologically oriented action). In fact, only the two polar opposites will be utilized in this study, which analyzes in particular forms of political action, although ideologically oriented action is mentioned because its consideration will contribute to the understanding of the other two levels.

The term "strategy" refers, then, to a type of collective political action that is highly organized. In it, beliefs and behavior reveal a high level of specification of goals as well as a high level of awareness of the relationships that exist between means and goals and between action and consequences. On the other hand, the term "forms of political action" refers to a type of collective political action in which the level of organization is low: in it, the identity of the political actor is diffusely and affectively defined, there is little specification of goals, and the degree of awareness of the connections between means and goals and between action and consequences is low. Rather, it is useful to define forms of political action as a set of generalized beliefs and dispositions for action in relation to the foundations of the social order.

In Table 4, the differences among the three levels of complexity are specified in relation to the elements of action. These differences are illustrated with some examples taken from nationalist and socialist politics.

Level I of complexity can be applied to all types of political force, but this would be a very poor conceptualization of the political action of a unified elite, or even of a very well-organized political movement. Level III, on the contrary, can only be profitably applied to these types of political force. It makes sense to describe the political action of elites with the language of the purposive model, while unorganized or weakly organized masses seem to be more adequately accounted for by the reactive model. Organized mass movements, finally, are fond of the rhetoric of purposive political action, but the extent to which this rhetoric corresponds to actual practice is an empirical problem. Political forces based on large aggregates, therefore, are likely to fluctuate between levels I and II, while elites—both established elites and organized counterelites—are likely to approach level III. In the following discussion, level III is applied to elites, and level I to the working class. The adequacy of the different levels in relation to the action of concrete groups is, of course, empirically variable, and it is important to avoid hypostatizing collective rationality. Level I seems to be the most appropriate one for the description of an emerging working class, but "higher" levels may be more adequate in situations in which this class is a highly organized social force.

ELITE STRATEGIES

Three ideal-typical elite strategies vis-à-vis the working class can be discerned: inclusion, exclusion, and co-optation. The successful implementation of these strategies leads to the establishment of liberal democracies, exclusionary dictatorships, and corporatist regimes. The first type of strategy, inclusion, was given a name different from that of the corresponding outcome, accommodation, in order to emphasize that in this case, more than in the others, the generation and maintenance of the outcome depend on the interaction between the elite and the working class as two relatively independent forces. In the other two cases, the initiative belongs almost exclusively to the elite, even though the forms of political action of the working class and environmental factors are also significant determinants of the outcome. Polarization, finally, is not the actualization of an elite strategy; rather, it is an objective outcome which results from political stalemate.

It should be emphasized again that these strategies are ideal types and that concrete policies implemented by governments and parties representing the elite or fractions of the elite are blends of one or more "pure" types. This seems to be especially so with respect to noninclusionary strategies. However, as was noted above, in relation to the blend of outcomes, it is usually possible to determine which is the dominant strategy underlying concrete policies. The other remark that was made in connection with outcomes also applies to strategies: they vary over time, after an initial stage in which exclusion is the most frequent strategy.

Inclusion, exclusion, and co-optation can be conveniently la-

Table 4. *Levels of Complexity of Political Action*

| | Diffuseness ⟵————————— |
| | Affectivity ⟵————————— |

	Levels of Complexity
	I *Forms of* *Political Action*
Elements of *Political Action*	
Identity of political actor	Actor is defined as a diffuse collectivity, e.g., "the people."
Goals	Diffuse goals and diffuse definition of opponents. Beliefs are expressed as demands or supports, acceptance or rejection, e.g., "justice," "liberation" as goals; "the rich" as opponents.
Means	Low level of awareness of the means-goals connection, e.g., "struggle" and "revolution" as universal and absolute means.
Consequences	Low level of awareness of the problem.

→ *Specificity*
→ *Neutrality*

II *Ideologically Oriented Action*	III *Strategy*
Actor is a collectivity or a section of it that is defined on the basis of specific membership criteria, e.g., "nation," "class."	Actor is either an organization—such as the government or an interest group—or a collectivity that is effectively led by an organization, such as a party. Examples: same as in II.
Beliefs are focused on more specific goals and more specific opponents, e.g., "national power," "socialism" as goals; "imperalism," "the capitalists" as opponents.	Goals are highly specified and ordered into short-run and long-run. Opponents are ordered according to the degree of antagonism. Action is consciously maximizing or "satisficing." Examples: same as in II, but more "realistic."
Greater specification, but connection is still diffuse. Specification of types of activity: e.g., "people's war" as opposed to "guerrilla" in insurrectionary movements.	High level of awareness of means-goals relationship. Examples: same as in II, but greater specification and awareness of the distinction between tactical and strategic levels.
Higher level of awareness, but the relationship is still diffuse.	High level of awareness. Specification of consequences as short- or long-term.

beled after prominent practitioners of each, the Disraelian, Bismarckián, and Peronist options. In order to illustrate these alternative strategies and to examine their interaction with the forms of political action of the working class in each example, the cases of Britain under Disraeli, Germany under Bismarck, and Argentina under Perón will be examined later. These examples have been selected because they correspond to typical configurations of factors in relatively industrialized countries at the point of development in which the working class becomes a significant political actor, either because of its mobilization or because of its availability as a power base. However, these three cases are not necessarily the most extreme or "pure" cases of implementation of each strategy, especially as far as exclusion and co-optation are concerned.

THE FORMS OF POLITICAL ACTION
OF THE WORKING CLASS

The phrase "forms of political action" was applied above to a low level of complexity of collective political action, in which diffuseness and affectivity are high. Forms of political action were also defined as a set of generalized beliefs and dispositions for action in relation to the foundations of the social order. The meaning of this definition will be clearer after the discussion in this section.

In principle, two explanatory remarks will be useful. First, the definition refers to generalized beliefs and dispositions for action, i.e., to abstract, diffuse, global ideas and propensities rather than to concrete, specific, focused ones. The goal in using this concept is to ascertain whether ideas and behavior indicate support for or opposition to the social order, i.e., to make a judgment on the legitimacy of the status quo for the working class.

In the second place, the foundations of the social order are mentioned in the definition. This specification implies that both ideas and propensities for action are being evaluated from the point of view of the consequences that the actualization of these ideas and behavior would have in relation to the central institutional characteristics of the social order. An evaluation of this type presupposes, of course, a prior definition of the foundations of the social order, i.e., the specification of thresholds in relation to which support and opposition can be assessed.

These thresholds of legitimacy are contextually specific: the same beliefs and behavior can be legitimate in a given context and illegitimate in a different one. It is important to note that thresholds can be manifest or latent; the first type refers to "formal" rules, i.e., to prescriptions which are formulated and transmitted regardless of their actual validity. It is the second type of thresholds with which I am concerned: "latent" thresholds are those that correspond to the objectively central characteristics of the social order, regardless of whether they have been explicitly formulated as rules. Norms regarding political corruption, for instance, are usually a "manifest" threshold, for corruption is formally illegitimate in all societies; however, moderate levels of corruption are "objectively" legitimate in many societies. The acquisition of political power by different sectors of the elite through the use of force is formally illegitimate in all countries, but military coups are actually a legitimate mechanism for the transfer of power in many praetorian polities—the Latin American ones, for instance. Manifest rules embody the consciousness that the members of a society are supposed to have about the "ideal" operation of their social system. And it is not necessary to state that this consciousness may not be an adequate representation of the actual operation of the social order.

The "central" characteristics of the social order can be defined as the necessary characteristics, i.e., those objective norms without which the social order would not be what it is. It is not very difficult to point out some of these central characteristics in the economy and the polity of societies facing the issue of incorporating the working class into the political system. As far as the economy is concerned, an obvious necessary characteristic of capitalism is the centralization of the control of the means of production—or, what is the same, the existence of a free labor market in the specific sense that was discussed in Chapter 1. Therefore, those beliefs and predispositions for action which, if actualized, would lead to the suppression of this trait can be considered to be beyond the threshold of legitimacy for capitalist institutions. On the other hand, latent thresholds for behavior also vary according to the degree of pluralism that exists in the polity: the more monistic the regime, the more limited the scope of legitimate behavior. The generalization that seems possible in relation to the effect of the pluralism-monism dimension on the scope of legitimate behavior is that the utilization of violence by subordinate strata is beyond the threshold of legitimacy in all societies—even in those contexts in which "collective bargaining by riot" by the lower classes is a recurrent form of behavior.

It should be emphasized, finally, that the evaluation of ideas and behavior from the point of view of their objective consequences for the social order, if actualized, does not imply that correspondence between these potential consequences and the actual functions that forms of political action have in relation to the social order is assumed. For instance the fact that in some societies anti–status quo beliefs and/or forms of behavior are widespread, or even prevalent, does not imply that the existence of these forms of political action is dysfunctional for the existing social order.

THE LEGITIMACY OF BELIEFS
AND THE LEGITIMACY OF BEHAVIOR

In analyzing political action from the point of view of its legitimacy, it is very important to make a distinction that is not always clear in the literature on collective political action, be it academic or nonacademic. This is the distinction between the legitimacy of beliefs and the legitimacy of behavior. Very frequently a high correlation between both variables is assumed. It is commonly expected that if people are socialized into anti–status quo beliefs, they will be available for anti–status quo behavior or, conversely, that whenever individuals carry out anti–status quo activities, they are likely to hold anti–status quo beliefs as well.

In reality, beliefs and behavior can vary independently, and empirical examples of all the possible combinations abound. There are, of course, cases of association between ideas and behavior: the combination of legitimate ideas and legitimate behavior is, almost everywhere and at all times, the most frequent form of political action, and revolutions are examples of collective action in which a significant segment of the population displays both ideas and behavior which are antagonistic toward the social order. However, revolutions, those situations in which, in Trotsky's terms, there is a "direct interference of the masses in historic events,"[4] are a relatively infrequent phenomenon in human history. And, furthermore, it would be wrong to assume that all or most of the people who have participated in revolutionary upheavals held anti–status quo beliefs.

Let us look now at cases of lack of correspondence between ideas and behavior. The combination of anti–status quo behavior and beliefs that do not oppose the foundations of the social order is best illustrated by jacqueries and similar instances of peasant rebellion. In many cases these upheavals have occurred in defense of the traditional social order—either feudalism or a centralized agrarian bureaucracy—in which the peasantry was the subordinate class. Thus, Mousnier, in a study of peasant uprisings in seventeenth-century France, China, and Russia, has concluded:

[The French peasants] want respect for the traditional customs, privileges, and liberties of the provinces and districts, a return to the old taxes . . . there is usually no demand affecting the system of seignorial property and the feudal political system. . . . The program of the Russian peasants in the Time of Troubles seems also to have been rather a return to a customary condition of things, somewhat idealized. Prisoners themselves, too, of respect for custom, and with the mentality of ritualistic cultivators, the peasants do not seem to have sought either the abolition of Tsarism or the transformation of the domanial and seignorial regime.[5]

Finally, the case of collective action in which beliefs that contradict the foundations of the social order and behavior that conforms to the rules are combined is best exemplified by the social base of contemporary mass revolutionary parties in advanced capitalist societies, such as communist parties in France and Italy. Moderation of behavior is not, of course, an indicator of the absence of revolutionary commitment—the view that revolutionaries are those who engage in continuous illegitimate behavior would be infantile—but there are instances in the history of these two parties (the postwar period in both countries and May of 1968 in France) in which the statement that they failed to pursue more revolutionary options seems plausible. Besides other factors that would provide an explanation for this behavior—such as Soviet global policies, realistic prospects of success, and Michelsian mechanisms—the moderation of the social base of these parties seems to be a central factor.

If beliefs and behavior, considered from the point of view of the objective consequences of their actualization in relation to the foundations of the social order, can vary independently, then their combination generates a typology of forms of political action (see Table 5). In what follows, the two dimensions will be considered as continua. Their extreme points will be called consent-dissent, in relation to beliefs, and compliance-radicalism, in relation to behavior. The first category in each pair is, in fact, defined residually: these categories simply indicate the absence of dissent or radicalism, rather than effective political socialization or active support for the status quo.[6]

These types refer, it should be stressed again, to individual political action. Aggregates are, therefore, likely to be heterogeneous. Forms of political action, however, do not occur at random in the social structure: different classes and strata are more prone to develop specific combinations of beliefs and behavior than others. In

Table 5. *Typology of Forms of Political Action*

Beliefs

		Consent	Dissent
	Compliance	I	III
Behavior			
	Radicalism	II	IV

most societies, for instance, peasants and urban marginals have wavered between types I and II, and industrial workers have tended to fit type III. In organizations and political movements, finally, the degree of consistency between the forms of political action of the leadership and of the rank and file is also empirically variable. The relationship between forms of political action and more complex levels, such as ideologically oriented action, is also problematic. There are some obvious affinities between these types and political ideologies, but it should be kept in mind that forms of political action are no more than diffuse and affective orientations. *They are a set of structurally determined propensities.* As such, they are a central factor in the diffusion of ideologies and the formation of mass organizations. But the latter do not flow automatically from these structurally determined propensities. What Lenin and other practitioners of revolution knew very well—that the revolutionary organizations of the lower classes come to their social bases largely from without, and that "revolutionary situations" and actual revolutions are two very different things—can be generalized to all relationships between structure and collective action. Neither ideology nor organization are spontaneous outgrowths of class positions, and structural conduciveness is only one of the factors, the "opportunity from below" ingredient, in the genesis of political movements. The "resource mobilization" approach is right in its contention that the link between the existence of grievances and the activation of social groups is problematic, for discontent does not lead necessarily to mobilization, and group dissatisfaction can be produced by political activists. It is also right in its insistence on the role of organizations and outside actors in the production of social movements.[7] How-

**Table 6. Typology of Forms of Political Action
of the Working Class**

Dissent

		Low	High
	Low	Acquiescence I	Reformism III
Radicalism			
	High	II Mobilization	IV Revolutionary action

ever, the existence of discontent as well as its pattern of distribution are significant, for discontent does not occur at random in the social structure. And, in my opinion, the assumption that there is always a reservoir of grievances among the lower classes is also empirically problematic.[8] The determination of the locus of discontent is essential for the understanding of the opportunities and constraints that exist for the formation of movements of different types.

The conversion of forms of political action into ideologically oriented action and strategy and the corresponding formation of group organizations is the result of a complex social process involving economic, political, and cultural constraints and opportunities, rather than of the abstract affinity between different levels of complexity of action. In fact, the same forms of political action can be channeled into different ideologies: individuals having the same combination of beliefs and predispositions for action can end up at opposite extremes of the political spectrum. On the other hand, as noted above, several of the forms of political action, and probably all, are represented in significant proportions within the set of supporters of a specific ideology or political movement.

It will be useful to specify further the typology presented above in relation to the working class and the legitimacy of capitalism. In the remainder of this study, dissent is operationalized as opposition to the private ownership of the means of production, and radicalism as a propensity to undertake modes of behavior that include violence or other forms of coercion. In Table 6, the types have been labeled with familiar designations.

The first situation, acquiescence, corresponds to both the stage of passive nonparticipation and integrated participation after incorporation. The contemporary American labor movement would be an example of the latter situation. As for mobilization, it refers to the case of working classes that engage in anti–status quo behavior but do not have an anti–status quo ideology; the action of the English working class during much of the nineteenth century corresponds to this pattern. Reformism and revolutionary action, finally, correspond to the classical variants in the European labor movement.

THE INTERPLAY AMONG ELITE STRATEGIES, FORMS OF POLITICAL ACTION, AND ENVIRONMENTAL FACTORS

Elite strategies and forms of political action are partially determined by each other and also by environmental factors. In this section, some tentative propositions linking these three sets of determinants will be presented.

The usual ceteris paribus is especially significant in connection with hypotheses about complex historical processes such as the incorporation of the working class into the political system: the collective action of elites and working classes is affected by contextually specific factors that are exogenous to the framework presented here. The most obvious of these is the organizational pattern—the size, strength, and effectiveness of interest groups and of political parties based on the elite and the working class, characteristics of the leadership of these entities, and the like. Since organization does not just flow from the social structure, its traits cannot be predicted from collective action and environmental factors. In any concrete situation, these will determine organizational structure and process only partially. The fact that, in a general framework of this type, organization is considered as an exogenous factor does not mean, of course, that it is less important than the propensities generated by the social structure. The relationship between the "general" and the "particular" is not one of hierarchical order; contextual variability does not imply lesser significance. In fact, the more developed the organizations, the more independent they are of their structural conditioning, and thus the more significant their causal weight. There are many other empirically variable factors besides organization: the salience of noneconomic cleavages (ethnic, religious, regional), the specific relationships with other societies, et cetera.

Let us begin by examining options available to the elite in different situations. Since the forms of political action of the working class are partially determined by factors other than elite strategies and environmental factors, it is useful to look at the former as constraints or opportunities for the implementation of elite strategies. Ceteris paribus, it can be hypothesized that the existence of an acquiescent working class will induce the elite to implement nonexclusionary strategies, either co-optation or inclusion. A mobilized working class, on the other hand, seems to be incompatible with co-optation, so the other two strategies appear more likely. In fact, there is an association between mobilization as a form of political action and the generation of inclusionary strategies by elites. A possible reason might be that, on the one hand, co-optation—whose central mechanism is the organizational control of the working class by the elite—is made difficult by mobilization and that, on the other, the prospect of accommodation is acceptable to the elite, due to the low level of dissent of the working class. And accommodation is, of course, less "costly" in the long run as a political formula than exclusion.

A reformist working class is the third case. In a situation of this type, co-optation is even more unlikely, due to the high level of dissent, and stable accommodation is not a realistic possibility. It would seem that either polarization or exclusion are the likely outcomes in this case. Finally, in a situation in which the working class is characterized by what I have called revolutionary action, the elite will tend to apply an exclusionary strategy, and the outcome will depend on the relation of forces.

Let us look now at the possible effect of elite strategies on forms of political action. As far as inclusion is concerned, it can be hypothesized that the implementation of this strategy is not likely to result in the growth of either dissent or radicalism in the working class—ceteris paribus, of course. Exclusionary strategies, on the other hand, are likely to produce an increase in both dissent and radicalism, even though the expression of these two tendencies can be effectively controlled by the threat of coercion. Moreover, it was stated above that the possibility that exclusion might modify the forms of political action in an adaptive direction cannot be rejected on theoretical grounds, even though there are no empirical cases of this effect. Finally, as for co-optation, it can be hypothesized that this strategy is not likely to produce per se an increase of either dissent or radicalism.

In considering the possible consequences of environmental factors, let us begin with groups other than the elite and the working class. It was mentioned above that the peasantry and the urban middle class, as well as some fractions of the latter, such as the intelligentsia, are significant as partners or leaders of coalitions or as power bases. Whether the peasantry and the urban middle classes ally with or come under the hegemony of parties that control any of the two main contenders is a crucial determinant of the outcome of the process of incorporation.

This is most obvious in cases of polarization or exclusion leading to revolution—nobody will quarrel with Lenin's estimate that no revolutionary breakthrough was possible in Russia without the Communists assuming, to a significant degree, control of the peasantry, for instance—but examples from other situations come quickly to mind. Thus, the establishment of exclusionary regimes in countries having a large peasantry has been generally facilitated by the hegemony of the agrarian elite over the peasantry; the success of accommodation would be unthinkable without the cooperation of urban middle classes; and it is the radicalization of these same classes toward the right that has provided a social base for exclusionary regimes arising in situations of high polarization. The existence of a revolutionary intelligentsia, finally, is a necessary condition for the crystallization of working-class dissent into a mass party and thus for the generation of polarization.

As for the systemic resources discussed above, their role as either opportunities or constraints for the implementation of the different outcomes is clear. Let us begin with the first of these resources, the existence of a surplus available for redistribution. In relation to elite strategies, it can be asserted that the availability of this resource is a necessary condition for the implementation of both inclusion and co-optation, for the generation and maintenance of legitimacy is likely to require the granting of economic rewards. The problem is, of course, that the availability of surplus is a function of the level of productivity of the economy and of pressures for alternative uses, such as the accumulation of capital. And, in the beginning of industrialization, the dilemma of accumulation versus redistribution is experienced even by highly productive economies. It is for this reason that long-term economic growth is a precondition for the success of either accommodation or co-optation. Therefore, redistribution is likely to have an adaptive effect on the forms of political action, and absence of redistribution is likely to facilitate a deviation from adaptation.

As for the second type of resources, the amount of coercive resources that exists in a society and the degree of centralization of coercion under state control determine the feasibility of exclusion as an alternative for the elite. In modern societies, the means of coercion are usually controlled by elites, but war, especially when it leads to defeat, is a situation particularly conducive to the decentralization of coercion; modern war entails the arming of a large proportion of the population, and defeat may lead to a drastic reduction of the level of effectiveness of the state. In that case, if the level of legitimacy of the social order is low, revolutionary outbreaks are likely to follow.

The consequences of cultural factors, finally, are obvious. Both the orientation of the elite toward any of the three strategies and the propensities of the working class toward dissent and radicalism are partially determined by political culture. The correspondence between the different outcomes and cultural characteristics—such as the predominance of either a "participant" or a "subject" type of political culture as well as patterns of trust, cooperation, and an ideological or pragmatic style of problem solving—is clear. These culturally transmitted orientations operate as either constraints or opportunities for the institutionalization of each of the four outcomes, since they affect the choice of strategy by the elite and the choice of form of political action by the working class.

There are many intriguing regularities in the covariation between cultural factors and the outcome of the process of incorporation, and the causal mechanisms involved are not fully understood. For example, it is interesting to note that there is a correlation between Catholicism and polarization as an outcome of the process of incorporation. On the one hand, most mass communist parties in the West have arisen in Latin-Catholic countries—Finland, which was a part of the Russian Empire, is an exception—and on the other, there is an association between the predominance of Catholicism in a society and the frequency of authoritarian regimes. Factors of a structural nature can be proposed in order to explain this pattern (the delayed industrialization-syncratism-hegemonic crisis syndrome is discussed later), but one is left with the impression that there is still a cultural residue; the Weberian question is still with us. Deutsch has speculated that there are "protoindustrial" and "antiindustrial" cultures and that Hispanic and Islamic civilizations belong to the latter type.[9] The question could be raised in relation to the political realm: are there, for instance, "protocommunist" cultures?

Finally, a brief remark on belief systems. The ideologies that are operative in a society at a given moment—either because they are endogenous or because they are available internationally—play a role in the determination of the outcome. Elite behavior has been affected at various times by the influence of ideologies such as liberalism, fascism, nationalism, and populism, and the same is true for the working class in relation to the different varieties of socialism and to nationalism and populism. The factors involved are whether an ideology exists (socialism, for instance, was not available as a codified system during the period of Chartist agitation in England), whether the ideology is perceived as effective (vide the varying appeal of fascism for the elites of the Third World before and during World War II), and whether there are mechanisms that facilitate the spread of the ideology in question in a specific society (the existence of carriers and propagandists or the incidence of international diffusion channels). Even though an initial affinity between the aims of the ideology and the goals of either the elite or the working class should exist, the ideology could have an independent effect of its own once it is institutionalized. Ideologies are not simply the rationalization of instrumental goals; once established, they become cognitive frameworks that shape attitudes and behavior.

4. Three Cases: Disraelian Britain, Bismarckian Germany, and Peronist Argentina

In order to illustrate the interplay between elite strategies and forms of political action, three cases will be briefly examined. This application of the conceptual framework to concrete situations provides some evidence for the propositions advanced in the previous chapter. These cases exemplify different patterns of correspondence between elite strategies and forms of political action. They are the extension of the franchise in Britain in the 1860s, the exclusion of the socialists in Germany in the 1880s, and the development of a labor movement under state control in Argentina in the 1940s. As was noted above, these situations do not necessarily correspond to "pure" or extreme patterns. They have been chosen because they exemplify typical relationships between elites and working classes in countries belonging to different waves of industrialization.

Britain provides the classic example of accommodation. The examination of the period leading to the enactment of the Second Reform Bill shows the interaction between an elite which was unified behind an inclusionary strategy and a mobilized working class. The emphasis put on Disraeli's views is simply due to the fact that they represent an articulate presentation of the inclusionary option by a government leader. In fact, the policy was supported by all the significant segments of the elite.

The case of Germany under Bismarck illustrates the interaction between an elite inclined toward exclusion and a working class whose form of political action was reformism, even though it was perceived as potentially revolutionary by much of the elite in a country belonging to the second wave of industrialization. The selection of this example does not imply that Bismarckian Germany was an extreme case of exclusion: repression of opposition was very light by our contemporary standards and was carried out on the basis of very precise rules. In spite of its leaders, Imperial Germany was part of liberal Europe.

Argentina under Perón, finally, is an example of the application
of a co-optive elite strategy vis-à-vis an initially acquiescent working
class in a country belonging to the third wave of industrialization.
This case was preferred over other very good illustrations, such as
Brazil under Vargas and modern Mexico, for two reasons: because
of Argentina's higher level of modernization and because this example provides a useful background for the analysis of survey data in
Part II.

Discussion of each of these well-known cases focuses on elite
strategies and forms of political action. Less attention will be given
to environmental factors and to general background characteristics.

MOBILIZATION AND THE DISRAELIAN OPTION

It is in nineteenth-century Britain that the crises of incorporation
of the classes generated by industrialization were solved through accommodation for the first time. Both the bourgeoisie and the working class were included in the political system as a result of an
exchange of the acceptance of independent participation for the
granting of legitimacy. This process reflected the ability of established elites, whose composition was changing in the meantime, to
adapt to social change rather than to resist it.

In a well-known sequence, accommodation was reached first between the agrarian aristocracy and the new bourgeoisie. The relation
of forces within the elite changed over time, and the bourgeoisie
gradually became the hegemonic sector. On the other hand, the systematic extension of civil, political, and social rights reached the
working class, which was granted participation as an independent
political force before exclusion could lead to the institutionalization
of opposition to the social order.[1] The milestones of this process were
the reform acts of 1862, 1867, and 1884, which gradually extended
the franchise. Trade union rights were recognized through several
pieces of legislation, among them the Trade Union Act of 1871,
which legitimized unions, and the Protection of Property Act of
1875, in which peaceful picketing was expressly legalized. Finally,
labor legislation enacted after 1867, such as the factory acts of 1874
and 1875 as well as several other acts also approved in the early seventies, constituted a significant aspect of the inclusionary strategy.

Strategies and Forms of Political Action

It is particularly interesting to look at the period leading to the
Second Reform Act of 1867, which was regarded by contemporaries

as the critical point in the process of democratization—a "leap in the dark"—and especially to the role played by the Conservative Party, which was assumed to represent traditional agrarian interests, and its leader, Disraeli.

The issue of the extension of the franchise to the working class had been at the center of the British political agenda since the 1830s. Both universal manhood suffrage and vote by ballot had been the main Chartist demands in the thirties and forties, and electoral reform had been the focus of working-class and radical mobilization ever since. In 1865, the working class–based Reform League was established, and large-scale agitation, triggered in part by unemployment and cholera, took place in 1866 and 1867. A vivid description of the situation is offered by Briggs:

> In July, 1866 there were riots and disturbances in London
> . . . the railings of Hyde Park were torn down . . . and Life
> Guards had to be summoned to the assistance of the police.
> . . . Winter brought no relief. To add to the distress, cholera,
> the regular harbinger of political excitement, made another of
> its dramatic reappearances, and fenian disturbances . . . created
> additional alarm. The deteriorating social and economic situa-
> tion favoured a sharp spasm of political radicalism, and "the
> people" were showing as clearly as they could that the reform
> issue could be trifled with no longer.[2]

Mass demonstrations and riots took place, and within the reform movement there was talk about resorting to direct action.[3] The situation was perceived as very serious by segments of the elite who feared that, unless working-class demands were met, an upheaval might erupt. Harrison, who considers the most important factor behind electoral reform to have been the intensity of working-class agitation, notes: "In the end, all the most influential men of property and power were persuaded that they must make a substantial concession in order to break up the agitation and remove the danger that prolonged intransigence, accompanied by police violence, would cause the popular forces to assume a truly menacing character."[4]

Concern about reform, however, was not new among elite leaders. In fact, the issue had been debated in Parliament since the early fifties, and the cause was championed not only by the liberals but also, since 1859, by conservatives as well. A bipartisan consensus emerged, and reform became "the flag and shibboleth of the new nation against the old," as Blake has put it.[5] It is particularly significant that the incorporation of the working class would be favored by the conservatives, whose main base of support was the landed aristocracy. This attitude was, among the most lucid Tories, a realistic evaluation of the consequences of modernization, and it signaled a deliberate orientation toward adaptation to those consequences. In Smith's words, "It was increasingly apparent, in the generation after Waterloo, that old-fashioned Church and King Toryism must find a *modus vivendi* with the forces of the industrial age, from a head-on collision with which it could reap only disaster. It was not through a blind and uncompromising resistance to the pressures created by the advance of the manufacturing and commercial bourgeoisie and the urban proletariat that Tories could best preserve the essentials of the society they were organized to defend."[6]

This willingness was explicit in Disraeli, who became aware of three facts. The first of these was that the social order would not be threatened if the working class was incorporated into the political system, for the British proletariat was not "dangerous." In 1859 he had said: "I have no apprehension . . . that if you had manhood suffrage tomorrow the honest, brave, and good-natured people of England would resort to pillage, incendiarism, and massacre."[7] This expectation was correct, for workers were not contesting the legitimacy of the social order, in spite of their high level of mobilization and their participation in acts of violence. The working-class movement was seeking a role in the existing institutions rather than supporting their overthrow. As Briggs writes, quoting Dicey, ". . . large numbers of the working class were in no sense levellers. They looked up to their betters as to 'a sort of divine Olympus, beautiful, sacred, above all things *intelligible*.' . . . So long as social attitudes of this kind persisted, changes in the constitution would not produce the disastrous consequences their opponents suggested."[8] In the language of the times, the working class was "loyal": "Their heads were not full with the 'boundless utopia of revolutionary expectations,' and they would answer to 'good will' shown by their 'betters.'"[9] In the second place, Disraeli became aware that if the working class were to pose a threat to the social order, it would be the excluded working class, for exclusion would generate dissent and revolution. In Smith's words, "Disraeli was deeply impressed with the dangers inherent in the abandonment of the working classes to the vicissitudes of an industrial society governed by the tenets of individualism and political economy, and struck by the gulf between the 'two nations' of rich and poor which he portrayed in *Sybill*, and the restoration of social cohesion was from the first among his major political themes."[10] Third, Disraeli noticed that the inclusion of a nonrevolutionary working class and the ensuing generalization of legitimacy would in fact strengthen the social and political order. As early as 1840, he had remarked: "... a union between the Conservative Party and the Radical masses offers the only means by which we can preserve the empire. Their interests are identical; united they form the nation."[11]

Against this background the Second Reform Act was discussed. The original bill, which was introduced by the minority conservative government, proposed a limited expansion of the franchise. The original provisions are summarized by Briggs:

> The franchise in the boroughs was to be based on personal rating; all householders paying their own rates and possessing a residential qualification of two years were to be given votes. Lodgers and those rate payers who compounded their rates with their weekly rents were not to be given votes. The county franchise was to be based on a voting qualification of fifteen pounds rental. In addition, special franchises were to be introduced for special groups. . . . Dual votes were going to be conferred on those individuals who possessed special as well as property qualifications.[12]

In the debates that followed the presentation of the bill, these provisions were transformed beyond recognition. Different amendments, proposed by Gladstone, were initially rejected by the conservatives, who had, by the way, also defeated a liberal reform bill the year before. However, other amendments, which were proposed later by radical members of Parliament, were quickly accepted. The period of residential qualification was reduced, and the distinction between compounders and direct rate payers was abolished. Finally, special franchises were dropped by Disraeli. The outcome of the debate was complete household suffrage.[13]

This competition between the parties for a more radical reform bill looks paradoxical. As noted above, Harrison has argued in this connection that the enactment of the bill and the progressive widening of the franchise as the discussion proceeded were not the result of the elite's enlightenment; on the contrary, these would have been concessions, forced upon the elite by the intensity of working-class mobilization.[14] A critical event convincing the elite that it should yield would have been the mass demonstration in Hyde Park, which took place while the bill was under consideration, in spite of the government's prohibition.[15]

When it was clear that the Reform League would go ahead with the preparations for the banned meeting, troops were brought into

London, and special constables were recruited.[16] The government did not dare to enforce the prohibition when more than 100,000 workers marched into the park. Harrison's description of the meeting conveys the degree of radicalism of the working class:

> At about 6:00 p.m. [on May 6, 1867], the Clarkenwell Branch of the Reform League appeared at the gates of the Park carrying a red flag surmounted with a cap of liberty. Half an hour later there were between 100,000 and 150,000 people in the Park. The leaders of the League entered to the sound of great cheering and proceeded to address the crowd from no less than ten separate platforms. . . . From one platform the call was given for a great national convention to prepare a Reform Bill. If their demands were rejected 300,000 men should be brought into London from the North and no man return until either the Commons passed the bill or "until England has found its new Cromwell to turn out the men who had misrepresented the people in St. Stephens."[17]

This meeting was interpreted by all the political actors as a test of the relation of forces, and, needless to say, the humiliation of the government was complete. Harrison's interpretation, however, is not shared by other scholars, who have pointed to the effect of other factors. Briggs, for one, denies that either external pressures or unlimited opportunism prompted the conservatives to introduce the bill.[18] Cowling has shown that much of the debate in Parliament can be understood on the basis of short-term political considerations: the attitudes of both parties in relation to the different stipulations of the bill, as well as to proposals for redistributions, were guided by estimates of the effect of these new rules on the number of seats each party would win in the following election.[19]

Finally, even if the plausibility of Harrison's argument is accepted, the fact remains that inclusion was not the only strategy available to the elite and that both parties preferred compromise over confrontation with the working class. The elite perceived that the form of political action of the labor movement was what I call mobilization, i.e., radicalism that was not correlated with a high level of dissent. This combination made inclusion possible.

The implementation of an inclusionary strategy would be, in Gladstone's words, a gesture of "good will" reinforcing "self-help" orientations toward social mobility among the workers[20] and thus strengthening the social order. As for the role of the conservatives, it is important to note that they not only agreed with the liberals on the need for an inclusionary strategy, but also that they took the initiative at a critical point in the process of incorporation. This does not mean that the Tory Democracy argument, according to which the Second Reform Act is part of the implementation of a Disraelian grand design, is correct.[21]

Environmental Factors

We have seen, therefore, that the inclusionary strategy of the British elite was made possible by the specific form of political action that the working class had at that time, but it was also facilitated by environmental factors. In the first place, as far as other classes and strata are concerned, the fact that the middle class had already been incorporated into the political system through accommodation was obviously of central importance, and it provided a successful model for the resolution of the conflict.

Second, the role of systemic resources as constraints and opportunities is clear. Thus, redistribution of income was made possible by the availability of a surplus for that purpose: per capita real income quadrupled in Britain during the nineteenth century.[22] As far as wages are concerned, there are conflicting interpretations of their evolution during the first half of the century, but the picture after 1860 is unambiguous. Real wages increased by 40 percent from 1862 to 1875, sagged during the depression, and climbed again in the eighties. In 1900, real wages were 84 percent higher than in 1850.[23] The sharp decline of the infant mortality rate and changes in the pattern of consumption during the same period also indicate the improvement in the standard of living of the working class.[24]

With respect to the coercive apparatus, Harrison's argument suggests the possibility that available coercive resources would have been inadequate to support an exclusionary policy vis-à-vis the working class. This would have been, obviously, a short-term constraint only. As far as cultural factors are concerned, finally, it is redundant to state that the political culture that was being institutionalized in Britain at that time produced an affinity with accommodation and that the general tenets of liberal ideology, as well as working-class religious beliefs, also contributed toward shaping the outcome of the process of incorporation. The relatively low level of articulation and diffusion of Marxist and other socialist ideologies in the period was also a relevant factor.

In summary, the context in which accommodation arose in Britain was characterized by a "fused" elite, in which the bourgeoisie was becoming hegemonic, and a working class which, in spite of its radicalism, had a low level of dissent. The stability of accommodation was made possible by continued economic growth, and other environmental factors also contributed to the generation and institutionalization of the outcome. The long-term consequence of the incorporation of the working class through accommodation, finally, was the generation of a legitimate regime whose ability to manage internal conflict has been relatively high.

REFORMISM AND THE BISMARCKIAN OPTION

The development of Germany is a typical instance of affinity between late industrialization and exclusion. The fact that the unification of Germany was carried out under Prussian leadership had two consequences for the process of incorporation of the classes generated by industrialization. The first effect was that, whatever the constitutional facade, the political regime would be traditional bureaucratic absolutism. The second consequence was that the interests of the socially backward and economically inefficient Junkers would have paramount influence on government policies. The "marriage of rye and iron," a classic case of syncratic development, was accepted by the weak bourgeoisie. The substance of the agreement was that the industrialization of Germany would be carried out in such a way that the Junker interest would be protected and that the political hegemony of the Junkers would not be challeged. The effects were, for the economy, development based on agrarian tariffs and the expansion of heavy industries (including military) and, for the polity, the preservation of authoritarianism.[25] The German bourgeoisie preferred to become a junior partner of the anticapitalist and antidemocratic landed elite rather than to head a proindustry and liberal coalition that would contest Junker hegemony. A factor contributing to this choice was the fear of a socialist working class.

Once the crisis of incorporation of the bourgeoisie was "solved" in this manner, the working class faced an exclusionary alliance of the superordinate classes. The elite strategy was basically exclusionary, even though the German empire was not an extreme example of the application of coercion vis-à-vis the working class, and elite policies included significant welfare aspects. In order to illustrate the counterpoint between strategies and the forms of political action, it is interesting to look at the Bismarckian period and particularly at the characteristics and consequences of the antisocialist laws that were in force from 1878 to 1890.

Strategies and Forms of Political Action

In the early empire, the working class was viewed by the elite as a dangerous segment of society whose exclusion from the political system seemed to be the only reasonable course of action. This was the predominant evaluation even before the Social Democratic Party emerged as a major political force. The Junkers' image of the German proletariat has been vividly summarized by Lidtke: "Encumbered with archaic values and ancient arrogance, many Junkers viewed the members of the 'fourth estate' as the unfortunate by-product of an undesirable industrial capitalism. Given their social values and their traditional eminence, the Junkers found it difficult to see by what means the fourth estate could be integrated into German society."[26]

As for the bourgeoisie, it preferred to join the Junkers in a superordinate alliance in which the bourgeois interest would not be maximized rather than to bid for hegemony and risk opening Pandora's box: "With the memory of 1848 still fresh in their minds, the bourgeois liberals drew back from unleashing the full force of the radical elements in German society."[27]

This attitude, however, was not entirely determined by the internal structural factors. The Paris Commune, which took place when Germany had become a unified nation, contributed in creating among possessing classes in Europe the fear that a proletarian revolution was not only possible but also imminent. The millenarian socialist rhetoric about the significance of the Commune was taken very seriously by the German elite. We can only imagine the bourgeois and Junker reaction to statements such as the one made by Bebel in the north German Reichstag: "And though Paris [i.e., the Commune] is suppressed at the moment, I would like to remind you that the battle in Paris is merely a small skirmish of outposts, that the decisive events are still to come, and that within a few decades the battle cry of the Paris proletariat—'War on the palaces, peace for the huts, down with misery and idleness'—will be the battle cry of the whole European proletariat."[28]

The identification of the Social Democrats with the Communards was one of the central rhetorical resources that Bismarck used in the Reichstag in 1878. By manipulating the emotional connotation that the ghost of the Commune had for German superordinate classes, he presented the suppression of the socialists as an act of self-defense.[29]

Bismarck perceived the Socialist Party as a fierce subversive organization. The support of the immediate interests of the workers by the socialists was seen by him as a diversionary tactic that the party used in order to hide its true aims. His views are presented by Busch, the chancellor's biographer and apologist, in the following terms: "The Social Democrats of Liebknecht's party did not care about ameliorating the working man's lot, but about destroying the ruling and proprietary classes with fire and sword. Above all, they were Nihilists, and therefore it became necessary to put them down, in sheer defense of the State and of society at large."[30]

This definition of the working class and the Socialist Party as a threat rendered accommodation impossible. The outcome of democratization, Bismarck feared, would be revolution and, eventually, a military dictatorship. Roth writes: "He hoped that a strong authoritarian system could indefinitely prevent the revolutionary potential from becoming active; he considered it much too dangerous to make concessions to the masses, trying to integrate them into the political process. . . . To Bismarck every step in the direction of genuine mass participation in politics meant a strengthening of the revolutionary force which would first produce chaos and then Caesarist dictatorship."[31] Bismarck was, however, aware that traditional absolutism was not viable. According to Rosenberg, ". . . Bismarck considered it to be . . . essential that the old Prussian aristocracy should adapt itself to the new order. The Junker must learn that the German Empire could not be governed by the same methods that were employed in the working of an estate to the East of the Elbe."[32] In Taylor's words, "Bismarck recognized that the Junkers could survive only by putting themselves at the head of national Germany."[33] The "solution" was a compromise with the bourgeoisie to exclude the working class in the context of an authoritarian regime based on low participation and the rule of (authoritarian) law.[34] Taylor's formula is fitting: the terms of the agreement were that military power would remain in the hands of the Junkers, economic power would gradually be wielded by the bourgeoisie, and the power of the state would safely be held by Bismarck himself.[35] As for the working class and the Socialist Party, repression would be the lot reserved to them. The compromise between the Junkers and the bourgeoisie would permit the attainment of "national unity" and would at the same time "raise a strong bulwark against the 'Red' revolution"[36] through the preservation of unequal suffrage—the three-class system—and the antisocialist laws.

Bismarck's reasons for wanting to crush the Social Democrats were, however, complex. Besides the basic inconsistency between socialist values and the institutions of authoritarian Germany, there was also, as Lidtke has remarked, a desire to use the antisocialist issue in order to weaken the liberals, whose liberalism was not only political but also economic: "The economic crash of 1873 and the continuous slump in the subsequent years had created serious doubts among many Germans about the practicality of economic liberalism."[37] Pushed by Junkers and industrialists, Bismarck was seeking to pass protective tariffs. And the introduction of antisocialist proposals would allow him to "confront the free traders on an issue of patriotism and the defense of German society, while at the same time seeking to weaken them politically to clear the way for tariff legislation."[38]

Even though the elite strategy under Bismarck was primarily exclusionary, it also contained a secondary co-optive aspect that was manifested in the attempt to implement preventive modernization through the enactment of welfare legislation. The focal point of exclusion was the antisocialist laws. Prompted by two attempts on the emperor's life—which had not been carried out by party members—Bismarck introduced legislation "against the publicly dangerous endeavors of social democracy." This legislation was passed in 1878, and the laws were in force until 1890. They prohibited all societies "which aim at the overthrow of the existing political or social order through social-democratic, socialistic, or communistic endeavors."[39] Meetings expressing aims of this type were to be dissolved, and socialist publications were to be banned.

The law was quickly implemented. Grebing notes that ". . . the organizations of the party were disbanded, nearly all its papers banned, and an estimated number of 1,500 persons sentenced to terms of imprisonment and hard labor. Nine hundred persons were expelled, and many people were forced to emigrate."[40] As for the significance of these figures, the size of the party and of its sphere of influence can be estimated on the basis of the 1877 election. In that year, the party polled nearly half a million votes, or 9 percent of the total. The proportion of leaders or active members who were jailed or sent into exile was, however, high. Furthermore, the suppression of the socialist press was widespread: within eight months after the law was passed, 127 periodical publications and 278 nonperiodical ones had been banned.[41]

Even though the party was persecuted, however, the law did not prevent individual Social Democrats from running for office, and the party representation in the Reichstag was not only maintained but increased in size. Bismarck tried to close this loophole, but he was unable to get a parliamentary majority. In fact, he was even willing to disenfranchise the Social Democrats. He declared that ". . . if the law is to be effective, then it is impossible in the long run to allow any citizen legally proved a Socialist to retain the suffrage, the right to run for office, and the enjoyment of the privileges of a member of the Reichstag."[42]

The law was also applied to labor organizations. Socialist trade unions were immediately abolished. Lidtke notes that a "faint suspicion that Social Democrats were associated with a trade union was sufficient reason for its suppression."[43] Nonsocialist unions, however, were permitted. And labor organizations under socialist leadership reemerged in the eighties, even though their political activities were limited by the threat of dissolution.[44] Nonpolitical associations were also affected by repression: "Educational societies, glee clubs, entertainment clubs, mutual welfare societies, consumers' cooperatives—none was exempt of harassment if the police had the slightest suspicion of socialist affiliation."[45]

In summary, through the application of limited coercion, life was made miserable for several thousands of party militants. The law failed, however, to achieve its purpose: not only did the Social Democratic Party survive, but its organization was strengthened and its character as the institutional center of social dissent was solidified.

Before considering the objective consequences of exclusion, it will be useful to make some reference to the other aspect of Bismarckian policies, namely welfare legislation. It is possible that Bismarck's interest in social welfare was genuine, perhaps a reflection of precapitalist "noblesse oblige" values. His championing of social security and other protective measures, however, was directly related to the antisocialist campaign. He expected that Social Democratic influence among the working class could be obliterated through a combination of coercion and "state socialism."

The system of social insurance initiated by Bismarck in 1881 was the first in the world. And accident and health insurance, as well as old-age pensions, were established by legislation introduced from 1883 to 1889. The practical significance of these measures, however, was very limited. Old-age pensions, for instance, "were payable only after the seventieth year, an age relatively few people reached in this period of low life expectancy."[46] Furthermore, Bismarck resisted social reform in those areas not directly related to the ability to work. He opposed measures such as factory inspections, limitations on the length of the work day, and the establishment of minimum wages, i.e., all the reforms that would later be supported by William II. Bismarckian reform, finally, cost the German state nothing. As A. J. P. Taylor has remarked, "Bismarck's method was peculiarly ingenious: he consoled the German workers for their absence of liberty partly by providing security at the expense of the employer, more by making them provide security for themselves out of their own pocket."[47]

This legislation was part and parcel of the antisocialist offensive. "Of course, Bismarck did not promote social reform out of love for the German workers," Taylor writes. "Sympathy and affection had never been his strong points. His object was to make the workers less discontented, or, to use a harsher phrase, more subservient."[48] Quite simplistically, he expected that a modest investment in welfare, coupled with the antisocialist laws, would suffice in order to detach the working class from the Social Democratic Party and thus avoid a revolution. In fact, he was willing to make even greater sacrifices. He told Busch that, as his "last trump," he contemplated raising taxes on tobacco and liquor: "If the result [will] enable us to secure the future of our operatives . . . the money will be well invested, for by spending it thus we may avert a social revolution which may break out fifty years hence, or ten, and which however short a time it [may] last, will assuredly swallow up infinitely larger sums than those we now propose to spend."[49]

It is interesting to note that, even though these reforms do not qualify as co-optation according to my definition of that term—they did not involve the organizational control of a participant working class by the elite or by the state—Bismarck seems to have envisaged, as his ultimate goal, the constitution of a corporatist state: "Bismarck wanted to make the workers feel more dependent on the state, and therefore on him. Ultimately he wanted to put the politicians out of business. He talked of ending the representation of individual voters and of substituting for it 'corporative associations,' based on the insurance system."[50]

Social reform was not more successful than repression in arresting the growth of the Socialist Party. This was due in part to the workers' ideological rejection of the state and in part to the very limited practical impact of these laws on their daily life. In Holborn's terms, "In their eyes a government that discriminated against the working class through the anti-socialist law could not be credited with humane designs in offering the insurance laws. The practical value of these laws could only appear after they had been operative for a number of years. Moreover the laws did not deal with those problems that were central to the workers in their wretched circumstances. More than anything else they wanted improved working conditions and higher wages."[51]

Let us look now at the consequences of persecution for the party itself. The growth of the socialist vote was spectacular. Socialist candidates polled 7.5 percent of the vote in 1878 and 6 percent in

1881, but their share increased thereafter with minor fluctuations, up to the point in which the party became the largest political force in Germany. In 1890, the last year in which the antisocialist law was effective, its candidates obtained almost 20 percent of the vote.[52] To a large extent, the growth of the party was a consequence of exclusion. In Taylor's assessment, "the Social Democratic party had been little more than a sect until the passing of the anti-socialist law, then every working man regarded himself as persecuted and was not to be bought off by insurance against accidents."[53]

The party organization strengthened during the period of persecution. As Holborn writes, "in contrast to the old parties, it was not a mere contraption for winning elections. . . . Its function was the infusion of communal ideas into its members, something neither state nor church was capable of doing any longer. The party became a state within the state."[54] Local units arose throughout the country, and "a proliferating network of political, economic, and cultural organizations"[55] appeared at the surface. A party organ was published in Zurich and smuggled into Germany by an illegal distribution network, the Red Postal Service, which delivered the newspaper to over one hundred localities.[56] The result was the gradual development of a socialist subculture. In Roth's words, "the labor movement came to offer to masses of workers a way of life which was significantly different from that of other groups, especially those explicitly supporting the prevailing political and social system."[57]

Marxist ideology, finally, became solidly entrenched in the party during the period of persecution. If the Gotha program of 1875, which was adopted when the different socialist groups merged into a unified party, cannot be properly considered Marxist—vide Marx's devastating critique—the Erfurt program of 1891 definitely was, as Engels himself attested. The turning point in this process was the St. Gall Congress of 1887 in which the Marxist leadership under Bebel achieved full control of the party.

In order to evaluate the consequences of the institutionalization of the determinist and evolutionist variety of Marxism that was propagated by the party leaders, it is important not to dismiss this ideology as innocuous "reformism." Roth states that the reformist aspects were prominent, at least in part, because "it became tactically relevant for the party leadership during the anti-socialist legislation . . . the party had to abandon, in popular agitation, its self-identification as a revolutionary body and to emphasize its character as a parliamentary reform party."[58] Roth has also pointed out that the apparent paradox of the coexistence of a revolutionary ideology and a moderate practice becomes understandable when one looks at the combination of coercion and permissiveness that prevailed in Imperial Germany. On the one hand, the existence of a parliamentary outlet generated incentives for moderation; on the other, the repressive nature of the German state contributed toward shaping the leaders' deterministic view of social development, "which seemed to point a way out by offering 'scientific' proof that the contemporary society was . . . doomed to destruction, leaving the proletariat to become the founder of a millennium."[59]

This combination of dissent and compliance that I am calling reformism was an effective weapon. It was the moderation of the party which limited the intensity of coercion, thus permitting the organization and propaganda to develop. The consequence was, of course, the socialization of the rank and file, and of a large segment of the working class, into Marxist ideology. This is how forms of political action became ideologically oriented action, and a stable value cleavage was generated in German society. Whatever the degree of "vulgarity" of the brand of Marxism that was propagated by the party, it included the basic tenets of anticapitalist ideology. The concept of exploitation—i.e., the idea that, in Otto Bauer's words, "the wealth of the propertied classes derives from . . . the unpaid labor of the working class"[60]—was a central component of that ideology. Beyond its surface moderation, then, the Social Democratic Party became an effective engine of value cleavage. The combination of low radicalism and high dissent generated a revolutionary potential that later could be activated by changes in environmental factors.

Environmental Factors

The fact that neither the peasantry, which was under Junker hegemony, nor the urban middle classes were allied to the working class was a very significant element in the relation of forces that led to exclusion. There existed, however, a small segment of the middle classes whose contribution to the organization of the party and the diffusion of Marxist ideology was crucial: the socialist intelligentsia.

The configuration of systemic resources also contributed to the exclusionary outcome. In the first place, it is doubtful that a central precondition for accommodation, i.e., the availability of a surplus for redistribution, was present. During the period under analysis, the German economy was expanding rapidly, but real wages did not increase significantly. They dropped from 1875 to 1881 and then rose slowly, and in 1887 real wages were only 2 percent higher than in 1875.[61] This pattern suggests that the inclusion of a potentially militant working class would have been regarded by the elite as inconsistent with rapid accumulation of capital. Second, the fact that a centralized bureaucratic and coercive apparatus existed was another factor that made exclusion possible. Cultural factors, finally, were also significant. Traditional authoritarianism was undoubtedly one of the independent determinants of the strategy of the elite, and it perhaps contributed as well to the organizational efficiency of the socialists. The availability of a fully developed Marxist ideology and of a group of effective carriers and propagandists made possible, of course, the generation of value cleavage in German society. Therefore, environmental factors had in Germany an effect opposite to that in Britain: these factors contributed in Disraelian England toward accommodation, and in Germany they were conducive to exclusion.

This outcome in Bismarckian Germany resulted from the interaction between a fragmented and thus Bonapartist-prone elite, in which the bourgeoisie was not hegemonic, and a reformist working class, as well as from the specific configuration of environmental factors. The stability of the regime rested mainly on coercion, for the attempt to legitimize the social order through the application of positive controls—the protective and welfare legislation—failed. The long-term consequence of exclusion, finally, was the crystallization of value cleavage in German society.

ACQUIESCENCE AND THE PERONIST OPTION

The dynamics of the Peronist regime in Argentina is a classic illustration of the shortcomings of corporatism as a solution to the crisis of incorporation of the working class. A discussion of the interaction between co-optive elite strategy and a labor movement whose form of political action was what I have called acquiescence, set against a background of environmental factors which did not facilitate the institutionalization of co-optation, will reveal the intrinsic pull of corporatism toward polarization and exclusion. It will be useful to begin the discussion with some general references to the modernization of Argentina.[62] This will also provide a background for the analysis of the data in Part II.

The economic and social development of Argentina from the middle of the nineteenth century to 1930 resembled, in some aspects, the evolution of the "open spaces" or "lands of recent settlement," such as Australia or Canada. The economy was geared toward trade with Britain, and although agricultural production was controlled by the domestic elite, transportation and packing facilities were developed by foreign capital. As in these other cases, manpower was supplied by mass European immigration.

The area that later became Argentina was a peripheral segment of the Spanish Empire, both in terms of its economic significance and of the size of its population. The creole population which existed before mass immigration was small and concentrated in the interior, the part of the country that was less suited for labor-extensive agriculture. Argentina developed, therefore, unevenly: the modern center was directly linked to the European economy and inhabited mostly by European immigrants; the traditional periphery, whose economy was labor-intensive agriculture, either linked to the internal market or subsistence production, was inhabited mostly by Spanish and mestizo populations. Much of the periphery was socially traditionalized as a consequence of the growth of the center. Imported European manufactures displaced local handicrafts, and market-oriented areas reverted to subsistence farming.

Besides this internal discontinuity, there were three other important differences between Argentina and lands of recent settlement. In the first place, land, the most important economic and political resource, was monopolized by the elite, so a large middle class of independent farmers did not develop: most European immigrants stayed in the cities. This was the reason for the early high rate of urbanization. Second, the relative impact of immigration was different from that in open spaces. The ratio of immigrants to the preexisting population was very high—higher than in the United States, as Germani has pointed out[63]—and the composition of the immigrant pool was also different. Most immigrants were of southern European origin and thus were carriers of cultures different from those of most immigrants settling in open spaces. Finally, the Argentine political system differed from the pattern found in the areas of recent settlement. Even though Argentina was, between the 1860s and 1930, a relatively stable liberal democracy, the landed elite was reluctant to include into the political system the new classes and strata that were generated by the economic and social transformation of the country. The struggle for universal and secret manhood ballot, which was led by the middle-class Radical Party, was protracted, in spite of the fact that the "universality" of electoral reform would be very relative due to the fact that foreigners, who made up most of the "modern" classes, did not vote.[64] Universal suffrage was finally granted in 1912, and the following election was won by the radicals.

Prior to 1930, the foreign origin of a large proportion of the working class contributed toward diminishing the political impact of the anti−status quo ideology of the labor movement. Even though it was largely reformist and its rate of unionization was low, in comparison with the post-1945 period, the labor movement was the carrier of anarchist and socialist, and later communist, traditions. The Socialist Party, which was founded in the late nineteenth century, was a significant political force in the modern sector of Argentina prior to Peronism; this party was represented in Congress since the beginning of the century. In 1930, socialists polled 8 percent of the vote at the national level, but the percentage in the city of Buenos Aires, the industrial center of the country, was 28 percent.

The pattern of economic and political development of Argentina that prevailed during the period of so-called "externally led growth" came to an end with the depression. Liberal democracy and European immigration ended altogether with the expansion of the export economy. The evolution of the country after 1930 has been radically different. It has been characterized by inefficient industrialization—import substitution developed as a consequence of the automatic protection generated first by the depression and the war, and then by populist governments—and an alternation of unstable authoritarian and corporatist regimes.

The rapid development of light and intermediate manufactures resulted in the generation of new sectors in the bourgeoisie and the working class. The new bourgeoisie was mostly of immigrant origin, and much of it was the product of upward mobility from the working and lower middle classes. The interests of these new industrialists were different from those of the landed elite and the preexisting bourgeoisie—much of which was engaged in activities that were a forward linkage of agriculture: their relative inefficiency made them dependent on protection, and their need for massive foreign inputs made them consumers of the surplus generated by agriculture.

The new working class, on the other hand, was generated by migration from the traditional periphery. In a few years, most of the "old" European working class in the center had disappeared—via upward mobility—and was replaced by recent migrants, many of whom had participated in different types of precapitalist social relations as landless laborers, sharecroppers, and independent peasants. Germani has estimated that, in 1947, migrants made up 73 percent of the working class in greater Buenos Aires and that most of them had arrived after 1938.[65]

The political system faced the problem of integrating these two classes. Peronism was the movement through which an attempt at inclusion and value generalization took place. Even though co-optation was the dominant elite strategy, exclusionary aspects were salient as well. In the following pages, Peronist policies toward the working class are briefly discussed.

Strategies and Forms of Political Action

Up to 1943, when the right-wing military coup from which Peronism sprang took place, neither the existing trade unions nor the traditional left had been successful in influencing the "new" working class. This inability was not only the result of coercion, which had been uninterruptedly applied since 1930, but also of the cultural gulf that separated the old Marxist and anarchist organizations from the recent migrants. Perón was aware of this situation, but he was at any rate still obsessed by the "danger" that the existence of an available mass, as well as the "old" labor movement, posed for the social order. He was perceptive enough, however, to realize that if the working class could conceivably provide a mass base for socialists or communists, this class was also available for corporatist inclusion. Further, his policies suggest that he was aware that, for this goal to be achieved, both coercion and economic rewards would be needed, and that the organizational control of the working class by the state was the key mechanism that should be employed. Even though Perón's words were not the best indicator of his underlying purposes, the following statements, made when he was secretary of labor, look like a programmatic foundation for subsequent policies:

> The working masses, which have not been organized, represent a dangerous panorama, since the inorganic mass is unquestionably the most dangerous one. . . . Modern experience demonstrates that the best organized working masses are . . . those who can best be guided and led in all respects. The absence of a well-determined social policy has produced this amorphous mass in our country.[66]

> We have defended the unity and harmonization (*compenetración*) of purposes among employers, workers and the State as the only means to combat the true social enemies, which are represented by false politics, alien ideologies . . . , false apostles who penetrate the labor movement in order to thrive on deceit and betrayal of the masses, and the hidden, disturbing forces from the international political field.[67]

In order for the radicalization of the masses to be prevented, their organization under government control, as well as the granting of economic rewards, should be the "insurance," while coercion should be available as a "reinsurance":

> In order to avoid that the masses who have received the neces-
> sary and logical [amount of] social justice do not go beyond
> that level in their claims, the first remedy would be the organi-
> zation of these masses. . . . This would be the insurance. . . .
> Still, the State would organize the reinsurance, which is the
> authority necessary to keep people in their places . . . because
> the State has the instrument that, if necessary, would make
> things fit (*en quicio*) through force, and would not allow them
> to overflow.[68]

The coercive aspect of this strategy was prevalent in the beginning, right after the military coup, but was much less salient later
once positive controls were successfully implemented. During the
military regime of 1943–1946, one of the two CGT's (trade union
federations, Confederación General del Trabajo) was banned, and
many unions were "intervened," i.e., seized by the government.
Leftist union leaders and political militants were jailed, and strikes
were suppressed.[69]

Even though significant elements of coercion persisted throughout the constitutional administrations of 1946–1955, there was
more pluralism in Argentina under the Peronist regime than in most
military governments after 1930. Competitive elections were held,
opposition parties could function, and there was limited freedom of
the press. But civil and political freedoms were restricted. Opposition party leaders were jailed, and many of them went into exile.
There were thousands of political prisoners, and the use of torture
by the police was widespread. Some opposition newspapers were
taken over by the government, and freedom of speech was hampered
by the "contempt law"—*ley de desacato*—which made it a crime to
"offend the dignity" of public officials, "whether the statement refers directly to the person or by allusion to him or the government
organization of which he forms part."[70] Pluralism was also limited
by the laws against "treason," sabotage, and espionage as well as by
other pieces of legislation. As far as the labor movement is concerned, opposition trade unionists were persecuted, and strikes not
supported by the government were declared illegal and subsequently
repressed.[71]

These coercive aspects were, however, a secondary aspect of
Perón's policy—just the "reinsurance"—for co-optation depends

mostly on positive controls. The most salient of these controls were the granting of protective legislation and redistribution of income.

In the first place, protective and welfare legislation of different types was enacted: restrictions were placed on the employers' ability to dismiss workers; severance compensation to be paid by the employers, was established; the stability of union officials was protected; the eight-hour day, which was prevalent already, was generalized to all occupations; limitations on the work of women and children were imposed; paid vacations were made mandatory; the social security system was expanded; and health insurance was established for many occupations.

Second, the real income of the working class increased steadily. The most spectacular provision was the decree of December 1945, which required all businesses to pay their employees not only a minimum wage but also a thirteenth-month bonus. The following figures give an idea of the redistribution of income that took place: average urban real wages increased from a base of 100 in 1943 to 112 in 1946—when Perón was elected president—to 140 in 1947, and to a peak of 181 in 1949. In 1955, when the regime was overthrown, the index was still 163. GNP per capita, on the other hand, increased more modestly. It rose sharply between 1943 and 1947—30 percent—but declined afterwards, and in 1955 was only 16 percent higher than in 1943.[72]

Finally, support for the government among the most underprivileged strata of the population was enhanced by the well-publicized charitable activities of the Eva Perón Foundation, which erected schools and hospitals and made direct gifts to poor families—these ranging from substantial contributions to such token activities as the giving of holiday food and toys.

In order to understand the effect of these rewards, the change in the composition of the working class should be remembered. Even though most pieces of labor legislation promulgated by Perón had been pursued by the preexisting labor movement for a long time, they appeared to the new members of the working class as gifts spontaneously bestowed upon them by Perón. Recent migrants, for whom the organizations, ideologies, and goals of the labor movement were totally foreign, were startled by the granting of rights and rewards for which they had not fought and of whose need they had probably not been aware. We can only imagine the psychological impact that such measures as paid vacations or the thirteenth-month bonus had on individuals who, in many cases, had never enjoyed a vacation, either paid or unpaid, or even participated in a stable wage relationship. In terms of their short-term effectiveness, these Peronist policies were a brilliant example of preventive modernization. As could be expected, these measures also generated enthusiastic support for the regime among most members of the "old" working class, trade union leaders included. It is a well established fact that the two segments of the labor movement, the old and the new, participated in the social base of Peronism.[73]

Besides economic rewards, another more subtle type of positive control should be mentioned: psychological gratification. The previously nonmobilized migrants from the periphery as well as the "old" workers experienced not only collective social mobility and political inclusion; they were also symbolically integrated into the national community. This was a central aspect of the process of value generalization that was taking place. This symbolic incorporation was, of course, salient in Peronist ideology. Workers were glorified by Peronist propaganda, Perón himself was called "the first worker," May Day became a national holiday, et cetera. But the most important factor was the emphasis on the expansion of those forms of participation whose symbolic content was high. Union leaders became not only congressmen but also ministers and diplomats; middle-class resorts were made available to the workers and first-class hotels were bought by the unions for the use of their members; and popular music was played in opera houses.

After having examined the negative and positive sanctions in Peronist policies, we may turn to their organizational infrastructure. As stated above, organizational control was the key aspect of the strategy. The establishment of a corporatist relationship between the working class and the state presupposed two processes: the organization of the "inorganic mass" and the placing of organizations under government control.

The growth of unionization from 1943 onward was impressive. According to Murmis and Portantiero, the number of organized workers jumped from 441,000 in 1941 and 528,000 in 1945 to 1.5 million in 1947—after Perón became president—and 3 million in 1951.[74] Perón himself led unionization drives and forced employers to recognize and bargain with labor organizations. The goal of placing labor organizations under government control can be discerned in the legislation regulating the structure of the labor movement. The central piece of this legislation was a Law of Professional Associations, which stated that unions, in order to represent workers, had to be expressly recognized by the government. Even though the law declared that unions could be freely established "without necessity of previous authorization, always provided their objectives are not contrary to the morality, laws and fundamental institutions of the nation," it also specified that "those organizations which do not possess *personería gremial* (trade union personality), granted by the government, cannot act as professional associations of the workers." Only organizations with "trade union personality" could "represent the interest of the workers in dealings with the employers and the state . . . participate in collective bargaining . . . participate in political activities . . . conduct their meetings and assemblies in closed halls without previous permission . . . ," et cetera. Where rival unions existed, recognition could be transferred from one union to another "even if its membership is smaller." Finally, in order to facilitate vertical control, the labor movement was hierarchically organized.[75]

Perón used these legal instruments generously. Unions whose leadership was hostile to the government were destroyed through the simple mechanism of shifting recognition to new organizations that were created under government sponsorship. A second device Perón used was to take advantage of the government control of the collective bargaining process in order to reward those leaders who were compliant and to punish those who resisted. As Germani puts it, "unions which did not demonstrate their predisposition to collaborate could obtain nothing in labor conflicts, legislation, social services, et cetera."[76]

These policies aimed at the effective control of the labor movement by the government. The actual practice of Peronism, however, was at variance with the provisions of corporatist legislation. It is true that the leaders of the CGT and of the large unions held their posts at the pleasure of the government, but the rank and file were not so easily controlled, as the several major conflicts that erupted from the late forties onward indicate.[77] In fact, the evolution of the labor movement from the forties to the seventies can be understood as a shift from acquiescence to mobilization, and it is precisely the organizational infrastructure created by Perón that transformed the increasingly independent working class into one of the central political forces in Argentine society.

Environmental Factors

In the last instance, workers' acceptance of corporatist controls depended on the ability of the regime to prevent discontent, and this in turn presupposed that the standard of living of the working class would rise, or at least would not deteriorate after the initial increase. Furthermore, it should be noted that satisfaction thresholds were bound to rise over time, as a consequence of the fading of preurban and preindustrial standards of comparison among new workers and also because of the industrial and political experience that the working class, old and new, was acquiring. Beyond these subjective factors, however, there was a limit on the ability of the regime to improve or maintain the level of wages: the relative inefficiency of the Argentine economy. Redistribution in the initial period was made possible by the postwar boom. Through taxation, exchange policies, and the nationalization of foreign trade, the regime appropriated a significant part of the surplus generated by agricultural exports and utilized these funds to subsidize import-substituting industrialization—regardless of its efficiency—and to redistribute income to the working class. In the late forties and early fifties, it became increasingly clear that the stage of expansion based on "easy" import substitution was over. As the surplus grew more slowly, the conflict between accumulation and distribution surfaced. And the Peronist coalition, based on the acceptance of a corporatist formula by an inefficient bourgeoisie and an increasingly mobilized working class, began to shatter. Therefore, a crucial systemic resource, the existence of a surplus available for redistribution, provided at different stages an opportunity and a constraint for the development of Peronism.

The role of the other two systemic resources will be considered briefly. In the first place, the existence of a centralized coercive apparatus contributed to the success of co-optation, as was noted above. But this factor also cuts both ways. The overthrow of Peronism was made possible by the imperfect control that Perón had, in the mid-fifties, of the armed forces. As for cultural factors, finally, it is possible that traditional rural authoritarianism, as well as the Catholic-Latin type of political culture, played a significant role in shaping both the co-optive strategy and the initially acquiescent response. Available belief systems also contributed to the outcome. Fascist, nationalist, and corporatist ideologies were carried and propagated by an articulate segment of the intelligentsia with good elite connections; and the availability of the working class was facilitated by the barriers to the diffusion of traditional leftist ideologies.

Finally, a reference to the political action of classes and strata other than the elite and the working class. Since there is no significant peasantry in Argentina, the most important of these was the urban middle class, most of which was anti-Peronist. This class was unable to prevent the establishment of Peronism—even though Perón won the 1946 election by a relatively narrow margin—but it provided a mass base for the regime that came to power after the 1955 coup.

Thus, Peronism, an instance of failed corporatism, illustrates the preconditions for co-optation, the prerequisites for its stability, and its long-term consequences. Peronism arose in a situation in which a fragmented elite (in which industrialists were not hegemonic) was prone to Bonapartism, and its rise was made possible by initial working-class acquiescence. Its persistence would have required continuous redistribution. Its unintended consequence, finally, was the conversion of an "inorganic" working class into a formidable political force. Peronism is an extreme instance of what in Chapter 2 was called the intrinsic weakness of corporatism. The objective outcome of the incorporation of the working class under state control was precisely the magnification of the threat that Perón wanted to reduce. When he was overthrown, the terms of the political equation had changed radically. The existence of a mobilized working class—in the context of a very unstable economy—contributed toward generating an exclusionary elite strategy. Since 1955, exclusion has been the prevailing outcome of the crisis of incorporation, with the exception of the brief Peronist interlude of 1973–1976, which reversed Marx's humorous hypothesis about what happens when tragedies are repeated in history.

CONCLUSION

This brief discussion of Victorian England, Imperial Germany, and Peronist Argentina has illustrated the interplay between elite strategies and forms of political action in the generation of the outcomes of the crisis of incorporation of the working class. The examination of these cases supports hypotheses concerning patterns of correspondence between elite strategies and forms of political action. Whenever the environmental factors that are relevant for the institutionalization of each outcome are present—the availability of a surplus for redistribution, in particular, seems to be crucial—the interaction between mobilization and an inclusionary strategy seems to lead to accommodation. The same can be stated about reformism and an exclusionary strategy in relation to exclusion—even though polarization is also a likely outcome in that case—and about acquiescence and a co-optive strategy in relation to corporatism.

The discussion of these three cases has also made it clear that the prerequisites for the stability of each type of outcome are different. While the accommodation agreement, i.e., the exchange of pluralism for legitimacy, seems to have a high level of stability, the other two outcomes are intrinsically fragile. Exclusion seems incapable of generating legitimacy unless a totalitarian organization emerges, so the continuity of this outcome is likely to depend on sheer coercion. The maintenance of legitimacy in co-optation, finally, presupposes the continuous availability of a surplus for redistribution, for otherwise co-optation will tend to shift toward polarization and exclusion due to the likely mobilization of the working class. The long-term consequences of the establishment of each outcome are, therefore, very different: while accommodation tends to preserve and increase pluralism and legitimacy, exclusion is likely to lead to a deepening of cleavages, thus reducing the likelihood of the achievement of a legitimate political formula. Co-optation is, finally, a paternalistic arrangement that merely puts off the solution of "the social question." Thus, elite strategies and forms of political action are only partially determined by each other and by environmental factors. Some major structural characteristics of the society are associated with the establishment of the different outcomes, and some of these correlates are explored in the next chapter.

5. Structural Correlates of Outcomes

In this chapter, some very tentative generalizations about the structural correlates of outcomes will be discussed.[1]

When the emergence and consolidation of the different outcomes are examined, a pattern stands out: there is a covariation between the frequency of occurrence of the different patterns and the timing of industrialization. When a closer look is taken, it seems that two correlates of the timing of industrialization—namely, degree of dualism and degree of alienation of control of economic resources—are associated with elite strategies, forms of political action, and some of the environmental factors. These three variables, timing of industrialization, dualism, and alienation of control, are intercorrelated even though their association is not perfect—Scandinavian countries, for instance, are nondualistic second-wave industrializers—but each of them seems to contribute toward the establishment of the different outcomes.

"Timing of industrialization" refers to the relative order of entry into the industrial world. As for "dualism," I mean the coexistence in the social structure of a significant "traditional" sector together with the "modern" capitalist sector. "Traditionality" in this context may denote either a qualitative or a quantitative discontinuity. The former type corresponds to the case in which precapitalist social relations persist, and the latter is a productivity differential within the capitalist sector. Thus, dualism is used here in a purely descriptive sense in order to denote a heterogeneous social structure. The second structural correlate of timing of industrialization, alienation of control of economic resources, is a central aspect of imperialism or dependency. I prefer to use that expression here, for it conveys a more specific meaning.

The covariation referred to above can be summarized as follows. Accommodation, as an outcome of the crisis of incorporation of the working class, seems to be associated with early industrialization, exclusiveness of capitalist social relations, and retention of control of the most significant economic resources by the domestic bourgeoisie (at least up to the point in social development in which the crisis of incorporation of the working class has been solved). Deviation from accommodation, on the other hand, is correlated with lateness of industrialization, a dualistic social structure, and a high level of alienation of the control of economic resources. Second-wave industrializers have been prone to polarization and exclusion, while third-wave countries seem to have an affinity with exclusion and co-optation.

The association between lateness and dualism and the "reactionary route" of capitalist development underlies Moore's comparative analysis.[2] Schmitter has written about the "elective affinity" between the corporatist-authoritarian modal path of development and delayed industrialization and external dependency,[3] and O'Donnell has linked the emergence of the Latin American regimes that he calls bureaucratic-authoritarian with the "deepening" of import substitution on the basis of the large-scale participation of multinational firms.[4] Since the outcome of the crisis of incorporation of the working class is a central component in the development of these nondemocratic patterns, the discussion of elite strategies, forms of political action, and environmental factors will be useful for the clarification of the political consequences of timing of industrialization and of its structural correlates.

TIMING OF INDUSTRIALIZATION AND OUTCOMES

In his analysis of European industrialization, Gerschenkron distinguished between early and late industrializers.[5] Hirschman extended this conceptualization to Latin America and defined a third category: the "late-late" industrializing nations.[6] If this reasoning is applied, those capitalist countries in which large-scale industrialization has so far taken place—say, countries in which the percentage of the active population in the secondary sector and the percentage of the GNP generated by manufacturing are at least 20 percent—can be grouped into three categories. The first one corresponds to early industrializers such as Britain *as well as* their offshoots, the "lands of recent settlement" in North America and Oceania. The second group is made up of the second-wave industrializers, i.e., those nations that became industrial societies in the second half of the nineteenth century and the beginning of the twentieth in competition with Britain and other early industrializers: Germany, Italy, Russia, Japan, and several other countries in Europe. The third wave of industrialization, finally, comprises those countries which made the transition into industrial society after the depression. If the manufacturing enclaves in Southeast Asia are excepted, these are mostly Latin American nations: Argentina, Uruguay, and Chile are the cases in which the process is most advanced. Other countries, such as Mexico or Brazil, which have significant manufacturing sectors even though their aggregate level of industrialization is not high, due to the existence of internal discontinuities, should also be included in this group.

The criteria specified above are not totally precise, for some countries cannot be so easily categorized. Even though in most societies industrialization occurred in spurts rather than as a continuous process, infinite gradations could be introduced. The classification is, however, useful for examining the relationship between the timing of industrialization and outcomes of the crisis of incorporation.

Contrary to optimistic expectations about the political consequences of economic development, countries of delayed industrialization have been prone to outcomes other than accommodation. Stable industrial democracies based on the exchange of pluralism for the legitimacy of capitalism have been established in early industrializers and their offshoots—and, as we will see later, also in other countries in which significant "qualitative" dualism was not present because a precapitalist landed elite did not exist or was eliminated as a central power contender. In the other countries of delayed industrialization, on the other hand, the only variety of democracy that has been stable has been the preindustrial "whig" type, which proved incapable of absorbing a high level of participation.

Second-wave industrializers have been prone to polarization and exclusion, and in many of these countries—pre-1945 Germany, Italy, Spain, and even France—modern political history is a sequence of cycles of both outcomes. Liberal democracy has been institutionalized in postwar Germany and Japan only after preindustrial antidemocratic residuals (such as landed elites) were removed through revolutions carried out by occupying powers. In all second-wave industrializers except Russia, exclusionary regimes checked the revolutionary impulses that were generated by polarization. As for co-optation, its rhetoric rather than its reality is what appeared in second-wave industrializers, at least as far as the working class was concerned.

It was in countries belonging to the third wave that the substance of co-optation emerged—many times without its rhetoric—alongside exclusion and polarization. Schmitter's hypothesis about the affinity between delayed industrialization and corporatism is supported by the evidence concerning third-wave industrializers, such as Mexico—an example of corporatism under a liberal democratic guise—and partially by the cases of Argentina and Brazil. The history of the latter two countries since industrialization is a counterpoint between co-optation and exclusion. However, other third-wave industrializers, such as Chile and perhaps Uruguay, fit a pattern similar to the one of second-wave societies. The reason is that these countries, especially Chile, generated a value cleavage, and the existence of significant working-class dissent is incompatible with corporatism, in the specific sense in which I am using this term. These apparent exceptions illustrate two preconditions for corporatism: bourgeois peripherality within the elite and working-class acquiescence. When the bourgeoisie is hegemonic, it will prefer accommodation; and when the working class is not acquiescent, the polarization-exclusion route will be followed.

It is interesting to note in this connection that the threshold for the breakdown of polarized liberal democracy is lower among third-wave industrializers than among second-wave countries. In nations of the second wave in which polarized democracies gave way to exclusionary regimes during the interwar period—Italy, Germany and Spain, as well as France—the existence of a mass militant left rendered the possibility of a revolutionary outcome to polarization credible. In these countries, the exclusionary response took place after current or past instances of widespread working-class mobilization, or even uprisings, or seizure of power by the left: extensive agitation in Italy and France, revolutionary episodes in post–World War I Germany, and Popular Front governments in Spain and France. Unstable liberal democracy is more fragile, on the other hand, in third-wave industrializers. The establishment of exclusionary regimes in countries such as Argentina, Brazil, and Uruguay in the sixties and seventies has not been the response to credible revolutionary threats, for in these cases the working class was at most mobilized. Chile, where the sequence of polarization/leftwing government/exclusionary reaction seems to be a replay of second-wave cases such as Spain a generation before, is of course another matter. In most third-wave industrializers, then, exclusionary responses have been triggered by much lower levels of polarization than in countries of the second wave.

TIMING OF INDUSTRIALIZATION, ORDER OF CRISES, AND POWER CONTENDERS

The relationship between the timing of industrialization and the probability of occurrence of the outcomes is mediated by differences in the characteristics of the contenders for power. Two of these differences that have an immediate bearing on the process of incorporation are: first, the order of crises, i.e., the order in which the two main crises of incorporation, the one related to the bourgeoisie and the other related to the working class, took place; second, differences in the relation of forces among contenders for power.

Let us consider the order of crises first. As Germani has pointed out, in the countries of early industrialization the issue of incorporating the bourgeoisie tended to precede, both in its inception and its solution, the issue of incorporating the working class.[7] Therefore, the first crisis was "solved"—and in a way that enhanced the legitimacy of the social order—before the second crisis reached its maximum level of intensity. The crisis of incorporation of the bourgeoisie did not exist, of course, in lands of recent settlement, which were born capitalist.

In countries belonging to the second wave of industrialization, on the other hand, both crises tended to be closer in time, so that the contest for power was actually a three-way conflict among agrarian elites, the industrial bourgeoisie, and the working class. Finally, in third-wave countries, the crises are even closer, but the crisis of incorporation of the working class seems to be more salient. The incorporation of the bourgeoisie might not even be a political problem in cases where the central economic resources are controlled by external actors, and therefore the domestic bourgeoisie is not an internal contender for power.

The second major difference pointed out above has to do with the relation of forces among contenders for power. This difference is especially significant at the level of superordinate classes. Three generalizations can be made in this regard. The first one has to do with dualism: the timing of industrialization is associated with the relative strength of preindustrial elites and, correspondingly, with the relative weakness of the industrial bourgeoisie. In the second place, timing of industrialization is correlated with an increasing relevance of external economic actors, which, in countries belonging to the third-wave, can become a central fraction of the elite. Finally, timing of industrialization is associated with an increasing autonomy of the state vis-à-vis superordinate groups—i.e., Bonapartism. This autonomy of the state manifests itself as a propensity toward bureaucratic monism, either civilian or military. The common consequence of these three relationships is that timing of industrialization is positively associated with an increasing peripherality of the domestic bourgeoisie.

In countries of early industrialization, entrepreneurs prevailed, early in the process, over landed aristocracies—either as a result of fusion or of confrontation—and became the most powerful ruling stratum both economically and politically. In second-wave industrializers, on the other hand, traditional agrarian elites survived as the most powerful component of the superordinate classes, retaining significant economic power and the control of the state apparatus. The industrial bourgeoisie became in these countries a minor partner of landed elites. As industralization proceeded, a gradual shift in the balance of power took place, but for a long period landed elites retained a considerable ability to protect their interests—Russia is an exception, of course, for the revolution took place when the bourgeoisie was still extremely weak. Among third-wave industrializers, finally, domestic industrialists are even more peripheral vis-à-vis traditional aristocracies, foreign capital, and the state bureaucracy, the military bureaucracy in particular. The issue of incorporating the bourgeoisie into the political system has generally been solved in most of these countries through the control of the bourgeoisie by the state, i.e., what I have called co-optation.

These differences in the characteristics of superordinate strata in the three waves of industrialization are related to the resulting elite strategies vis-à-vis the working class. After an initial stage in which exclusionary strategies prevailed in most societies, elites in countries of early industrialization have been prone to inclusion; second-wave elites have wavered between inclusion and exclusion, and most third-wave elites have tended toward exclusion or co-optation.

The choice between alternative strategies in second- and third-wave countries has depended to a large extent on the forms of political action of the working class. In second-wave industrializers, instances of exclusion have been the elite response to a working class that was either revolutionary or was perceived as such, while cases of inclusion generally reflected a relation of forces in which polarization was intense enough to make inclusion without value generalization appear less costly to the established elites than exclusion. In third-wave industrializers, finally, elites tended to implement a co-optive strategy whenever the working class was acquiescent and to resort to exclusion when the working class deviated from acquiescence.

These references bring us to the relationship between timing of industrialization and forms of political action. The evidence suggests that the revolutionary potential of the working class varies in a curvilinear manner with timing of industrialization. In countries belonging to the first wave, the working class was prone to mobilization before its inclusion into the political system. In the specific case of Britain, which was discussed above as a typical example of the interaction between inclusion and mobilization, the working class was activated in pursuing its demand for political participation, and it even engaged in violent behavior, but this radicalism was not the reflection of an underlying anti–status quo ideology. It is in countries belonging to the second wave, on the other hand, that forms of political action I call reformist were more likely to prevail. Even though the support for revolutionary ideologies was seldom actualized as revolutionary behavior, the existence of a value cleavage in these societies rendered inclusion an unlikely outcome of the crisis of incorporation. This propensity to support a revolutionary ideology was, in part, the result of the exclusionary behavior of established elites, as was shown in the discussion of the classic example of Germany, where the "marriage of rye and iron" left little room for the accommodation of the working class.

In most third-wave industrializers, finally, the working class has been prone to acquiescence and mobilization (Chile is the obvious exception). Acquiescence has been, in part, a response to the strategy of established elites who not only included the working class into the political system under government control, but also implemented a policy of preemptive modernization: in many cases, the working class was granted benefits it did not have to fight for. The example of Peronist Argentina, discussed above, illustrates the correspondence between co-optation and acquiescence and shows very well the intrinsic limitations of this type of solution to the crisis of incorporation of the working class.

Timing of industrialization is also associated with variations in characteristics of two of the systemic resources, namely economic and cultural ones. First, the existence of a surplus available for redistribution to the working class is affected by two factors in countries of late industrialization: dualism and the incidence of external factors. These two correlates of timing of industrialization will be discussed below, but their effect on the size of the surplus can be mentioned here. Dualism increases the number of contenders for power, for it means, in its pure form, that no social strata are destroyed by modernization and that most groups are fragmented. The consequence is greater competition for the utilization of the surplus, and this fact affects the size of that portion of the surplus that established elites can redistribute among industrial workers. Second, the size of the surplus is also affected by external economic actors in countries of late industrialization: trade, investment, and aid policies of external firms and governments will produce net subtractions from or additions to the surplus available for redistribution. The impact of these external actors was much less or insignificant in countries of early industrialization.

In relation to cultural factors, finally, three generalizations can be made. First, the political culture of late industrializers tends to be less conducive to accommodation than the political culture of early industrializers. This is also a manifestation of dualism. Late industrializers are likely to have the type of social structure and culture that is most resistant to both industrialization and democracy. Second, another consequence of dualism is the fragmentation of political culture. Different political traditions coexist in countries of late industrialization, and none of these is hegemonic. Third, the stock of relevant ideologies is affected by external factors. In different waves of industrialization, the different belief systems in whose framework the goals of the two main contenders for power were formulated—such as liberalism, nationalism, fascism, varieties of socialism, or populism—had different degrees of availability, prestige, and material reinforcement. A cursory inspection of intellectual history since the 1870s shows that the spectrum of relevant ideologies that competed for the provision of cognitive frameworks and models of "the good society" varied in almost every decade, both in terms of its composition and the relative influence of each ideology.

These differences in elite strategies, forms of political action, and environmental factors are reflected in the covariation between timing of industrialization and outcomes of the process of incorporation.

DUALISM AND OUTCOMES

As indicated above, the term "dualism" refers to the existence of either a qualitative or a quantitative discontinuity in the social structure. As a consequence of this discontinuity, a "traditional" and a "modern" sector coexist. The first type of discontinuity entails the failure of capitalist social relations, i.e., wage relations, to become exclusive in the primary and secondary sectors of the economy. The second type arises when a low-high productivity complex develops within a society or sector of a society which is structurally capitalist.

In countries of delayed industrialization, precapitalist social strata have tended to persist in spite of the development of capitalism. Therefore, in most third-wave industrializers, a precapitalist sector of variable size and composition remains. Many times this sector is the product of the reversion of previously developed areas toward subsistence agriculture and other traditional social relations, rather than a consequence of the lack of penetration of capitalism.

This phenomenon has been interpreted either as a transitional stage in the process of modernization, i.e., a reflection of the discontinuous character of development, or as a specific type of social structure in which precapitalist social relations are "combined" with the capitalist ones as a necessary component, rather than their being a residual or an anomaly. The first type of conceptualization can be traced to Marx, who in a famous passage hailed the establishment of British rule in India, for he expected that this process would lead to the dissolution of the particularly contumacious type of precapitalist social relations that made up the "Asiatic mode of production."[8] Lenin's analysis of Russia as a case of "uneven development" also belongs to this tradition. In this line of interpretation, dualism appears as a consequence of the weakness of the capitalist impulse and/or of the resistance of the traditional social structure.

As for the second interpretation, the earliest example can be found in Trotsky's remarks about Russia being a case of "combined development" in which modernization took place in such a way that advanced and backward forms of social life coexisted.[9] Contemporary examples are the economic literature on dualism, as well as conceptualizations such as that of Organski on "syncratic development"[10] and much of the Latin American "dependency" literature.[11] According to this interpretation, the articulation between modern and traditional sectors is explained in functional terms: the existence of precapitalist social relations would contribute to the operation of the capitalist sector. The term dualism refers, then, to the spatial consequences of accumulation and will be used here as a shorthand for "uneven and sometimes combined development." It does not imply a hypothesis of "separation" between modern and traditional sectors.

Either of the two explanations of dualism can be valid in particular cases, but neither is correct in general. The combination hypothesis is plausible in situations in which a labor-intensive capitalist sector coexists with a precapitalist one which functions as a labor reserve. Typical examples are the latifundio-minifundio complex and the coexistence of modern manufacturing and traditional handicrafts. In all the other cases, the claim of functional complementarity does not seem to be warranted. As for the weak impulse/

strong resistance hypothesis, it is partially supported by the fact that there is some association between the type of preindustrial social structure and political system that existed in a country and the probability that this country will be a latecomer to industrialization and will become a dual society. Many dualistic societies, for instance, have been generated either in second-wave centralized agrarian bureaucracies, such as Russia and Prussia—and the resistance of societies of this type to modernization is well known—or in third-wave Latin American countries in which industrialization took place under the control of landed elites, or at least under the constraints imposed by the need to protect the landed interest. In fact, Moore's analysis[12] and the copious literature on differences between Western and Eastern European feudalism suggest the possibility that the correlations referred to above between dualism and timing of industrialization, on the one hand, and dualism and the outcomes of the process of incorporation, on the other, are spurious. The propensities toward both industrialization and liberal democracy could mainly be the consequence of the type of social structure and of political system that existed in the preindustrial period.

The second form of dualism, i.e., a quantitative discontinuity within the capitalist sector, exists to some extent in all societies regardless of their level of development. The coexistence of highly productive economic units with marginal ones has been noticed in advanced and backward societies alike, and this is the source of the differentiation of industrial social classes into distinct fractions. It is in countries belonging to the third wave of industrialization, however, that this type of dualism becomes particularly intense and thus significant in relation to the outcome of the process of incorporation of the working class. In this type of country, the discontinuity between "modern" and "traditional" industrialists and workers is greater than in previous waves of industrialization. As far as the working class is concerned, differentials between fractions in terms of income and security of employment are wide. In relation to the bourgeoisie, discontinuity tends to be associated with the locus of control: the "efficient" sector of industry is likely to be controlled by multinational corporations and their domestic associates, while the marginal one is likely to be operated by the domestic bourgeoisie. The articulation between the two sectors can be interpreted on the basis of the same hypotheses referred to above, i.e., weakness of the industrialization impulse and functional complementarity. The latter interpretation would be based on the hypothesis that the inefficient sector is functional for the operation of the highly productive one by providing a labor reserve or, in cases in which the two sectors compete, by setting higher prices and therefore providing a higher rate of return for the efficient sector.

There is an association between the exclusiveness of capitalist social relations and the frequency of accommodation as a solution to the crisis of incorporation of the working class. The classical discussion of the incompatibility between the survival of a precapitalist elite and the establishment of liberal democracy was made by Engels in his treatment of the Junkers and Bismarck.[13] The argument was elaborated further by Moore.[14] Accommodation has been institutionalized in those societies in which a landed elite whose power was based on serfdom or other precapitalist social relations did not exist or was eliminated. Dualism was absent in three situations— first, in countries in which serfdom had not existed or had disappeared before industrialization (e.g., the Scandinavian countries or Britain); second, in societies in which these elites were eliminated as central powerholders during industrialization (e.g., the United States after the Civil War) or after industrialization took place (e.g., Germany and Japan in the twentieth century); third, in the "new" societies without a precapitalist past (e.g., Australia or Canada).

We can only speculate about the linkages between dualism and deviation from accommodation. Whatever the nature of dualism, i.e., whether "qualitative" or "quantitative," its consequence on the social structure is the fragmentation of both elites and subordinate classes, the working class included. As was indicated above, at the superordinate level fragmentation generates Bonapartism, i.e., the relative autonomy of the state vis-à-vis the superordinate strata. This is an old theme which underlies Marx's analysis of the second empire in France.[15] In relation to Germany, Engels argued that the absolute monarchy in Prussia was necessary in order to hold the balance between the Junkers and the bourgeoisie, and that the Bismarckian state performed the same function between the propertied classes as a whole and the working class, even though Bonapartism gradually transformed the Junkers into capitalist producers.[16]

Elites unified by Bonapartist rule tend to deviate from inclusionary strategies toward the working class and to pursue either exclusionary or co-optive policies, depending on the forms of political action of the working class and on the endowment of systemic resources. Anderson has called Latin American societies with this pattern of elite fragmentation "syncratism," and Bonapartism a "living museum": "While, in the history of the West, revolutionary experiences or secular change have sequentially eliminated various forms of power capability, contemporary Latin American politics is something of a 'living museum,' in which all the forms of political authority of the Western historical experience continue to exist and operate, interacting one with another in a pageant that seems to violate all the rules of sequence and change involved in our understanding of the growth of Western civilization."[17]

As for the impact of dualism on the forms of political action, it can be hypothesized that it is the "quantitative" type of dualism that is especially significant. It produces a heterogeneous working class, and there is a positive correlation between the fragmentation of the working class and the diversity of its forms of political action. In spite of unifying pressures produced by the same elite strategies and environmental factors, the different fractions are likely to experience dissimilar social conditions, so that their forms of political action are likely to vary. This fact is an obstacle to the spread of dissent and to the transformation of the working class into a unified political force that would be capable of what I have called ideologically oriented action.

As for the relationship between dualism and environmental factors, the fact that dualism increases the number of political forces has consequences in relation to systemic resources. In the first place, fragmentation multiplies claims on the surplus, and this increases the pressures for alternative policies. Second, the fact that fragmentation is associated with an increasing autonomy of the state apparatus also makes it likely that there will be a substantial development of coercive resources, thus rendering exclusion more feasible. Finally, in relation to cultural factors, the fragmentation of social classes and political forces implies the fragmentation of the political culture and thus increases the number of socially grounded political ideologies competing for hegemony. This situation also contributes to outcomes other than accommodation.

LOCUS OF CONTROL OF ECONOMIC RESOURCES AND OUTCOMES

The timing of industrialization is also associated with the growing internal influence, both economic and political, of external factors. In the case of the first industrializing nation, Britain, autonomy was maximized by the control of the supply of raw materials and of foreign markets by British manufacturers. Second-wave industrializers, on the other hand, had to compete for markets and raw materials with countries industrialized earlier. The incidence of external factors is highest, however, among third-wave industrializers to the extent that their industrialization was basically externally induced. Even though trade dependency or foreign investment was significant in countries belonging to prior waves, it is among third-wave countries that this power may become central, i.e., that external actors may control a larger share of economic resources—as measured by percentages of the GNP or of the active population—than the domestic bourgeoisie, or a more strategic share—a more productive sector of the economy or the sector most efficient in international terms. The immediate consequence of a high level of control of economic resources by external actors is the paradox of the possibility of capitalism without capitalists, i.e., without a domestic bourgeoisie being a significant contender for power. A peripheral bourgeoisie is unlikely to become hegemonic, in the Gramscian sense, both in relation to other superordinate classes and in relation to the subordinate ones. And an external bourgeoisie is likely to have a relationship with the internal political system different from that of a domestic one. External economic actors are likely to define their interests more narrowly, both in terms of policy areas and of time span. They will, of course, mobilize their control of economic resources in order to exert political influence, but their political activity is likely to be focused on specific policies that affect them directly, and they will probably be oriented toward the maximization of short-term interests. For this reason, an external bourgeoisie is less likely to be a contender for hegemony. Once its interests are protected, it will probably be happy to leave the hegemonic battleground to other superordinate actors, namely the landed elite and/or the Bonapartist state.

The partial control of economic resources by external actors contributes to the weakness of the domestic bourgeoisie not only directly but also indirectly, for a high level of external economic influence is also conducive to the enhancement of the autonomy of the state and, at least in the case of some third-wave countries, to the strengthening of preindustrial elites.

In principle, the increasing internal influence of external factors in late waves of industrialization seems to contribute to the increasing scope of state activity. The need for government regulation or direct intervention in productive activities was limited in countries of early industrialization, once industrialization was underway. Second-wave countries, on the other hand, faced a different situation: the need to compete with early industrializers both in domestic and foreign markets enhanced the role of the state. In the third wave, finally, industrialization would have been unthinkable without tariff protection, exchange controls, and regulation of foreign investment.

As for the effect of external factors on the strength of landed elites, it can be asserted that in third-wave industrializers the power of landed elites was enhanced by the development of export economies, especially in those cases where the export economy was based on goods that were produced by the elite itself. In these countries, landed aristocracies became the strategic actor of modernization. Argentine, Brazilian, and Uruguayan elites fitted this pattern. The effect was different in countries such as Chile and other "enclave" situations, where the export sector was directly operated by external actors. In those cases, even though landed elites retained control of the state apparatus after the incorporation into world markets, their power cannot be compared to that of landed elites who were both economically and politically central, as was the case in the countries mentioned above.

Systemic resources, finally, are also affected by the incidence of external actors in countries of the third wave. Just as the size of the surplus internally available, either for redistribution or for accumulation, can be affected by international movements of surplus, the internal influence of external actors can be translated into net additions to or subtractions from the amount of coercive and cultural resources available in a society.

We can conclude, therefore, that, in a society facing the crisis of incorporation of the working class, a high level of external control of economic resources is likely to contribute toward weakening the domestic bourgeoisie and strengthening preindustrial elites and the state, and thus to lead to a configuration of forces conducive to a deviation from accommodation. However, the cases of Canada and Australia and, to a lesser extent, several Western European nations in the postwar period suggest that a significant degree of alienation of economic control is compatible with stable accommodation in contexts in which qualitative dualism is not present, and also in situations in which the crisis of incorporation was already solved.

Timing of industrialization, dualism, and control of economic resources by external actors are thus associated with variations in the characteristics of both the elite and the working class as well as those of the society at large. These variations, in turn, produce changes in elite strategies, forms of political action of the working class, and environmental factors and consequently influence the probability of occurrence of the different outcomes. More specifically, in latecomers, both elite strategies and environmental factors are conducive to outcomes other than accommodation. This pattern, in itself, is likely to produce, on the side of the working class, a pull in the same direction. Furthermore, in those latecomers which are at middle levels of development, the configuration of what I call structural properties is also likely to facilitate nonaccommodation outcomes, as the discussion in Part II will show.

PART II. STRUCTURAL PROPERTIES
AND FORMS OF POLITICAL ACTION

6. Structural Properties

In analyzing the process of incorporation of the working class into the political system from the point of view of the options available to the elite, the forms of political action of the working class appear as either an opportunity or a constraint for the implementation of different elite strategies. However, forms of political action are only partially determined by elite strategies and by the set of elements I have called environmental factors. There are other determinants, some of which are aspects of the political system, e.g., the characteristics of interest groups and political organizations, and others of which are exogenous. Among the latter, the different aspects of the position of the working class in the economy are of paramount importance.

The remainder of this book will be devoted to the analysis of the effect of workers' position in the economy on the forms of political action. Positions in the social structure can be broken down into analytically distinguishable dimensions that denote different aspects of the positions and their context. I will call these aspects structural properties. Four of these properties are: centrality, deprivation, integration, and marginalization. Most characteristics of the position in the economic system that appear in the literature as relevant factors in the determination of working-class political behavior can be subsumed into these four dimensions. Centrality and deprivation can be considered static properties, while integration and marginalization would be dynamic ones.

Centrality-peripherality refers to the position in the productive process. This is a complex dimension in which two axes of differentiation of the working class can be subsumed: the differentiation produced by the degree of modernization of the productive unit, and the hierarchical stratification of individuals within productive units. In relation to the first of these axes, two aspects are important. The first of these is the degree of development of the productivity of la-

bor—Marx's "development of productive forces"—which is correlated with changes in the complexity of the division of labor. The
second aspect is the degree of bureaucratization of the productive
unit, which can be indicated by size. These two levels of modernity
of productive units vary both between and within industries. As
for the hierarchical differentiation of individuals within productive
units, stratification on the basis of skill is the usual indicator. It is
possible, therefore, to rank industrial workers and other subordinate
strata according to their centrality. The more skilled the individual
and the more "modern" the workplace—in terms of its productiveness, the complexity of its division of labor, and/or its degree of bureaucratization—the more "central" the worker's position in the
economic system.

Deprivation is the second static property. It refers to the position in the system of consumption and can be indicated by income
or by other measures of standard of living. There is usually a negative correlation between deprivation and centrality, but this correlation is not perfect, so it is useful to distinguish between the two
dimensions.

The two dynamic properties are integration and marginalization. Integration, as this term will be used here, refers to the process
of inclusion of individuals into the working class; it is the process
through which marginalized individuals who have previously been
uprooted—typically from the agrarian precapitalist sector—are incorporated into the working class and the industrial world. The two
polar states between which this process takes place are marginality
and full integration. Indicators of integration would be variables
such as intergenerational mobility, amount of industrial experience,
seniority, and so on.

Marginalization is the opposite process: the ejection of individuals from the working class or the transition from relatively "central" social positions toward more "peripheral" ones. Measures of
downward mobility and of job insecurity are the typical indicators.

These four properties appear in the literature, both in the radical
theoretical tradition and in contemporary research, as causal factors
related to the political action of the working class. In the research
literature, the different properties are usually distinguished. In the
political and theoretical literature, on the other hand, structural
properties are frequently grouped into pairs, one of which is privileged as the determinant of working-class consciousness and behavior. These pairs are often made up of a static property, which is usually held to be the primary determinant, and a dynamic one, which
is generally considered to be a powerful precipitant. The focal point

of the debate has been, in revolutionary thought, the search for the locus of the revolutionary potential in a social system: inside, at the center, or outside, and at the bottom of the class structure. Ever since industrialization began, the political debate has been a dialogue between these two traditions, each one focusing on the presumed revolutionary efficacy of a different pair of structural properties.

The first of such pairs is deprivation and marginality, i.e., a low level of integration. Deprivation theory corresponds to the anarchist tradition from Bakunin onwards, but it also fits Mao's and Marcuse's theories of revolution. The second pair is centrality-marginalization and is found in Marxist thought, beginning with the mature Marx and carrying over into contemporary theoreticians of the "new working class." Bakunin, Marcuse, and Marx will be discussed in the next chapter. Mao's deprivation theory will not be examined, for its focus is not on the working class.

In this ideological debate, structural properties have usually been defined in the same way as in the contemporary research literature, so empirical evidence can be used in order to test hypotheses extracted from the theoretical tradition. Perhaps the only exception is the treatment of deprivation. The distinction that is made in contemporary social science between observed or "objective" deprivation and relative or "subjective" deprivation is not systematically found in revolutionary thought—even though Marx, in particular, was aware of it—perhaps because of the rationalistic bias among revolutionary theorists, who assumed that awareness of deprivation would more or less follow upon objective deprivation.

As far as the forms of political action are concerned, on the other hand, neither revolutionary political theory nor contemporary research on the determinants of working-class political action have distinguished systematically between the two dimensions that make up my typology: dissent and radicalism. Political traditions have been concerned with the factors that are supposed to determine class consciousness and/or revolutionary behavior, but the distinction between the two is generally not clear. In much of the research literature, on the other hand, the dependent variable is either the vote for the left or indicators of leftist attitudes. In my terminology, most of that literature is concerned with the specification of the conditions that determine deviation from acquiescence rather than with the prediction of the direction of that deviation.

As will be seen, contemporary research on the effect of structural properties on forms of political action is often as inconclusive as the revolutionary debate, except perhaps for marginalization. There are probably two reasons which explain this inconclusiveness. First, it is difficult to find stable relationships between an isolated structural property and political orientations and behavior. The analysis of interrelated structural properties should yield better results. Second, cross-national comparisons are influenced by the effect of uncontrolled contextual variables.

Most of the remainder of this study will analyze the effect of different configurations of structural properties in a context whose major characteristics will either be controlled or held constant. Two sets of survey data will be analyzed. These data originated in two studies of the Argentine working class, and contextual variations between the two sets of data are such that it is possible to examine the consequences of different combinations of structural properties.

7. Structural Properties in Classical Revolutionary Theories

This chapter will be an exploration of the origins, in modern revolutionary thought, of the debate about the relationship between structural properties and the forms of political action of the working class.

DEPRIVATION AND INTEGRATION
FROM BAKUNIN TO MARCUSE

Nineteenth-century anarchism is the most extreme case of deprivation theory. Bakunin, its most systematic expounder, did not expect the more skilled and less deprived sectors of the working class to have any revolutionary potential. In contrast with Marx, he considered the proletariat to be ideologically integrated into capitalist society. Bakunin was, in fact, the forerunner of the *embourgeoisement* hypothesis. In a characteristic statement of his views, he wrote: "To me the flower of the proletariat is not, as it is to the Marxists, the upper layer, the aristocracy of labor, those who are the most cultured, who earn more and live more comfortably than the other workers. . . . By virtue of its relative well-being and semibourgeois position, this upper layer of workers is unfortunately only too deeply saturated with all the political and social prejudices and all the narrow aspirations and pretensions of the bourgeoisie."[1]

In discussing the French working class, Bakunin noted that that class was corrupted by "the deleterious influence of bourgeois civilization."[2] It is among the poorer strata of the working class, he thought, that a revolutionary potential could be found, but this potential would be a function of deprivation rather than of centrality, i.e., of the fact that these workers participate in the productive process. He claimed that ". . . the great mass of toilers, . . . worn out by daily drudgery, is ignorant and miserable. This mass . . . is unconsciously socialistic. Instinctively, by virtue of its social position, it is socialistic in a more serious and real fashion than all the bourgeois and scientific Socialists put together."[3]

Bakunin, in fact, expected the foremost revolutionary agent to be the lumpenproletariat. In this category, it should be noted, he included not only what Marx and Engels called "the social scum, that passively rotting mass thrown off by the lowest layers of the old society,"[4] but also the unskilled and deprived strata of the working class as well as other uprooted and déclassé elements: "Marx speaks disdainfully of this *lumpenproletariat* . . . but in them, and only in them—and not in the bourgeois-minded strata of the working class—is crystalized the whole power and intelligence of the Social Revolution."[5]

The two defining characteristics of this revolutionary agent would be, in the first place, deprivation, and, secondarily, lack of integration into capitalist society. Bakunin deposited his revolutionary expectations in the "rabble" of the disinherited, also because they were free from cultural contamination: "By the *flower of the proletariat*, I mean above all that great mass, those millions of the uncultivated, the disinherited, the miserable, the illiterates, . . . I have in mind the 'riffraff,' that 'rabble' almost unpolluted by bourgeois civilization, which carries in its inner being and in its inspirations, in all the necessities and miseries of its collective life, all the seeds of the socialism of the future, and which alone is powerful enough today to inaugurate and bring to triumph the Social Revolution."[6]

Some of Bakunin's statements support the interpretation that he expected deprivation to generate what I am calling radicalism, i.e., anti–status quo behavior. Socialization into anti–status quo beliefs would provide an additional necessary factor. The combination of both would make revolution inevitable: ". . . poverty and degradation are not sufficient to generate the Social Revolution. They may call forth sporadic local rebellions, but not great and widespread mass uprisings. . . . It is indispensable that people be inspired by a universal idea . . . that they have a general idea of their rights, and a deep, passionate . . . belief in the validity of these rights. When the idea and this popular faith are joined to the kind of misery that leads to desperation then the Social Revolution is near and inevitable and no force on earth can stop it."[7]

The same theme has been echoed in contemporary revolutionary ideology by Marcuse. For him, the industrial working class in advanced industrial society has been socially and politically integrated. Two processes have taken place. First, the nature of work has changed, as a consequence of automation and of the increase in the number of white-collar occupations. Second, the emergence of a revolutionary consciousness has been stifled by the satisfaction of economic needs and by the efficient imposition of capitalist culture. As a result, he claims, even though the working class is still the revolutionary class "in itself," it has become "a conservative, even counter-revolutionary force" for itself.[8]

Opposition to the social order, for Marcuse, can only arise from without: among the outsiders to the productive process, both in the periphery and in the center of the capitalist system. These are, on the one hand, the poor of the Third World, the "wretched of the earth," and, on the other, the periphery of the center found in the ghettos and on campuses. The unifying characteristic of these three groups is their low integration. They are "free" from participation in highly productive economic activities and, to a large extent, from any productive process at all. For this reason, he expects them to be also free from economic and ideological pressures for integration. But only the "external proletariat" would be truly an authentic revolutionary force, for only there would the two "historical factors of revolution" coincide, the one objective (i.e., deprivation) and the other subjective (i.e., "political consciousness"). Even though much of the "agrarian proletariat" of the Third World participates in the productive process, its revolutionary potential would be determined by its deprivation and its marginality rather than by its productive nature as such: ". . . the external proletariat is a basic factor of potential change within the dominion of corporate capitalism. Here is the coincidence of the historical factors of revolution: this predominantly agrarian proletariat endures the dual oppression exercised by the indigenous ruling classes and those of the foreign metropoles. . . . Kept in abject material and mental deprivation, they depend on a military leadership."[9]

In advanced capitalist societies, on the contrary, Marcuse states that the "historical factors" are dissociated. While "political consciousness" might arise among the privileged marginals—students and the intelligentsia—deprivation and total marginality at the bottom of the society would engender a potential for revolt, i.e., radicalism, rather than for revolution: ". . . underneath the conservative popular base is the substratum of the outcasts and outsiders, the exploited and persecuted of other races and other colors, the unemployed and the unemployable. They exist outside the democratic process, their life is the most immediate and the most real need for ending intolerable conditions and institutions. Thus their opposition is revolutionary even if their consciousness is not."[10] In summary, both Bakunin and Marcuse expected deprivation and absence of integration to determine deviation from acquiescence. Centrality, on the other hand, when not associated with deprivation, would generate acquiescence.

CENTRALITY AND MARGINALIZATION IN MARX

The discussion of structural properties in Marx will be more extensive, due to the fact that in the Marxist corpus there is not an explicit and systematic argument concerning this issue. In order to develop an interpretation, different strands have to be linked. A more detailed analysis is also necessary because the prevailing version of Marx's theory of revolution makes him another theorist of deprivation. The most frequent argument in this regard is the "absolute immiserization" thesis, which can be summarized in two propositions. First, as capitalism develops, the real income of the working class declines; and second, when deprivation is intense and generalized, the proletariat will carry out a revolution. Schumpeter is a distinguished representative of this line of interpretation. He sees only the first of these propositions as empirically problematic: "Based as Marx's 'dialectic deduction' is on the growth of misery and oppression that will goad the masses into revolt, it is invalidated by the *non sequitur* that vitiates the argument which was to establish that inevitable growth of misery."[11]

On the other hand, orthodox Marxists, such as the Soviet economists who supported this interpretation, have insisted on the validity of the absolute immiserization thesis.[12] This argument should, of course, be distinguished from references to "relative immiserization," i.e., to the fact that as a consequence of the increase in the productivity of labor and of changes in the occupational structure, the share of industrial wages in the national income declines.

An analysis of this type would lead to the conclusion that there is no essential difference, in relation to the consequences of structural properties, between Marx and the anarchists. The reading of different texts suggests a different interpretation, and I conclude that the determinants are centrality and marginalization. The first is emphasized in the *Grundrisse*, and the second is more salient in *Capital*.

In the famous passage in the *Manifesto*, it is asserted that "of all the classes that stand face to face with the bourgeoisie today, the proletariat alone is a really revolutionary class."[13] Marx's views about the structural properties that would determine this revolutionary role, however, were not always the same. The young Marx was, without question, a theoretician of deprivation, and it is after what Althusser has called his *coupure épistemologique* that different forms of centrality in the social structure, as well as marginalization, began to be associated with the characterization of the proletariat as a revolutionary force.

In *The Holy Family*, deprivation and revolutionary potential were explicitly linked:

> [Private property drives itself towards its own dissolution]
> . . . only inasmuch as it produces the proletariat *as* proletariat, poverty which is conscious of its spiritual and physical poverty, dehumanization which is conscious of its dehumanization, and therefore self-abolishing . . . [Socialist writers do not ascribe this role to the proletariat] . . . because they regard the proletarians as *gods*. Rather the contrary. Since in the fully formed proletariat the abstraction of all humanity, even of the *semblance* of humanity, is practically complete; since the conditions of life of the proletariat sum up all the conditions of life of society today in their most inhuman form; since man has lost himself in the proletariat, yet at the same time has not only gained theoretical consciousness of that loss, but through urgent . . . absolute imperative *need*—the practical expression of *necessity*—is driven directly to revolt against this inhumanity, it follows that the proletariat can and must emancipate itself.[14]

For the mature Marx, on the other hand, centrality was paramount. If different texts are put together, Marx's argument about structural properties can be constructed as follows. The hypothetical determinants of the revolutionary potential of the proletariat would be two: first, the position in the social structure—basically, "productiveness," an aspect of centrality—and, second, changes that would be produced in that position as a consequence of the development of capitalism and that would induce or facilitate revolutionary action. Unlike anarchism, Marxist theory is not based on statements about the relationship between structural properties and forms of political action whose validity is considered to be general. Marx expected that the causal link between structural properties and revolutionary action would be activated at "high" levels of development of capitalism, in agreement with the proposition that "no social order ever perishes before all the productive forces [i.e., the highest possible level of productivity of labor] for which there is room in it have developed . . . therefore mankind always sets itself only such tasks as it can solve."[15] The famous passage in which Marx states that a revolution occurs when "the material productive forces of society come in conflict with the existing relations of production"[16] should be interpreted as predicting that the working class will become a revolutionary agent when the development of society, as measured by the level of productivity of labor, would render a revolution both possible and necessary for the further development of the productivity of labor. It is only at this point that Marx expected the working class to establish new relations of production, whose characteristics would have been incompatible with lower levels of productivity of labor.

Let us examine these determinants more closely. The first one was the position in the social structure. The central characteristic in this regard is an aspect of centrality that Marx calls "exploitation." Beyond its moral connotation, this term, as used by Marx, may be strictly defined. Exploitation means the alienation by a participant in the productive process of the control of the surplus that this individual has generated. Its indicator is the rate of exploitation, which is the ratio of surplus—profits, rents, and interest—to wages.[17] As the rate of exploitation is a measure of the share of "productive" labor, in the Marxist sense, in total income, there is a positive correlation between exploitation and productivity of labor, i.e., the higher the degree of development of productive forces, the higher the rate of exploitation. A worker in contemporary America is, then, more "exploited" in this sense than a worker in eighteenth-century Britain or in the Third World today. As Bukharin has pointed out in his very systematic discussion, the working class is the only subordinate class in capitalist society in which three characteristics—freedom from private property, exploitation, and productivity—coincide: the peasantry is not free from property, while the lumpenproletariat is neither exploited in the Marxist sense nor productive.[18]

The second set of determinants arises from the development of capitalism. They are basically three, two of them referring to the increasing centrality of the working class and the third one relating to its increasing marginalization. The two processes that increase the centrality of the working class are its progressive concentration into large units of production and the formation of a highly skilled proletariat as a consequence of automation. The third process, finally, would be a tendency toward the marginalization of an increasing proportion of the working class.

Let us look at each of these developments in greater detail. The meaning of the first one, the concentration of the working class into large factories, is clear. Marx expected that accumulation of capital would lead to types of a productive process in which the degree of "socialization of labor" would be very high and in which the internal differences in the working class would disappear due to the dissolution of traditional crafts. All these changes would facilitate collective political action.[19]

The effects of the second and third determinants, i.e., the generation of a very highly skilled working class in automated industry and the tendency to marginalize an increasing proportion of the working class are more complex. These are two aspects of the same process of dualization of the working class: the stratum of "workers-scientists" who would operate the automated sector, and the marginal mass of actual and potential members of the "labor reserve army." Let us look at the process of automation first.

In the *Grundrisse*, Marx refers to automation as "the last metamorphosis" of the productive process. The application of science to production, he predicted, would change the nature of work. Physical labor would tend to disappear, and "the human being [would come] to relate more as watchman and regulator to the productive process itself."[20] For him, the generalization of automation would be the manifestation of the underlying process of supercession of the division of labor between manual and intellectual labor. When science becomes a "direct productive force," two consequences would follow. First, workers would cease to be an ignorant mass, for the productive process itself would require them to master the scientific foundation of their work. Apparently, the possibility that very complex machinery could be operated by unskilled workers was not contemplated by Marx. Such a highly skilled working class, incidentally, would have a high standard of living, for its reproduction cost, the basic determinant of the wage level in Marxist economic theory, would be high. The other consequence of automation would be the creation of the preconditions for the progressive reduction of labor time.

In summary, then, Marx expected capitalism to reach a level of productivity of labor in which physical labor and the division of labor between manual and intellectual labor would tend to disappear, and in which a large amount of free time would be available to all the members of the society. It is at this point, and only at this point, that he expected capitalism to break down. This was so for two reasons. First, relations of production based on the division of labor—including the division of labor between the capitalist, in the dual role as organizer of the productive process and as supervisor of work, and the worker—would become "historically unnecessary" due to the characteristics of the automated productive process. Second, the establishment of relations of production based on the supersession of the division of labor and of exploitation, in the Marxist sense, would be objectively possible only when that level of development has been reached. It is at that point that the collective control of the productive process would exist in actuality, regardless of the legal or organizational norms prevailing in the society. For socialism, in the Marxist sense, presupposes the *objective* ability of the working class to control the productive process rather than the formal ownership of the means of production. It is at that moment, and only at that moment, that "the *surplus labour of the mass* has ceased to be the condition for the development of general wealth, just as the *non-labour of the few*, for the development of the general powers of the human head. With that, production based on exchange value breaks down, and the direct, material production process is stripped of the form of penury and antithesis."[21]

It is still unclear, however, how this transition is expected to take place, i.e., whether the dissolution of capitalist relations of production would be an evolutionary process of transformation of the division of labor or whether there would be a revolutionary rupture and, in the latter case, which sector of the working class would be the revolutionary agent. The general tenets of Marxist theory, however, suggest that it would be the working class in the automated sector that would "set itself the task" of eliminating the then "socially unnecessary" bourgeoisie. This interpretation is supported by passages such as the one that follows. Having noted that accumulation of capital produces a tendency "on the one side, to create disposable time, on the other, to convert it into surplus labor," Marx asserts: "The more this contradiction develops, the more does it become evident that the growth of the forces of production can no longer be bound up with the appropriation of alien labour, but that the mass of workers must themselves appropriate their own surplus labour."[22]

The underlying proposition is that automation would make it evident to the "workers-scientists" who exert actual control of the productive process that the capitalists' claim for the control of the surplus is not based on their contribution to production. This fact would not be manifest at prior stages of the division of labor because, among other reasons, the role of the capitalist would then still be a socially necessary one. Once the objective need and the objective possibility of the dissolution of capitalist relations of production are manifest, revolutionary consciousness is expected to follow.

These propositions raise many problems that cannot be discussed here. One of these problems has to do with the effect of countervailing forces. For instance, it follows from Marxist theory that a "labor reserve army" of workers-scientists would be generated in an automated society, and such an army could help to check, albeit temporarily, revolutionary tendencies among employed workers. A more fundamental problem has to do with the nature of the change to be produced in such a setting. If the foregoing interpretation is correct, Marx expected that the workers in the automated sector would establish socialism, i.e., turn over to the society as a whole the benefits of the high level of productivity. It is possible, however, to imagine alternative developments. If the process of automation implies a high level of differentiation of the working class, it could conceivably lead to a situation in which the workers in the automated sector become an autonomous social and political force. In that case, two alternatives to socialism in the Marxist sense appear possible: an alliance between workers in the automated sector and the capitalists in order to share the surplus—workers-scientists would then become a new "aristocracy of labor"—and the seizure and retention of control of the surplus by the workers in the automated sector, who would maintain the existing differentiation between themselves and the remainder of the subordinate classes. "Workers-scientists" would thus become a new ruling class.

Likewise, we are not concerned here with the empirical validity of Marx's propositions or with their political implications. With regard to the first of these issues, nevertheless, the existence of the association that Marx seems to have predicted between automation and changes in the skill of the labor force is as yet not apparent. As far as the forms of political action of workers in automated plants are concerned, most evidence so far suggests that these workers tend to fit the "acquiescent" category.[23] As for the political implications of the foregoing argument, it would seem that, if this interpretation is correct, Marx would not have considered either those societies where power has been conquered by communist parties or even today's advanced capitalist societies as yet "ripe" for a transition to socialism, for there are in none of these societies the objective conditions that he specified for the supercession of the division of labor.

The conclusion would be, therefore, that Marx proposed a link between different forms of centrality—productiveness, concentration in large plants, and a very high level of skill—and revolutionary action. He did not expect, however, this link to be activated until the evolution of productivity of labor reached the stage of generalized automation. The other consequence that he predicted capitalist accumulation would have is the increasing marginalization of the working class. This aspect of Marxist theory is well known, but it is important to link it to the centrality argument.

In a famous passage of *Capital*, Marx asserted that the development of productive forces under capitalism and the consequent increase in the organic composition and the centralization of capital generate a growing "labor reserve army." This is the "general law of capitalist accumulation."[24] This labor reserve army, which is distinguished by Marx from the lumpenproletariat, is made up of three strata: the "floating" one, which consists of those workers who are periodically attracted and repelled by the labor market; the "latent" segment, which is made up of the underemployed agrarian population; and, finally, the "stagnant" type, consisting of employed industrial workers who are in danger of being marginalized.[25] The labor reserve army would be a necessary component of the capitalist economy, and its size would vary with the phases of the economic cycle. The working class, therefore, would consist of three fractions: secure workers, employed workers whose probability of joining the labor reserve army is high, and marginalized workers. Secure workers, however, would also be affected by the size of the labor reserve, for this would be one of the factors determining the level of wages and working conditions. The development of capitalism would be associated, then, with an increasing insecurity for all segments of the working class.[26] In another well-known passage, the process of marginalization is explicitly linked to deviation from acquiescence. In an opening paragraph, Marx suggests that the growth of this pole of misery will cause the working class to revolt, i.e., in the terminology of forms of political action, to become mobilized: "Along with the constantly diminishing number of magnates of capital . . . grows the mass of misery, oppression, slavery, degradation, exploitation; but with this too grows the revolt of the working-class, a class always increasing in numbers, and disciplined, united, organised by the very mechanism of the process of capitalist production itself."[27]

This paragraph suggest that Marx did not expect the workers *already* marginalized, i.e., the "active" members of the labor reserve army, to revolt. Rather, it would be the employed workers—and most likely those workers whose insecurity was high—who would be radicalized. Up to now, Marx has referred to "revolt" rather than to "revolution." This is consistent with the general tenet that a transition to another mode of production was expected to occur only after capitalist social relations had increased productivity of labor up to the highest possible level. The fragments from the *Grundrisse* that were discussed above make it plausible to infer that this is the level of generalized automation. The passage continues as follows: "The monopoly of capital becomes a fetter upon the mode of production, which has sprung up and flourished along with, and under it.

Centralisation of the means of production and socialisation of labour at last reach a point where they become incompatible with their capitalist integument. This integument is burst asunder. The knell of capitalist private property sounds. The expropriators are expropriated."[28]

This passage of *Capital* apparently contradicts the texts examined above from the *Grundrisse*, for here Marx seems to link marginalization and deprivation with revolution.[29] The fragment is, however, clearly divided into two parts, and only in the first of these parts is a specific agent identified—the workers in danger of marginalization—and the action that is predicated is revolt rather than revolution. References to revolution, in the second part of the passage, are linked to global social processes—centralization of the means of production, socialization of labor—and no reference to either insecure or unemployed workers is made. It would appear, therefore, that this second part is not inconsistent with the interpretation of the *Grundrisse* discussed above. It is, of course, possible to link both arguments by stating that marginalization could be one of the factors precipitating the conversion of highly skilled workers employed in automated plants into a revolutionary agent, but this linkage is not made by Marx. In any case, my impression is that it is unwarranted to consider Marx, on the basis of this latter passage, a theoretician of deprivation.

Marx's views of the likely political behavior of very deprived strata provides further evidence that he did not expect deprivation per se to generate a revolutionary potential. He did not even consider the lumpenproletariat as a possible ally of the working class. The *Manifesto* states that even though the "dangerous class" might be "swept into the movement" by a revolution, a radicalization toward the right was more likely than radicalization toward the left: "Its conditions of life . . . prepare it [the lumpenproletariat] far more for the part of a bribed tool of reactionary intrigue."[30] In the same vein, Engels asserted: "It is an absolutely venal, an absolutely brazen crew."[31]

Even though my discussion focuses on the second proposition of the absolute immiserization argument, i.e., the relationship between misery and revolution, it will be useful to comment on the first hypothesis, i.e., the connection between the development of capitalism and the decline of real wages. It is clear that Marx predicted that the accumulation of capital would cause an increasing amount of poverty, but this is in relation to the process of marginalization discussed above. He did not expect the income of the employed workers to decline in *absolute* terms. References to an "absolute" type of immiserization in *Capital* and other works are always made in relation to specific situations and processes, such as the formation of the working class in the period of primitive accumulation, the generation of the labor reserve army, and the deterioration of the working conditions or standard of living of specific categories of workers and in particular social contexts. But there is no statement of a "tendency law" similar to Lassalle's "iron law of wages." It can be argued that the theory of immiserization is supported by the "law of capitalist accumulation": as the function of the labor reserve army is to depress the wages of the employed workers, the expansion of that army would cause wages to fall, up to the subsistence level. However, in Marxist economics, this depressing effect is only one of the factors entering in the determination of wages. Other variables have opposite consequences: the increasing reproduction cost of labor power, trade union activity, culturally determined standards,[32] and the capitalists' need to expand consumption. In relation to the latter, Marx argues: ". . . the production of *relative surplus-value* . . . requires the production of new consumption; requires that the consuming circle within circulation expands as did the productive circle previously. Firstly quantitative expansion of existing consumption; secondly: creation of new needs by propagating existing ones in a wide circle; *thirdly*: production of *new* needs and discovery and creation of new use values."[33]

In addition to the immiserization thesis, it is still possible to maintain that Marxism is a theory of deprivation, at least in some historical contexts, by turning to the opposite pole of the deprivation continuum. The result is the "labor aristocracy" argument. In order to account for the apparent acquiescence of industrial workers in mid-Victorian England, Engels advanced the thesis that this fact was the consequence of the formation of a "trade union aristocracy" which was better off than the remainder of the proletariat.[34] The term was later used by Lenin as a component of the theory of imperialism: the surplus generated by the colonies was used by the bourgeoisie, he argued, to "buy off" a segment of the working class.[35] This argument was interpreted by some scholars, such as Linz and Zeitlin, as indicating that the "labor aristocracy" is the skilled stratum.[36] The empirical referent, however, is not totally clear. As far as Engels is concerned, it seems that "labor aristocracy" denotes the traditional craftsmen rather than the skilled factory population. In Pelling's words: "It seems clear that he was thinking primarily of those crafts in which, by means of the system of apprenticeship and the control of entry into the system, the artisans secured an effective bargaining position *vis-à-vis* the employers."[37] This line of interpretation has persisted up to this day, as *embourgeoisement* theories indicate.

After this detour, I conclude that Marx expected centrality to be the primary determinant of deviation from acquiescence. Centrality is the dimension that underlies those characteristics of the working class which, according to him, would cause this class to be revolutionary: exploitation, in Marx's sense, productiveness, concentration, and qualification. Marginalization, when associated with centrality, would be a second determinant. There is some support for the hypothesis that, in this case, the direction of deviation from acquiescence would be radicalization. Finally, marginality as such, i.e., the final state of the marginalization process, is not expected to cause a deviation from acquiescence in a revolutionary direction, and deprivation per se is not supposed to cause a deviation from acquiescence.

After this incursion into the realm of classical revolutionary theory, the discussion can return to the two studies of the Argentine working class. In analyzing the samples of established and new workers, the relationship between the four structural properties and indicators of dissent and radicalism will be discussed. These findings are relevant in order to assess the validity of propositions derived from these theoretical traditions, but my analysis cannot be properly considered a test of these propositions because of the range of variation of structural properties in the context in which these studies were made. This range does not include very high or intense levels, especially as far as static properties are concerned.

8. Two Studies of the Argentine Working Class

Argentine society is an adequate environment for this analysis. Argentina is an industrial society—even though not an advanced one—in which the crisis of the incorporation of the working class is still unsolved. It is not possible to interview Chartists or nineteenth-century German Social Democrats, but it is possible to collect data from contemporary Argentine workers. Even though considerable space will be devoted to the discussion of those aspects of Argentine society relevant to the argument, no claim is made that Chapters 8–11 constitute a study of the Argentine working class as a whole. Typical as the samples are of specific working-class situations, they are not representative of the working class in general.

The first of these studies deals with the established working class: workers in the sugar industry of Tucumán in northwestern Argentina. Their degree of centrality was high—most workers in the sample are skilled and employed at large mills—and their exposure to marginalization processes was also high—even though different levels of job insecurity can be discerned in these data—due to the impact of a crisis that affected the sugar industry. The second study is a survey of new workers: recent migrants from northeastern Argentina into the cities of Buenos Aires and Rosario. These migrants had a low level of integration into the working class—most of them had been only recently incorporated into the industrial world as unskilled workers in construction and in small plants—and most lived in shantytowns in large urban areas, i.e., in a context in which opportunities for the experience of deprivation are thought to be high. Besides these two samples, reference will be made for comparative purposes to other data gathered in the same studies: samples of transient and permanent rural laborers in the established workers study, and urban unemployed and unskilled service personnel in the new workers study.

ARGENTINA IN THE SIXTIES:
EXCLUSION AND MOBILIZATION

There are three important peculiarities of Argentine modernization. Argentina was incorporated into world markets as an exporter of labor-extensive agricultural commodities; the country was settled on the basis of mass European immigration; and the economic, social, and political evolution of the society consisted of two very different stages as a result of the depression. Because of the first two traits, Argentina stands, together with Uruguay, apart from the rest of Latin America; the third characteristic, on the other hand, brings Argentina closer to the Latin American modal pattern of modernization.

Specialization in labor-extensive agriculture allowed Argentina to reach a relatively high level of development before the depression. Díaz-Alejandro notes that "as early as 1895 . . . the Argentine per capita income was about the same as those of Germany, Holland, and Belgium, and higher than those of Austria, Spain, Italy, Switzerland, Sweden and Norway."[1] The surplus generated by the agrarian sector made possible, from the beginning of this century, relatively high rates of urbanization and literacy in the central areas of the country. As for the second peculiarity, the fact that Argentina was a country of mass immigration had a direct bearing, prior to 1930, on the crises of incorporation of the classes generated by industrialization and helped to defuse the impact of the issue. Finally, the depression was a watershed in the evolution of Argentine society. Efficient linkage into the world economy and an expanding liberal democracy gave way to inefficient import substitution and unstable authoritarian and corporatist regimes, making it appear as if the country was reverting back to relatively more traditional forms of economic and political life.

In this section, the outcomes of the process of incorporation of the Argentine working class as well as the determinants and structural correlates of that process will be briefly discussed; further, I will make some general comments on the economic, social, and political situation of the country toward the late sixties, when the surveys to be analyzed in the following chapters were conducted.

Argentina is a third-wave industrializer, even though manufacturing started in the late nineteenth century, both as a "forward linkage" of export agriculture and as import substitution. The sugar industry, whose workers will be described below, belongs to the latter category. The degree of industrialization prior to the depression can be seen in the following figures: in 1900–1904, the manufacturing sector (construction included) already made up 24 percent of the active population, and in 1940–1944 with the process of substitution under way, the percentage was 27 percent.[2] Rather than increasing in size, the manufacturing sector changed its structure after the depression: it became more diversified and concentrated.

In relation to dualism, the only variety that has been significant in Argentina is the "continuous" one, i.e., the cleavage between the developed center and the backward periphery, in the context of a basically capitalist social structure. As for "qualitative" dualism, its relevance has been less in Argentina than in most other Latin American countries. Capitalist social relations became almost exclusive in the early twentieth century, except for such residuals as sharecropping and, especially in the periphery, subsistence agriculture.

The discontinuity between the central and the northern regions has been one of the basic characteristics of Argentine society since the beginning of modernization. The center has been the locus of labor-extensive agriculture linked to international markets, European immigration, urbanization, industrialization, political power, and cosmopolitan culture and ideologies. The northern periphery, in contrast, had an economy based on labor-intensive agriculture— either for the internal market or subsistence—a mostly premigratory population, lower rates of urbanization and industrialization— the sugar industry was the only large-scale manufacture—little political weight, and traditional culture and ideologies.

With the spread of import substitution, a new form of "continuous" dualism emerged, this time within the center. It is the discontinuity between the relatively efficient agrarian sector and the mostly inefficient industrial sector, whose survival is made possible by subsidies and tariffs that are among the highest in the world.

Finally, the external control of economic resources has been relatively low by Latin American standards. The most important productive resource, land, has remained in the hands of the domestic elite. Even though railroads and meat-packing houses were operated by foreign capital during the period of "externally led growth," external control was based on trade mechanisms rather than on direct ownership of the means of production. Foreign capital participated mainly in those industries that were a forward linkage of agriculture, and import substitution was initiated mostly by domestic entrepreneurs. Foreign investment in industry producing for the internal market, however, became very significant in the 1960s.

The generalizations proposed in Chapter 5 are valid in relation to the Argentine case. In relation to timing of industrialization, it was asserted that this dimension is related to two major characteristics of the crises of incorporation: order of presentation of the crises of incorporation of the bourgeoisie and of the working class, and differences in the relation of forces between superordinate strata. As in other third-wave industrializers, the incorporation of the industrial bourgeoisie and of the working class were simultaneous rather than sequential issues in postdepression Argentina. Both were present prior to 1930, but their significance was diminished not only because of the foreign origin of a very large proportion of the urban population, but also because the pre-1930 bourgeoisie was not distinct from the landed elite. Their unity was facilitated by the fact that most large-scale manufacturing before the depression was a forward linkage of agriculture. After the depression, a new bourgeoisie came into being, and the working class changed its composition substantially. Peronism attempted to incorporate both in the framework of the corporatist setting that was described in Chapter 4.

The relation of forces between superordinate strata in Argentina also corresponds to the pattern found in other countries of delayed industrialization. The landed elite has retained a considerable amount of power, and the domestic industrial bourgeoisie has been incapable of establishing its hegemony. The latter shared power during Peronism, i.e., through a coalition with the labor movement and within the framework of a corporatist and at times paternalistic state. This arrangement is intrinsically unstable and was doomed to failure in the context of a low-growth economy, as was noted in Chapter 4. The consequence of this stalemate between the export-oriented agrarian elite and the bourgeoisie generated by import substitution has been, as in other late industrializers, the relative autonomy of the state. Liberal democracy died in Argentina with the depression, and ever since, the country has been under Bonapartist rule, either authoritarian or corporatist—except for brief periods of limited democracy, which were closely monitored by the military.[3]

Before 1930 there was some fragmentation in the elite, either along functional lines—e.g., the conflict between breeders and fatteners in the central elite—or regional ones—conflicts between central and peripheral elites. The first type of cleavage was of secondary importance, and the second type resulted in the uncontested hegemony of the central elite, for peripheral fractions were either marginalized or brought into association with the central ones as junior partners in two ways. First, economic policies favorable to regional upper classes were implemented when there was no interest conflict with central elites. A good example is the generation of the sugar industry in the northwest, in the late nineteenth century, on the basis of protection and subsidies. Second, leading members of peripheral elites could reach high positions in the national political system.

With the advent of import substitution, elite fragmentation became more intense, for both agrarians and the new industrialists were competing for the same surplus, most of which originated in the agrarian sector. The bourgeoisie, even though incapable of establishing its hegemony over the society, wielded considerable power, at times in coalition with the working class. This fragmentation generated Bonapartism, for the conflict could only be moderated by an external force—the state—through the implementation of syncratic policies in Organski's sense.[4] Since the development of this stalemate, regimes favorable to each segment of the elite have alternated in power, but in most cases the economic policies pursued by these regimes have differed little, for syncratism has provided the parameters within which policies reflecting different balances of power have fluctuated.[5] Radical measures, such as land reform or the suppression of tariff barriers protecting inefficient industries, would have been beyond acceptable boundaries.

This background helps to make sense of elite strategies and forms of political action of the working class. From 1955, with the overthrow of Perón, to 1966–1970, when the surveys to be discussed in following sections were conducted, the Argentine polity wavered between polarization and authoritarianism. The elite response to working-class mobilization was exclusion, which ranged from "high," the imposition of military rule, to "low," the establishment of military-controlled civilian regimes. The latter were "elected" in elections in which the largest political force, Peronism, was not allowed to participate. These two types of exclusionary regime were extremely unstable. From 1955 to 1970, Argentina had eight presidents, only two of which had been elected; there were major military coups in 1955, 1962, and 1966, and countless minor ones. This pattern of unstable exclusion was the result of the combination of working-class mobilization and the unavailability of a surplus for redistribution toward the working class. The latter was not due to the usual causes—stagnation or intense accumulation—but to the fact that income was being redistributed in post-Peronist Argentina in the opposite direction.

From the overthrow of Perón to the establishment of the authoritarian regime in 1966, the level of mobilization of the Argentine working class was among the highest in the world at that time. General strikes, most of which were politically motivated—even when demands were of the "bread-and-butter" variety—were a common phenomenon. And seizures of factories, as in the "struggle plan" of 1964, as well as other forms of "collective bargaining by riot," in Hobsbawm's sense,[6] were not rare occurrences. Radicalism was not, however, coupled with dissent. The labor movement was overwhelmingly Peronist, and most unions were controlled by conservative leaders. The penetration of leftist ideologies into the working class was of little significance. Nonexclusionary elite strategies would have required redistribution of income. In post-Peronist Argentina, the economy grew. The GDP per capita increased at a yearly rate of 2.1 percent between 1956 and 1970, and for 1960–1970 the rate was 2.7 percent.[7] These figures hide the intense fluctuations that rocked Argentine society. The whole postwar period was characterized by very sharp "stop-go" cycles. Diaz-Alejandro estimates that, in the twenty-one years between 1945 and 1966, nine had negative rates of GDP growth, and nine showed positive rates above 6 percent.[8] In the ten years between 1957 and 1966, when the surveys were taken, four had negative rates, and five registered positive ones of 7 percent and over.[9] These fluctuations, which affected the standard of living of all social classes, coincided with a process of steady redistribution of income that began in the early fifties and was intensified after Perón was overthrown in 1955. In the struggle over surplus, the working class was definitely the loser. The share of manufacturing wages in the national income, which was 50 percent in 1952 and 44 percent in 1955, dropped to 39 percent in 1958, 32 percent in 1963, and 36 percent in 1966. In 1969, the share was still 36 percent.[10] This process of redistribution was, of course, inconsistent with accommodation or co-optation. The availability of a coercive apparatus under its control, on the other hand, rendered exclusion attractive as a strategy for the elite.

Finally, in order to complete the discussion of systemic resources, it should be noted that the instability of exclusion was not only due to the intensity of cleavages but also to the prevalence of a political culture that, as a reflection of the collective experience of the Argentines, was more conducive to the politicization of conflict and to a confrontational pattern of its resolution than to bargaining among political forces.

One of the consequences of this praetorian game is that there are winners and losers, and the peripheral players of all social classes tend to be the losers. The discontinuity between center and periphery, therefore, was bound to increase. Several peripheral regions had become inefficient single-product economies, and their survival depended on government subsidies. The combination of peripherality and inefficiency led to defeat for these regions, for neither their superordinate nor their subordinate classes and strata were capable of wielding the amount of power that would have been necessary in order to compete successfully for the allocation of the surplus with their more powerful counterparts in the center. The outcome was a series of crises of overproduction of commodities that could not be exported without heavy subsidies, the shutdown of enterprises that could not function without government financing, and mass unemployment and migration toward the center. This constituted a further step in the secular process of marginalization of the Argentine periphery. The two most important of these crises occurred in the sugar industry of Tucumán in the northwest and in the cotton economy of Chaco in the northeast. The two sets of data that will be analyzed in the remainder of this study concern the victims of these processes of marginalization of the periphery.

Finally, a brief comment on the political situation in the second half of the 1960s. In 1966, the liberal-democratic Illia administration was overthrown by a military coup led by General Onganía, and an authoritarian regime was established. Political parties were suppressed, and universities and some unions were placed under government control. There was, however, what Linz has called "limited pluralism."[11] That is, most interest groups could function, the opposition was not actively persecuted, there was limited freedom of the press, and anti–status quo ideas, including those of the radical left, could circulate to a significant extent.

The initial reaction of the labor movement and of Peronism in general to the new regime was cautious consent. The most powerful union leaders cooperated openly with the government, in spite of the fact that strikes were harshly repressed. Discontent grew gradually, however, among the working and middle classes as a response not only to political exclusion but also to the "stabilizing" economic policies of the regime. The consequence was the eruption of a series of mass mobilizations and riots, from 1969 onward, in Córdoba, Rosario, and other cities of the interior, but not in Buenos Aires. Students and the middle class, as well as industrial workers, participated in these events. At the same time, the guerrilla groups forming in different segments of the radical intelligentsia came to the surface. Some of these groups were developing inside Peronism as a consequence of the radicalization of its middle-class component, which had become more significant after the overthrow of Perón and the desertion of the industrial bourgeoisie from the coalition.[12] Other organizations, prone to the "nonpeaceful road," were growing in the Marxist left. Induced by working-class mobilization into believing that the revolution was at hand, two segments of the middle class, the right wing, represented by the military, and the radical intelligentsia, were preparing the stage for the terror of the seventies, in which thousands of people lost their lives—in most cases as the consequence of state violence.

The late sixties were, therefore, a period of steady deviation from acquiescence. Under the stern facade of authoritarianism, radical propensities were growing among workers and in the middle class. For the first time in contemporary Argentina, the state was losing the monopoly of force; violence from above was beginning to elicit mobilization from below. Dissent, in the sense in which I am using this term, developed mostly in the intellectual and professional strata of the middle classes, in which different blends of socialism, left-wing nationalism, and Marxist versions of Peronism were gaining ground. The left made some significant inroads in the labor movement for the first time since the birth of Peronism, but the bulk of the working class remained loyal to Perón. However, the nature of that relationship had changed drastically. The labor movement was now not only organized but also relatively autonomous. It bargained and entered into coalitions with other forces, but would not be manipulated by them—and much less so by the state. The labor movement was also more heterogeneous. A differentiation had taken place between the unions more independent of Perón's leadership and those that were more orthodox.[13] As a consequence of Perón's exile, the demise of corporatist integration, and the experience of collective mobilization, trade unions were now one of the major power contenders in Argentine society.

The first of the surveys to be analyzed here, the study of sugar workers in Tucumán, was taken in 1966 immediately following the coup and during the "expectant" phase of the relationship between the labor movement and the new regime. The second one, the study of workers who had migrated from Chaco into Buenos Aires and Rosario, was taken in the period 1968–1970 when the phase of high polarization was beginning. The interviews in Rosario were conducted after the disturbances there had taken place.

The issue of the reliability of answers to questions on political attitudes and behavior in an authoritarian context may be raised. This problem is especially significant in relation to the Tucumán study, for interviews there were conducted within the framework of a study of the sugar industry that was being carried out by a government planning agency.

It is not possible, of course, to conduct a direct test that would permit a conclusion on the reliability of these interviews. There are, however, four reasons that lead me to think that self-censorship on the part of the respondents was not a significant factor. First, there was limited pluralism in the Onganía regime. There was nothing approaching the atmosphere of fear and suspicion that prevails in more coercive situations, such as the one that Argentines experienced in the late seventies. Furthermore, the repression of political opinions is not fostered by Argentine culture. Second, in both surveys, a large percentage of the respondents gave anti–status quo answers. And almost all these questions dealt with generalized orientations rather than with attitudes that could be specifically interpreted as indicating support for or opposition to the government, especially among relatively unsophisticated respondents. Third, within the framework of the established workers study, I conducted several extensive interviews with union leaders and developed informal contacts with some of them. My impression was that these people, including the ones who had anti–status quo or antigovernment attitudes, were frank and candid. Finally, the distributions of anti–status quo answers to political questions are associated with background variables of different types, and in some cases the relationships are relatively strong, for the standards of survey analysis.

ESTABLISHED WORKERS: THE TUCUMÁN STUDY

In the study of the sugar industry of Tucumán, representative samples of factory and rural workers, both permanent and transient, were interviewed in October and November of 1966.[14] The analysis focuses on the sample of 147 permanent factory workers, most of whom were skilled, working in large plants, and highly integrated into the working class. These workers had different degrees of exposure to the process of marginalization that the sugar industry was undergoing at that time.

The city of Tucumán is located in the northwest, the region of oldest settlement in Argentina and a relatively developed area in colonial times. Since the emergence of the export economy, however, the northwest has become a part of the periphery. The impact of European immigration in that area was limited and was concentrated in the large cities. Tucumán was not, however, a marginal section of the periphery, due to the establishment of the sugar industry in the late nineteenth century. The suitability of this industry for the analysis of the effects of centrality, integration, and marginalization springs from three of its characteristics: its organization into large enterprises, its gradual expansion up to the point that Tucumán became a single-product economy, and the long-term contraction of its personnel.

This industry combines industrial and agricultural activities. When the survey was taken, the mills, which are located near the farming areas in which the sugar cane is produced, ranged in size from 390 to 1,953 workers.[15] The median size was 579 in 1966, and five mills had more than 800 workers. These plants ranged in terms of efficiency from relatively modern to very traditional. Most permanent factory workers were skilled, while transient labor was mostly unskilled. In the sample, 80 percent of the former were skilled, while the percentage among transient workers was only 17 percent.

Even though most factories were located in a semirural environment, none was really isolated, for the mills are concentrated in a relatively small area, and four or five are close to the city of Tucumán (population in 1960: 270,000). Workers live in company housing, and most mills have developed factory towns. The sugar cane processed at the mills is produced both by independent farmers and on large farms operated by the companies owning the mills.[16] An important aspect of the sugar industry is its seasonal character: factories and farms hire seasonal laborers at harvest time and work with a smaller labor force during the rest of the year. This arrangement presupposes the existence of a labor reserve, which is made up of either independent peasants—the minifundio operators, both in Tucumán and in neighboring provinces—or a floating migrant population.

The second characteristic of the sugar industry is that it developed to the point that Tucumán became a single-product economy. In order to indicate the central role of this industry in provincial society, a few data will suffice. In the industrial sector, in 1966 the twenty-seven mills employed 17,711 workers, 31 percent of which were permanent. The number of permanent workers corresponds to 29 percent of the industrial labor force in Tucumán, according to the economic census of 1964.[17] The percentage of the labor force working on sugar farms is not known, but it is enough, in order to show the significance of this product, to point out that estimates of the number of sugar farms in the 1960s ranged from 13,000 to 20,000.[18] These limits would correspond to from 63 percent to 100 percent of the total number of farms that existed in the province.

Finally, a third characteristic of this industry is the long-term trend toward the reduction of its personnel. Permanent employment had been contracting steadily during the previous thirty years due to the introduction of labor-saving technology and the vulnerability to crises of overproduction. The crisis produced by the record harvest of 1965 was particularly important, and in 1966, eight of the twenty-seven mills were forced to close. Over 5,000 factory workers, or 28 percent of the total, were unemployed. This, it should be remembered, was in the context of a very unstable economy. The impact of the crisis will be further discussed below.

A first remarkable aspect of the workers in this sample is their very high level of integration into the sugar industry and into the working class. Almost all (92 percent) the permanent factory workers in the sample were born in Tucumán. Most of them were children of sugar workers, and the greater part of their work careers was related to the sugar industry. Seventy percent of the permanent industrial workers reported that their father's current or last job was in the sugar industry, and the percentage whose father was working or had worked in the same mill is 62 percent. In most cases, fathers working in the sugar industry had been factory workers: the percentage is 52 percent, but it rises to 61 percent among skilled workers. And 32 percent of the fathers had been skilled. Another effect of the single-product economy is that 70 percent of those respondents in the sample who have working sons indicated that their sons are employed in the sugar industry—in 89 percent of the cases, in the same mill as their fathers. When the workers who had sons were asked which kind of job they would desire for them, the percentage who preferred their sons to become skilled workers was higher than the percentage of those preferring a profession—36 percent to 29 percent.

This very high level of integration is also evident in the work careers. In spite of the fact that only 31 percent of the workers in the study were older than forty, 50 percent of them had twenty years or more of seniority in their current jobs. Furthermore, 64 percent had worked only in the sugar industry throughout their careers, and only 3 percent had done so for less than 60 percent of their careers. On the other hand, only 14 percent of the workers reported to have ever worked in industries other than sugar. And the exposure of the respondents to nonindustrial environments was minimal. Only 12 percent had worked in nonmanual occupations, only 7 percent had ever had regular employment in nonsugar agriculture, and only 3 percent had been seasonal laborers at harvest time. Most of these workers, therefore, had known only the large factory as a work place and the working-class community as a social environment.

Unfortunately, direct information is lacking about the income received by the individuals included in the study. On the basis of data on wages established by collective agreements for a random sample of ten industries, however, I estimate that wages in the sugar industry did not differ substantially from average industrial wages in Argentina at that time, especially as far as skilled workers were concerned.[19] The relative income comparisons that the social structure of the sugar industry facilitated, however, were always favorable to sugar factory workers: the respondents in the sample, living in relatively isolated occupational communities, had higher incomes and enjoyed a higher standard of living than all the other strata with which they were likely to interact or compare themselves: transient industrial workers, permanent and transient rural laborers, and minifundio operators. Opportunities for comparison with workers in other industries or with white collar employees were more limited, except for the workers of the few mills located near the city of Tucumán.

The relatively privileged status enjoyed by the permanent factory workers can be perceived on the basis of the deprivation indicator that is available in this study: quality of housing. An index was developed which combines information about the materials used in houses for walls and roof and about the type of stove (see Appendix). For a house to be considered "good," it had to have masonry, brick, or concrete walls, a tile, brick, or cement roof, and an electric, gas, or kerosene stove. The percentage of industrial workers having this type of housing was 53 percent. The corresponding percentages for rural laborers were 19 percent for the permanent workers and 12 percent for the transient ones. As could be expected, quality of housing is associated with skill. While 56 percent of the skilled workers had "good" housing, the percentage among the unskilled was 37 percent.[20] Ownership of appliances is another available indicator. Its distribution is similar to that of quality of housing. While 55 percent of the permanent factory workers had a radio set and a refrigerator, the corresponding percentages among rural workers were 14 percent for permanent laborers and 5 percent for the transient ones.

Education, finally, can also be considered an indicator of deprivation. Only 13 percent of the factory workers had finished fewer than three years of school, and 36 percent of them had completed the seventh grade. This level of schooling had been attained by only 9 percent of the permanent rural workers and by 10 percent of the transient rural ones.

It is against this background that the impact of the 1965 crisis can be fully appreciated. The Tucumán sugar industry is an extreme case of inefficient import substitution: it could survive only through tariff protection and government regulation and subsidies. This situation was a consequence of two facts: Argentina as a whole is a marginal producer of sugar, and, within Argentina itself, a more effi-

cient sugar industry arose in the northern provinces of Salta and Ju-
juy.[21] As the industry expanded and the relative inefficiency of Tucumán increased, the scope of government control grew steadily. The
state eventually regulated and financed every stage of the productive
process. Even the size of the output and the criteria for distribution
of gains between manufacturers and farmers were decided by the
government rather than by market mechanisms. The public sponsorship of backwardness reached its limit when, under the Peronist
administration, a "regulating fund," whose purpose was the subsidi-
zation of the less productive firms by the more productive ones, was
established.[22] It was possible, therefore, for almost all producers to
survive, regardless of their performance.

With the overproduction crisis of 1965, the indebtedness of
some firms to the federal and provincial governments, as well as to
farmers and to their workers, reached critical levels. After the military coup of June 28, 1966, government policy toward the sugar industry changed. In August, just before the survey was administered,
it was announced that seven of the bankrupt mills would be closed
and that their subsequent fate—either definitive closing or "transformation"—would be decided a posteriori. In addition, an eighth
mill shut down. As far as the personnel of these factories was concerned, the initial policy was that the permanent workers' basic
wages would be paid for a year and that, in order to receive the supplementary benefits, these workers would perform the tasks to be
assigned to them, either inside or outside the mills. Factory workers
were later employed in public works at reduced wages and without
supplementary benefits.[23] It was announced, finally, that a plan of
economic diversification would be formulated.

The future looked somber for workers in closed mills. They
were still getting paid and living in company housing, but their
short-term prospect was either idleness or unskilled work in public
projects such as digging ditches. In the long run, unemployment
seemed a more realistic prospect than nebulous diversification plans,
even though the hope that mills would be allowed to reopen was
still lingering (and, in fact, some of these mills reopened later).

In addition to the mills that had been closed, there was a group
of "threatened" mills made up of those plants that, while still functioning, were in danger, due to their critical financial status. On the
basis of information from different sources, it was ascertained that
nine mills belonged to this category. This fact was not necessarily
known by the workers or by the general public, but workers at active
plants experienced a feeling of diffuse insecurity that affected even
the personnel of the mills that could be classified as "safe."

The safety that workers in the latter mills could feel, on the other hand, was relative also for totally different reasons. They could become the victims of progress rather than of backwardness, as was the case with their counterparts in closed factories. Unemployment was also caused by the introduction of labor-saving technology, for there was a double process: reduction of the total size of the industrial work force and decline in the proportion of permanent industrial workers.[24] Job insecurity was, therefore, pervasive, even though different segments of the working class experienced its consequences differently. For workers in inefficient mills, the threat was unemployment, and for workers in secure mills, it was the shift from permanent to transient labor.

A few data will suffice to describe the crippling consequences of this crisis. In 1968, only seventeen mills were functioning, down from twenty-seven in 1966. And data on the occupational structure of the agrarian sector show an interesting phenomenon. From 1960 to 1969, the population living on farms in Tucumán decreased by 4 percent, but the personnel employed in agriculture decreased by 30 percent. This suggests that one of the consequences of the crisis was the retrogression toward precapitalist agriculture. Emigration was, as could be expected, a second consequence. The population of the province in the 1970 census was 18 percent less than was projected on the basis of the 1960 census.

As could be expected, sugar workers were highly dissatisfied with their lot: 95 percent of them considered their wages low, 53 percent thought their job was unstable, and 52 percent claimed that work in the sugar industry was hard or dangerous.[25] Factory workers were keenly aware of the nature of the crisis and of the repertoire of possible solutions. When asked, in an open-ended question, about the nature of the problem of the sugar industry,[26] only 25 percent of the respondents mentioned the immediate repercussions of the crisis—unemployment, delays in the payment of wages, and the like—and 47 percent referred to issues related to overproduction, inefficiency, and other global or "mediate" aspects of the situation.[27] In the second open-ended question, they were asked what they thought should be done to solve the crisis.[28] Almost a third—32 percent—replied in terms of diversification or modernization. Among rural laborers, on the other hand, the percentage giving these "progressive" answers was only 17 percent among permanent workers and 13 percent among the transient ones.[29] Several questions focused on mobility aspirations. Forty-six percent of the factory workers indicated that they would like to have a nonsugar job, and 92 percent reported interest in becoming self-employed. Most of them were, however, aware of the barriers to mobility posed by single production and stagnation. Fifty-three percent of those who would like to have a nonsugar job considered the likelihood of getting such job low or nonexistent. As for the likelihood of becoming self-employed, only 9 percent of that 92 percent considered their chances good.[30] And 79 percent of the sample thought that it was difficult, very difficult, or impossible for the son of a worker to become a doctor or a law-yer.[31] Most of these workers combined, therefore, a quite realistic evaluation of the crisis, a desire to escape its consequences through mobility, and an awareness of being locked into their social position.

Sugar workers were strongly organized. The union Federación Obrera de Trabajadores de la Industria Azucarera, or FOTIA, was es-tablished during the Peronist regime. Since its inception, the FOTIA has been very militant, for while the permanent crisis of the sugar industry was conducive to the generation of intermittent conflict, the existence of relatively isolated occupational communities and the organization of the industry into a few large mills facilitated a very high level of organizational cohesion.[32]

The high level of participation in the union can be ascertained on the basis of the following data: all the permanent factory workers in the study were members of the FOTIA, 96 percent had voted in union elections, and 23 percent were or had been union officials. Among those who were not or had never been officials, 58 percent had attended at least one union meeting in the previous month, and 19 percent had attended two or more meetings.[33] The union was sol-idly Peronist, and was enrolled in the minority "orthodox" faction of the Peronist labor movement. The central and, in most cases, the lo-cal leadership was actively Peronist. However, three or four local unions were under Trotskyist or communist leadership.

An indication of the militant character of the FOTIA is the fact that, even though the union had been organized by the Peronist gov-ernment, it turned out to be one of the labor organizations less ame-nable to corporatist controls. As early as 1949, it declared a strike which was supported by the other unions in Tucumán. This was one of the most important labor conflicts during the Peronist regime. As a consequence, the FOTIA was "intervened."[34] After Peronism, its "trade union personality" was withdrawn in 1961 and after 1966.

In the mid-sixties, the degree of labor militancy in this industry was among the highest in Argentina. Strikes, "hunger" marches, mass demonstrations, and even factory seizures were current events, as Sigal's excellent discussion shows.[35] Some of these actions were highly radical, e.g., the seizure of the Bella Vista mill in 1965 and its operation under union control. In 1966, when the survey was taken, mobilization focused, up to August, on collective bargaining. After the closure of the mills by the recently installed authoritarian regime, on August 2, job security and the provision of jobs for the unemployed became, of course, the paramount issue. That year there were sugar strikes in May and October, in addition to general strikes in June and December and countless conflicts at the factory level.[36] Such was the climate in which our interviews were conducted. These actions involved not only the workers, but also the whole population of the factory towns. Underlying these events was a "moral economy" mentality, in Thompson's sense,[37] this time operating in a capitalist, industrial setting. The closure of mills was, to be sure, an extraordinary event, but such intense mobilization was a regular aspect of collective bargaining in the sugar industry, both during the negotiating phase and after collective agreements were signed. The most frequent event that triggered collective action was the failure by management to fulfill contractual obligations, such as regular payment of wages or payment of stipulated increases.

The relationship between the FOTIA and the management was complex. The manifest conflict between union and management co-existed with an alliance vis-à-vis the government, for the immediate interests of workers and mill owners coincided. The two sought the maintenance and expansion of government subsidies and other forms of protection for inefficient firms.[38] Much of the mobilization was collective bargaining by riot—even though, of course, it cannot be assumed that this was consciously understood by the rank and file and the middle-level leadership, whose radicalism was probably "authentic." For this reason, mobilization was not only a bargaining tactic deliberately used by the union leadership in order to impress management and the government; once a mobilizational political culture is institutionalized, the stage is set for radicalizing "pressures from below," and leaders become prisoners of their own tactics.

Workers were not the only group that had adopted a mobilizational style of conflict management. The sugar industry in the early sixties was a typical example of mass praetorianism at the local level. As workers went to strike and seized factories, mill owners threatened with lock-outs, bankruptcy, and the ensuing social turmoil, and farmers demonstrated and warned of an impending agrarian rebellion. This collective upheaval aimed at extracting resources from the federal government. Lacking other bases of power, social strata in the periphery could only, in competition for the scarce surplus with strata in the center, mobilize their numbers and conjure up the specter of revolt. Radicalization is the power of the weak, of those who, lacking the ability to apply positive sanctions or impose their will through the application of negative ones, can only refuse to comply with public order.

The FOTIA leadership was, however, fully aware of the long-term lack of viability of the sugar industry. Union documents and statements emphasized that diversification of the regional economy was the solution to the crisis. So, when the seven mills were closed by the government in August of 1966, the FOTIA's initial reaction was cautious. The union stated its disagreement with the fact that mills had been closed before alternative employment opportunities were made available, but without opposing frontally the government policy. The response became more militant later, when it was clear that at that time there was no comprehensive diversification plan that would generate enough jobs to absorb the unemployment created by the closure of the mills.[39]

Tucumán was a solidly Peronist province. In the presidential election of 1963, the percentage of blank votes[40] was higher than the national average (27 percent versus 21 percent), and in the 1965 congressional election, in which Peronist candidates were allowed to run, the two largest Peronist groups polled 41 percent of the vote.[41]

Support for Peronism was probably wider among sugar workers than in the general population. Information about the respondents' electoral choices is not available, but the questionnaire included a question about Perón's epoch: whether the workers' situation was better then and, if that was the case, in what way.[42] Eighty-five percent of the respondents in the sample of factory workers considered the situation better, and the remainder did not answer—only one individual answered negatively. The reasons offered cast light on the instrumental nature of acquiescence to corporatism in a mobilized working class: more than half of those responding that the situation was better referred exclusively to factors directly associated with their work, such as existence of jobs, wage level, and observance of collective agreements. Only 7 percent, on the other hand, mentioned Perón's personality or behavior, without making a direct association with the work situation.[43]

The relationship between these workers and the political system was, predictably, one of alienated participation. Ninety-six percent had voted in the previous election—voting is compulsory in Argentina in spite of the secondary importance of popular elections as a mechanism for the selection of office holders—and 84 percent considered, curiously enough, that workers' voting was effective or useful.[44] On the other hand, when asked for their opinion about the administration of justice, 82 percent asserted that courts favor the upper classes rather than being equal for everybody.[45] Finally, 76 percent of these workers, when shown a list of social groups and asked which of these groups should have more power, mentioned the working class.[46]

On the basis of the foregoing discussion, it should be clear why the Tucumán study offers an ideal context for the examination of the effects of centrality, integration, and marginalization on the forms of political action. Not only did these workers have relatively high levels of these structural properties, but contextual factors also facilitated the expression of dissent and radicalism: the organization of the industry into occupational communities, the high level of unionization and the militant character of the union, and the mobilizational political culture.

NEW WORKERS: THE BUENOS AIRES—ROSARIO STUDY

The second set of data originated in a study of recent migrants in two large urban areas: Buenos Aires and Rosario. This was one of the surveys administered by the Marginality Project, directed by J. Nun. Interviews in Buenos Aires took place in 1968–1969 and in Rosario in 1969–1970 (see Appendix for a description of the project). A sample of 223 migrants from the northeastern province of Chaco, arrived since 1962, were interviewed. Sixty-five percent of the individuals in the sample were working in construction and manufacturing, 22 percent had unskilled service jobs, and the remainder were unemployed. The analysis in later chapters focuses almost exclusively on the first group, i.e., construction and manufacturing workers, but here the complete sample is described.

These migrants differed from the sugar workers in Tucumán. They were less integrated into the productive process and were located in an environment that is conducive to the experience of objective deprivation: 77 percent of them were living in shantytowns in cities with large middle- and established working-class populations. Their centrality, as measured by their position in the productive process, was lower than that of the sugar workers. Most employed migrants in this sample were unskilled laborers working in small plants or work sites. And the level of insecurity of those who were employed was lower than that of Tucumán workers. There is, however, a common trait underlying these differences. These are two studies of the victims of inefficient regional economies, two instances, perhaps the most important ones, of the widening of dualism in Argentine society as a consequence of the retrogression of the periphery. Like Tucumán, Chaco was a case of monoculture—in this case centered on cotton—experiencing an acute crisis of overproduction in the late 1960s. And the cause of this crisis, as in Tucumán, was the relative inefficiency of Chaco as well as the development of substitutes.

Unlike other areas of the periphery, such as Tucumán, the Argentine northeast is a region of recent settlement.[47] The first non-Indian inhabitants arrived in the late nineteenth century. The society that developed was ethnically mixed; both European immigrants and Creoles from neighboring provinces settled in Chaco.

Since the beginning of the century, monoculture was a central trait of the economy of the province. Forestry—the exploitation of quebracho wood, mostly for the extraction of tannin—was the first dominant activity,[48] but cotton, whose expansion began after World War I, gradually became the most important crop. In Argentina, cotton is produced on family farms, and most farmers in Chaco are squatters on government land. Half of the cultivated area consists of medium-sized farms, and the other half is made up of minifundia.[49] Many of the minifundio operators are semiproletarians, who hire themselves out seasonally as cotton pickers and lumbermen.

Cotton farming expanded until the late 1950s. The centrality of this crop in the provincial economy can be indicated by the fact that in 1960, 81 percent of the area cultivated with annual crops was devoted to cotton.[50] A crisis became apparent at the end of the 1950s. It was caused by the competition of artificial fibers and by the impossibility to export. According to a technical study, average yields in Chaco were among the lowest in the world.[51]

As in the case of Tucumán, the consequences were pervasive. From 1960 to 1967, the area cultivated with cotton decreased by 56 percent.[52] Farmers turned to cereals, i.e., to extensive crops that require more land and less labor than cotton. The effect was mass unemployment and emigration of minifundio operators, semiproletarians, and rural laborers. The speed of the process is impressive. From 1960 to 1965, 34 percent of the farms with fewer than twenty-five hectares disappeared.[53] And according to the 1970 census, the difference between the population actually counted and the expected one—i.e., the population that Chaco should have had on the basis of its population in 1960 and the rate of population growth—was 19 percent.[54] A source estimated that, in 1966 and the first half of 1967, 50,000 persons emigrated.[55] This would amount to 9 percent of the population of the province in 1960. Continuing a secular process, these migrants were expelled toward the big cities, such as Buenos Aires and Rosario.

In the sample itself, most of the respondents had been, while in

Chaco, either rural wage earners, transient in most cases, or mini-fundio operators, i.e., precapitalist peasants. Most of their fathers (77 percent) worked in agriculture. Most of the 42 percent who were independent, and the size of whose farms was known, were minifundio operators; and most of the 35 percent who were dependent had permanent rural employment. The proportion of respondents whose fathers were industrial workers is minimal (2 percent), and most of those fathers having urban occupations were probably engaged in low-productivity or marginal services.[56] As for the migrants themselves, their integration into agriculture can be indicated by the fact that only 11 percent of them had work careers without rural jobs. Fifty-seven percent, on the other hand, spent their entire career in Chaco working exclusively in agriculture. Most respondents had been wage laborers, either transient or permanent, and a large percentage had been involved in precapitalist minifundio agriculture.[57]

The crisis forced a large proportion of the rural workers and farmers to look for urban employment in Chaco. When asked about their last occupation prior to migration, more than one-fourth of the migrants in the sample reported having had nonagrarian occupations, more than half of them in construction and manufacturing. The remainder were still involved in agriculture: more than half of the people in the sample had been wage laborers before emigrating, 43 percent of the total on a transient basis.[58] Even though 55 percent of the migrants had had no urban experience before leaving the province, 13 percent had lived in one of the four cities whose population is 10,000 or more for at least half of the time after the age of twelve.[59] The industrial experience of those migrants who had had manufacturing jobs probably took place in small shops and factories. In 1964 industrial establishments in Chaco with fewer than twenty-five employees accounted for 48 percent of employment in manufacturing.[60] In general, workers in the sample spent their premigration lives in quite traditional environments: 76 percent of them, for instance, indicated that they had never had contact with machines in their work. Many of the migrants, however, had been exposed to urban and industrial life, and most of them also to capitalist social relations, albeit intermittently.

We can assess the impact of structural changes on individual careers. Seventy-five percent of the respondents had premigration work careers spanning more than ten years, and 37 percent had worked in Chaco for more than twenty years. The inspection of work careers permits us to visualize the two main processes of structural change that took place in Chaco after the incorporation of these people into the labor market: the expansion of inefficient, protected capitalism and its crisis, i.e., the retrogression of the province toward less modern forms of social life.

The first of these processes, the expansion of capitalist social relations, can be seen in the mobility from independent agriculture—mostly precapitalist minifundio—to wage labor. While only 35 percent of the respondents' fathers had been rural wage earners (when their children were from twelve to sixteen years of age), 71 percent of the respondents had been rural wage earners at some point in their careers, and 51 percent of them reported that dependent agriculture was their last occupation in Chaco. A similar process can be seen in relation to nonagrarian occupations. Only 40 percent of the fathers working in cities were dependent, while 85 percent of the respondents working in the same setting prior to migration were involved in wage relationships.

The second process, the crisis of inefficient capitalism and the subsequent marginalization of the area, is indicated by three types of mobility. The first of them is the shift within the agrarian sector from permanent to transient positions. Only 13 percent of the fathers were rural transient laborers, but 32 percent of the sons in the sample had this type of employment exclusively throughout their agrarian careers, and 43 percent had a job with these characteristics before emigrating. The extent of the regional crisis can also be indicated by the process of urbanization without industrialization. Only 16 percent of the fathers were employed in urban activities when their sons in the study entered the labor force, but 27 percent of these sons listed urban jobs as their last ones in Chaco. Finally, the third type of process that shows the intensity of the crisis is the growth of unemployment. I reported above the last occupation the respondents had in the province, but when asked about their employment status prior to emigration, 47 percent of them reported to have been unemployed at that point. Understandably, only 10 percent described their situation then as "good."

The migration process itself is a typical case of "push" migration. When asked for their reasons for leaving the province,[61] only 10 percent of the respondents reported that their decision was caused by an orientation toward personal advancement or by a desire to know other places. On the other hand, 57 percent referred to the lack of jobs or to the unstable character of the jobs that could be found, 13 percent to the harshness of living conditions, and so on. And almost half of the respondents considered that, when they left Chaco, their decision was definitive.

The points of arrival, greater Buenos Aires and greater Rosario (with populations in 1970 of 8.35 million and 0.8 million respectively), were major industrial centers. The proportion of the active population working in manufacturing and construction was 43 percent in the Buenos Aires area and 37 percent in the Rosario area.[62]

The experience of these migrants shows that it was possible for marginals from the periphery to insert themselves in the economy of the center rather quickly: 37 percent of the respondents had been able to find a job within the first week after their arrival, and 8 percent had even secured a job before migrating. On the other hand, only 19 percent had faced unemployment for more than four weeks.

The expectations of these recent migrants were very low, a reflection of their prior experience of deprivation and insecurity. When asked which type of job they were seeking after their arrival, over half of those answering replied that they would accept any. The percentage of migrants interested in a construction job—27 percent—was much higher than the percentage of those seeking an industrial one—12 percent. These expectations were realistic. Forty-one percent of the respondents began their postmigration careers as construction workers, and only 21 percent did so as workers in manufacturing. Construction operates as a mechanism of absorption; in both cities, the percentage of the active population employed in construction was only 7 percent.[63] When the survey was conducted, on the other hand, 31 percent of the migrants were still working in construction, and 34 percent had manufacturing jobs. As for the remainder, 21 percent of the respondents began their careers in Buenos Aires and Rosario as unskilled service workmen, and 17 percent by doing odd jobs of different types (*changas* in Argentine slang).

Small plants also operated as entry gates to the industrial world. The probability that these migrants would be hired by small firms was higher in the beginning of the postmigration careers. Only 12 percent were hired initially by firms whose plants had more than 100 workers; when the survey was taken, the percentage for the whole sample was twice as large, and the percentage for the total employed population was still much higher (44 percent in greater Buenos Aires and 39 percent in Santa Fe province, where Rosario is located).[64] This greater probability for these migrants to be employed initially in small plants is explained by the fact that construction firms are smaller.

When asked how the initial job was obtained, 65 percent of the respondents referred to networks of relatives, friends, and neighbors. This suggests that migrants were immediately absorbed into a community that was probably made up of migrants like themselves and also of people from the same area. They were unlikely, therefore, to have experienced high levels of isolation or anomie.

The examination of occupational careers from the time of migration to the moment when the interviews were made reveals that the absorption of migrants into the urban economy was a relatively smooth process. Even though one-third of the respondents had experienced unemployment for at least three weeks at some point, only 8 percent had been unemployed for three months or more. Furthermore, almost half of the migrants—48 percent—reported having had only one occupation in the city,[65] and the percentage who had had to change occupation three times or more was only 14 percent. This percentage, however, was only 1 percent among individuals working in manufacturing and construction when the survey was conducted. As for jobs, however, the turnover rate was substantial: only 30 percent of the respondents had had only one job after migrating, and almost one-third had had three or more jobs.

It was reported above that 41 percent of the respondents obtained their first job in construction, and 21 percent did so in manufacturing. The exposure of these migrants to both types of industrial occupation increased in their subsequent careers, especially in relation to construction. When the survey was conducted, 63 percent of the individuals included in the study had had construction jobs—29 percent exclusively—and 48 percent had had industrial jobs—but only 18 percent exclusively. And even though 29 percent of the migrants had worked in large enterprises—100 employees or more—only 9 percent had been skilled manufacturing workers.

As stated above, 31 percent of the migrants were working in construction, and 34 percent were in manufacturing. One-third of the latter was working in a very traditional industry, meat packing, and the next largest group, one-fourth, was employed in the metal industry. As for skill, construction is the only industry which employed a large proportion of skilled workers: 42 percent of the total. Most migrants in manufacturing, on the other hand, were unskilled. There was one skilled worker in meat packing, four in the metal industry, and nine in other sectors.

As for size, construction is organized into small units—67 percent of the respondents worked in sites employing up to 25 workers—while manufacturing establishments are larger: all but one of the migrants in meat packing were employed by plants having more than 500 workers, and almost half of the metalworkers had jobs in firms with a labor force of more than 100. Other manufacturing sectors seemed to have smaller plants; almost half of the respondents in other industries worked in units employing less than 25 operatives.

On the other hand, 22 percent of the migrants were working in nonfactory services: 4 percent were self-employed, and the rest had unskilled service occupations (they were cleaning personnel, stevedores, porters, waiters, and so on). Many of these workers were employed by government agencies. Finally, 14 percent of the individuals in the sample were unemployed when the survey was taken. According to available evidence, the rate of unemployment among the respondents was approximately three times as large as that in the active population of Buenos Aires and Rosario.[66] Even though unemployment statistics are not very accurate, the size of the difference corroborates the common-sense expectation that recent members of the urban labor force are more susceptible to unemployment than established ones. A possible reason is that many unemployed in the sample were likely to have had their latest job in construction, a not very stable occupation.

These three groups of migrants had different degrees of integration into the urban and industrial world. Variations in this regard were substantial. Service workers and their industrial counterparts had had comparable amounts of residence time in the city of arrival—the percentage which had arrived less than two years before the survey was conducted was 29 percent for the former and 32 percent for the latter—but their exposure to the industrial world, especially to manufacturing, was much less. As much as 48 percent of the service workers had had experience in construction, but only 23 percent had been in manufacturing. The respective percentages for the migrants who were industrial workers when the interviews were conducted are 67 percent and 60 percent. The unemployed, on the other hand, were more likely to have been recent migrants—61 percent had been in the city of arrival for less than two years—and their exposure to manufacturing had been almost as low as that of the service workers (29 percent). Given the function of construction as an entry mechanism, however, their likelihood of having had a construction job was high: 68 percent—in fact as high as that of industrial workers. The relatively lower exposure of service workers to construction suggests that there was a service "track" operating in the urban economy.

Some additional information about the characteristics of the unemployed will be useful in order to clarify further the situation of the migrants in general. As we have seen, more than two-thirds of them had had construction jobs in the past. Almost half of these workers had been unemployed for less than a month, and also almost half of them were being supported by their relatives, while 30 percent were subsisting on odd jobs of different types. They were, therefore, part of the labor force and were not starving, in spite of the absence of unemployment compensation.

The expectations of these unemployed workers were quite modest. Forty-three percent claimed to be seeking "any" job they could get, and when asked about the monthly wage level they were aiming at, 42 percent indicated amounts of less than 30,000 pesos ($85.71). Sixty-nine percent of the employed workers in the sample were earning more than this figure. Another difference between the unemployed and the other migrants was their lower level of education. The workers in this sample had, in general, less education than the industrial workers in the Tucumán study, but the unemployed were the least educated: 35 percent of them were illiterate—as compared to 24 percent of the industrial workers and 19 percent of the service workers—and only 10 percent had completed the seventh grade as compared to 15 percent of the industrial workers and, curiously, 29 percent of the service workers.

As for deprivation indicators, information on wages and quality of housing, the variable that was used in the Tucumán study, was also available. The usefulness of the income indicator is limited, due to the fact that interviews were made over a two-year period and in a highly inflationary economy.[67] The data show, however, some interesting differences between groups. Only 24 percent of industrial workers were earning less than 30,000 pesos per month—this amount would correspond to $85.71, according to the average free exchange rate from 1968 to 1970[68]—while one-third was making 40,000 pesos—$114.29—or more. Service workers' wages were lower: 52 percent of the respondents in this category were earning less than 30,000 pesos, and only 24 percent were making 40,000 pesos or more. However, a comparison of standards of living as measured by quality of housing reveals service workers to be slightly better off than industrial workers.

Income varied according to skill and sector of industry. In relation to skill, only 25 percent of the unskilled in the sample were earning 40,000 pesos or more, but the corresponding percentage among the skilled was 53 percent. The income differential associated with skill, however, varies according to the sector of industry. In order to give an idea of intersectoral differences, it will be useful to compare statistical data for several industries. Average hourly wages established by collective agreements in several industries, as well as income differentials associated with skill, are shown in Table 7. These data are for 1964, the latest year for which this comparative information was available. Besides the construction, meat-packing, and metal industries, which are represented in this study, the averages for the ten-industry random sample that was referred to in the previous section was included, as well as data for two industries

Table 7. *Average Hourly Wages by Skill, and Income Differential between Skill Categories for Selected Sectors of Industry, Argentina, 1964*

| Sector | Wages in Pesos | | % Difference |
	Skilled	Unskilled	
Construction	74.6	55.0	36
Metal	71.7	58.7	22
Meat-packing	56.4	46.1	22
Ten-industry sample	61.4	50.0	23
Textiles (cotton)	54.6	47.8	14
Light and power	72.4	58.8	23
Sugar	63.4	53.1	19

NOTE: The average free exchange rate in 1964 was $1.00 = 139.88 pesos (Banco Central de la República Argentina, in Scobie, *Argentina*, p. 309). Figures in the table here are based on CONADE-CEPAL, *Distribución del ingreso y cuentas nacionales*, Vol. 5.

located at the two poles of the distribution within manufacturing, textiles and electricity (which is useful for showing the diversity of standards of living within the working class) and for the sugar industry.

As Table 7 indicates, interindustry wage differentials were more significant for skilled than for unskilled workers. In the sectors discriminated in this study, wages were lowest in meat-packing, even though the difference between that sector and the average for unskilled workers in the ten-industry sample was not very significant. Skilled construction workers were, on the other hand, the best paid in the sample. Their wages, furthermore, were higher than those of skilled workers in any other sector, including electricity and, of course, sugar. But only 20 percent of the industrial workers in the sample were skilled and working in construction. Most migrants in construction were unskilled, and their wages, while lower than those of skilled workers in all sectors except for textiles, were not very different from those of the average unskilled worker. Due to the different qualification structure of the two populations under study, average wages were probably higher in the Tucumán sample, 80 percent of whose workers were skilled. Income differentials associated with skill, finally, were more significant in construction than in manufacturing. The income received by most migrants once in Buenos Aires and Rosario was higher than that in Chaco. In the first place, almost half of the workers in the sample were unemployed before migrating. Second, available estimates of the typical income earned by small farmers and seasonal cotton pickers indicate that urban wages were much higher.[69]

Compared with the workers in the Tucumán sample, these migrants had a lower standard of living as measured by the housing indicator. As reported above, 77 percent were living in shantytowns. The percentages were 75 percent for industrial workers, 69 percent for service workers, and a full 100 percent for the unemployed. Most of the remainder lived in working-class neighborhoods. As in the other study, an index of quality of housing is available (the index is described in the Appendix). In this case, the index combines information about materials used for walls, roof, and floors. The cutoff point between "good" and "bad" housing is lower than in the Tucumán study: the index varies from 0 to 3, and only the top score corresponds to a house that would be comparable to a "good" one in the Tucumán index. The distribution is, however, so skewed that if the cutoff point is 1.5, only 36 percent of the respondents—and 38 percent of the industrial workers—have scores above that point.[70] Quality of housing, finally, is strongly associated with skill.[71]

To complete the discussion of structural properties, a comment on insecurity is in order. These migrants did not experience the uncertainty and danger that were prevalent among workers in the Tucumán study. Only 6 percent of the workers in industry and 3 percent of those in services responded negatively when asked if they felt secure in their jobs (for the text of the question, see Appendix). This was so in spite of the fact that 30 percent of the industrial workers and 24 percent of the service workers reported layoffs at their firms, and that 42 percent of the former and 22 percent of the latter expected layoffs in the future (for the text of the question, see Appendix).

Unlike the established workers of Tucumán, these migrants had a very high level of satisfaction. When asked how satisfied they were with having migrated, 78 percent of them reported to be "happy" or "very happy," and only 3 percent claimed to be "unhappy." Seventy-seven percent said that they would migrate again.[72] They were also satisfied with their jobs: 74 percent of the industrial workers considered their jobs to be "good" or "very good."[73] When asked for causes of dissatisfaction, 27 percent of the employed migrants did not find any, even though 31 percent mentioned the level of wages, and 61 percent felt they were earning less than they deserved.[74] As a reflection of their successful adaptation to the new environment, these migrants felt much less blocked than the established workers in Tucumán: 91 percent of the industrial workers in this sample stated that they would like to become self-employed, and 48 percent of them considered that this change of status was likely or very likely, as compared to only 9 percent in the Tucumán sample.[75] Furthermore, the percentage considering it difficult, very difficult, or impossible for the son of a worker to obtain a degree in law, medicine, or engineering was 56 percent, as compared to 79 percent among the workers in the Tucumán sample in response to a similar question.[76]

The degree of unionization is a further difference between these migrants and the established workers of Tucumán. Migrants were weakly organized, taking into consideration the high level of unionization of the Argentine working class. Even though 45 percent of the dependent migrants in the sample reported being or having been union members, the percentage of those currently unionized among dependent workers in industry and services was 35 percent. In addition, only 9 percent of dependent workers reported they attended union meetings "always" or "frequently." Among industrial workers in particular, the percentage "always" attending union meetings was only 4 percent. Furthermore, when asked whether they remembered any strike, regardless of whether they had participated in it, 54 percent of the total sample responded negatively. Finally, one-third of the migrants did not know what the CGT, the central labor federation, was, and 31 percent had only a vague idea.

There was also a contrast between the political attitudes of the established workers of Tucumán and those of the working class of Buenos Aires and Rosario. The latter group had a low level of interest in politics. When asked if voting is important, 64 percent of the respondents answered affirmatively,[77] but other indicators pointed to low political involvement. In a question about how much interest they had in politics, two-thirds responded that they had none, and only 7 percent reported having "a lot." And when asked if it mattered to them whether elections were held again, 48 percent responded that it did not matter to them, and only 20 percent said it mattered a great deal.[78]

Concerning the extent of its support for Peronism, this sample is similar to the one of industrial workers in Tucumán: the Peronist government was rated as "very good" by 67 percent of the respondents, and "good" by an additional 24 percent.[79] This combined positive evaluation of 91 percent should be compared with percentages of respondents selecting the same alternatives in relation to three post-Peronist administrations. These varied between 7 percent and 17 percent. Last, when asked whether they sympathized with a political party, 43 percent reported having Peronist sympathies, and only 6 percent had sympathy for other parties.[80]

A comment on the political influences derived from the context is relevant. The points of arrival, Buenos Aires and Rosario were, together with Córdoba, the center of political activity in the country, and were also the main bulwarks of the Peronist movement. And the point of origin, Chaco, was also a stronghold of Peronism. In the election of 1965, the Peronist Unión Popular Party polled 41 percent of the total vote—the highest percentage in the country.[81]

A final aspect of Chaco should be mentioned: its structural conduciveness to radicalism. Three traits of the social structure of the province are among those generally associated with the generation of agrarian radicalism: the class system, the insecurity of tenure, and the pattern of settlement. First, small and middle independent peasants, such as those found in Chaco, seem to be more prone to agrarian radicalism than other rural classes.[82] Second, most peasants in Chaco were squatters, the radical predispositions of which are well known.[83] And third, a rural society of recent settlement and with a heterogeneous population, such as Chaco, should be more conducive to the actualization of a radical potential than other types of rural society, because these two characteristics—recent settlement and heterogeneity—would decrease the effectiveness of traditional cultural constraints on peasant mobilization.

Even though there have not been instances of mass mobilization such as peasant rebellions, the possibility that latent agrarian radicalism exists in Chaco cannot be discarded. Chaco is one of the few rural areas of Argentina where there is a long tradition of leftist political activity. During the period in which this study was conducted, radical rural organizations, the agrarian leagues, were being formed in that part of the country. Besides, instances of social banditry have been recorded. Shortly before this survey was conducted, the famous bandit Isidro Velázquez, who had become a folk hero among the lower classes, was killed by the police, and there were reports of widespread popular mourning.[84] Therefore, even though the actual exposure of the respondents to radical political influences is unknown, the possibility that they would have absorbed some form of radicalism while in Chaco should be taken into consideration.

The sample of migrants from Chaco consists, then, of individuals with low levels of centrality and of integration into the industrial world, who were placed in a context in which the potential for the awareness of deprivation was high. Their low levels of education and unionization, finally, make them a suitable group for the study of the effect of deprivation and marginality on the forms of political action.

9. Structural Modernization and Forms of Political Action: A Diachronic View

This chapter takes a preliminary look at the forms of political action of the different groups. Even though the subsequent analysis focuses on the two samples of industrial workers, some attention is also paid here to the other groups: permanent and transient rural workers in Tucumán, and service and unemployed workers in Buenos Aires and Rosario. To begin, I will discuss the operationalization of dissent and radicalism in terms of the available indicators. The distributions of these indicators for the six groups are presented afterward. As these groups can be ordered along a dimension that may be called degree of structural modernization, the results suggest a relationship between modernization and forms of political action. Subsequently, I analyze the effects of structural properties on dissent and radicalism in the two working class samples.

Let us begin with the indicators. I have conceptualized the political action of the working class in terms of the two dimensions that have been labeled dissent and radicalism, and have presented a typology in Chapter 3, Tables 5 and 6. These concepts were suggested to me by observing that the association between indicators of anti-status quo beliefs and of predispositions for radical action in the Tucumán sample was not very high. The four samples of the Tucumán study—the three that are considered in this chapter, plus a sample of transient factory workers excluded from the present discussion[1]—have been compared elsewhere (in an article written with M. Murmis[2]) in relation to two sets of questions. In the first place, there were items having to do with concerns with "mediate" aspects of the situation, i.e., factors that transcend the immediate working environment and are connected with the industry, the national economy, politics, development, and changes in the property of means of production. The last cluster, which can be considered an indicator of what I have called dissent, included questions about the desirability of transforming mills into workers' cooperatives and of expropriating large farms and factories. Second, there was a question about preferred courses of action for the union in case the management does not comply with collective agreements. The list of alternative courses of action included asking for government intervention, striking, seizing the mills, and applying pressure on the management without striking or seizing the mills. The analysis of the answers to these questions revealed that the strength of the association between radicalism and the different orientations varied in the different groups, so the most "radical" stratum included individuals with diverging ideas. Among those workers who considered that seizing the mills was the best course of action whenever management failed to abide by collective agreements, there were those oriented toward mediate goals and toward development, and with strong anticapitalist sentiment, and also those whose propensity for anti–status quo behavior was apparently unrelated to anti–status quo beliefs.[3] In my first formulation of the typology of forms of political action, in a paper dealing with labor participation in populist coalitions, the belief dimension was defined broadly as degree of autonomy.[4] The focus there was on the extent of differentiation between working-class beliefs and those of other classes. In later presentations, the dimension was specified further as consent/dissent with the social order. Working independently with partially different indicators in the established workers study, Sigal has organized responses to the crisis of the sugar industry into a typology that resembles the one presented here.[5]

The questionnaire in the Buenos Aires and Rosario study included similar or equivalent indicators of dissent and radicalism. As far as dissent is concerned, an index was constructed on the basis of questions that refer to the expropriation of farms and factories. In the two questionnaires, respondents who had previously expressed their disapproval of the existence of very large, individually owned farms were asked whether these farms should be taken away from their current owners. In the Tucumán study, this question was also administered to respondents who had previously expressed their disapproval of the fact that mill owners also owned farms. In the other question included in the dissent index, respondents were asked whether factories should be taken away from their current owners.[6] The responses to these items were coded as dichotomies ("yes/other") and combined in the index (for the text of the questions, see Appendix). The "high" category in the new dimension represents agreement with the expropriation of both farms and mills.[7]

It should be clear that even though this index indicates the existence of beliefs opposing private property of the means of production, it is not the operationalization of an ideology opposed to capitalism. Unless preferences about the subsequent fate of expropriated farms and factories are explored, no statement about the degree of articulation of an ideology can be made. In relation to farms, the goal most respondents probably had in mind was the reversion to family production, i.e., in this context, probably to precapitalist agriculture. And their conceptualization of the expropriation of factories, especially in Tucumán, was most likely nationalization along the lines of what can be called the "Argentine road to socialism," i.e., the nationalization of inefficient enterprises by a state whose main concern is the preservation of jobs rather than the increase of productivity.[8] If the index does not measure a specific ideology, nevertheless, it is a good indicator of what I mean by dissent as one of the dimensions of the forms of political action of the working class: a set of diffuse beliefs that would be, if converted into orientations toward action, in opposition to the central institutional characteristics of the social order. Rejection of private property of the means of production, however diffuse, indicates that the legitimacy of capitalism is low, regardless of whether the underlying orientation is backward-looking, aiming at the restoration of a traditional, precommercial social order in which the control of the means of production was decentralized, or forward-looking, oriented toward the actualization of a postcapitalist design. Finally, it is important to point out that, in spite of the lack of an institutionalized anticapitalist ideology, the desirability of capitalism was not an esoteric issue in Argentine political culture, the subculture of the lower classes included. Kirkpatrick administered a questionnaire to a representative sample of the Argentine population in 1965 which contained questions dealing with the expropriation of farms and the elimination of private property from key sectors in the economy. A large proportion of the lower strata in her sample agreed with these items.[9]

The indicators of a predisposition toward radical behavior are different in the two samples. The Tucumán study used the question about what the respondent thought the union should do when management failed to observe collective agreements. One of the alternatives offered (besides asking the government to intervene and/or striking), "to seize the factory as a signal of protest" (for the text of the question, see Appendix), was considered an indicator of high radicalism. As indicated in Chapter 8, mass mobilization, one of whose forms was the seizure of mills, was a typical occurrence. Also typical was the failure of management to comply with such basic contractual obligations as the regular payment of wages. The experience of new workers in Buenos Aires and Rosario, on the other hand, was more diverse, and most of these workers had probably never participated in collective activities of that type. It was also unlikely that they fully understood the language of direct action—"pressures," "strike," "seizure"—with which the workers in Tucumán were so familiar. For this reason, the indicator used in the Buenos Aires-Rosario study is equivalent but not identical to the one selected in Tucumán. Respondents were asked to select a course of action in response to a hypothetical situation: a scenario in which a group of workers felt hurt by measures taken by the management in relation to wages and work conditions. They were then shown pictures illustrating different types of reaction and asked to order these reactions in terms of their effectiveness (see Appendix). The pictures depicted three courses of action that workers affected by a grievance could take: (1) individual demand, illustrated by a worker discussing the content of a letter with a manager or supervisor; (2) collective demand, illustrated by the same worker discussing the letter with his workmates and then confronting the manager in their presence; and (3) collective mobilization, illustrated by a protagonist arousing his fellow workers and then organizing a militant demonstration. The selection of this third course of action was considered as an indicator of predisposition toward radical behavior (for a more detailed description, see Appendix).

The items used in the two studies are equivalent in the sense that in each case respondents were presented with a relatively similar stimulus and were asked to select a course of action out of a repertoire of potential responses available to them and meaningful in their environment. In both situations, the most militant course of action (considered an indicator of radicalism) implied the use of coercion, or at least its threat.

MODERNIZATION, DISSENT, AND RADICALISM

The six groups under consideration can be ranked along a traditionality-modernity continuum that can be called "degree of structural modernization," for it would represent different degrees of modernity of the social structure. We can compare samples of two agrarian classes, the transient laborers—i.e., landless peasants—and the permanent rural workers of Tucumán; two urban nonindustrial lower-class groups, the unemployed and service workers in Buenos Aires and Rosario; and two types of the industrial working class, the "new" workers in the migrants study and the "established" workers in Tucumán. These six groups represent most of the variability of subordinate classes that exist in societies undergoing the process of modernization. The "permanent" precapitalist peasantry would be the main missing group; therefore, they can be viewed, from a diachronic point of view, as "stages" in the transition of lower classes from a precapitalist to a capitalist social structure. These groups can be classified on the basis of the three contexts—agrarian, urban nonindustrial, and industrial—each of which represents a different threshold in the process of modernization, or a higher level of centrality in modern society. These levels are participation in capitalism, in the urban world, and in industry. Within each context, samples can be ranked in terms of integration. Transient rural workers, many of whom are precapitalist peasants for most of the year, are less integrated into capitalist social relations than permanent rural workers, for example. Table 8 shows these intergroup differences. "Low" and "high" refer to the degree of integration within each context.

These groups can also be ranked in terms of their potential for awareness of deprivation. The ranking would depend upon the type of deprivation hypothesis being tested: deprivation that is the result of an individual's comparing his or her present situation with past experiences, or deprivation due to intergroup comparisons in the present. The first type should be lower among migrants, for these individuals had substantially improved their standard of living after migration and were highly satisfied. Deprivation resulting from intergroup comparisons, however, should be higher in the migrant

Table 8. *Degree of Structural Modernization of the Six Samples*

| Context | Sample | Participation in | | |
		Capitalist Social Relations	Urban World	Industrial World
Agrarian	Transient	− (low)	−	−
	Permanent	+ (high)	−	−
Urban nonindustrial	Unemployed	−	+ (low)	−
	Services	+	+ (high)	−
Industrial	New	+	+	+ (low)
	Established	+	+ (*)	+ (high)

*Even though many mills were located in small factory towns, the environment of the sugar industry was by no means "rural" in a sociological sense.

Table 9. *Dissent and Radicalism of Subordinate Strata According to Their Degree of Structural Modernization*

	Rural Transient (N=60) %	Rural Permanent (N=36) %	Urban Unemployed (N=31) %
High dissent	15	11	39
High radicalism	20	17	23

NOTE: See Appendix for operationalization of variables and note on statistical significance.

samples, especially among the unemployed, due to the high conduciveness of the big-city context for comparisons with groups who are better off. This type of deprivation, on the other hand, should be low among industrial workers in the specific setting of the sugar industry for the two reasons discussed in Chapter 8: the concentration of these workers in factory towns, and their higher status vis-à-vis other subordinate groups with whom they were likely to interact. This latter type, finally, should be higher in the more "marginal" groups in each sector, the marginal group being likely to compare itself with other, more integrated strata in the same context.

The distributions of dissent and radicalism for the six groups are shown in Table 9. This table suggests that modernization and radicalism are independent and that the relationship between modernization and dissent is curvilinear. These propositions refer, of course, to magnitudes of respondents in each category of the variables rather than to intensities, which we cannot measure.

The first of these findings is unexpected. It could have been anticipated that the proportion of respondents with a high level of radicalism would be higher in rural groups or in the more marginal ones. These are the strata which one associates with instances of mass radicalism, such as jacqueries or urban riots. These results do not imply, of course, that deprivation and marginality are not operative, for a similar level of radicalism can be produced by different factors in the different groups. It would be possible, for instance, that the radicalism of the unemployed is produced by marginality, while the radicalism of the established workers may be a manifestation of the deliberate implementation of bargaining-by-riot tactics. The fact remains, however, that the degree of modernization of social positions is independent of the proportion of incumbents of these positions

Urban Services (N=48) %	Industrial New (N=144) %	Industrial Established (N=147) %
37	31	24
21	15	19

who have radical propensities. Therefore, whatever relationship exists has to be indirect. Variations in the level of radicalism would be produced by specific conditions whose effects are combined in such a way in the total samples that no meaningful differences among groups are registered. The effects of combinations of structural properties on radicalism will be examined later.

The curvilinear relationship between structural modernization and dissent can be interpreted in terms of variations of structural properties associated with the different social positions. But the hypothesis that differences are due to environmental variations should be discussed first, for the samples in the Buenos Aires and Rosario study have higher proportions of respondents with high dissent than the samples in the Tucumán study. It could be that differences in the level of dissent result from contextual differences.

There are three types of environmental effects that should be considered. The first of these is the difference in time: the Tucumán study was carried out at the end of 1966 while the interviews in Buenos Aires and Rosario were made in 1968–1970. The second possibility is that intergroup differences are determined by contextual variations with respect to political culture, ideologies, and activity. As the larger context, Argentine society, is constant, this second hypothesis leads to two different comparisons of local differences: Tucumán versus Buenos Aires and Rosario and, given the recent character of migration, Tucumán versus Chaco.

The first possibility would be, then, that variations in the level of dissent were produced by factors associated with environmental changes that took place from late 1966 to 1968–1970. It is my impression that this hypothesis should be rejected for three reasons. First, there were no major changes in the Argentine economy and polity between these dates. Second, if one looks specifically at variations in the forms of political action of the working class and of subordinate classes in general during that period, changes in the level of radicalism, indicated by the upsurge of urban disturbances that took place from 1969 onward, are much more noticeable than changes in the level of dissent. Third, scattered quantitative evidence suggests that intergroup differences were not affected by time. The comparison between the findings presented above and those of Kirkpatrick in her 1965 study disconfirms the hypothesis that a process of generalized increase in the level of working class dissent was taking place, for her results indicate that the Argentine lower classes in general had in 1965 a higher level of dissent than the Tucumán samples in 1966.[10] Data from the new workers study, finally, show no significant differences in levels of dissent—and of radicalism—between samples in Buenos Aires and Rosario, in spite of the fact that interviews in Rosario were carried out later than those in Buenos Aires.

The second hypothesis is that intergroup variations result from differences between the contexts in which the respondents lived, i.e., that Buenos Aires and Rosario were more conducive to the generation of anticapitalist orientations than Tucumán. Even though no direct evidence exists in this regard, I am inclined to reject this hypothesis as well. In principle, it is true that the magnitude of general leftist political activity was higher in Buenos Aires—I am not sure about Rosario—than in Tucumán, in terms of the number of active leftist militants, the circulation of leftist periodicals, et cetera. It is not clear, however, that differences in the level of dissent were due to this factor. To begin with, the exposure of the groups in the Tucumán study, the working class in particular, to anti–status quo ideological stimuli was very high. Political activity, especially leftist political activity, was also intense in Tucumán, and it was focused to a large extent on the industrial workers of the sugar industry. Further, it should be remembered that these workers had a high degree of political awareness and union participation. And the FOTIA, the sugar workers' union, was more militant in its demands and more radical in its behavior than most unions in Buenos Aires and Rosario—certainly much more so than the unions of the construction, meat packing, and metal industries, where most workers in the sample were working. Finally, the questioning of private ownership of the means of production was not an academic issue in Tucumán, where the crisis of inefficient capitalism was conducive to the development of generalized anticapitalist attitudes. In fact, references to land reform and the nationalization and cooperativization of mills were commonplace in political discourse there.

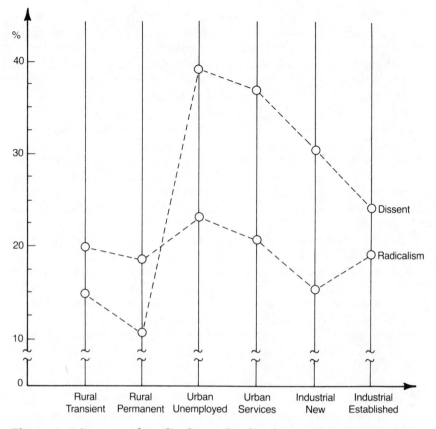

Figure 1. *Dissent and Radicalism of Subordinate Strata According to Their Degree of Structural Modernization*

On the other hand, there is no evidence that workers in the migrant samples had a high degree of exposure to anticapitalist ideology or to left-wing political activity. It should be remembered that the level of union participation and of political awareness among these workers was very low. Further, migrants living in shantytowns were relatively isolated from Marxist stimuli. Most leftist political activity at that time took place in non–working-class milieux, such as universities, organizations of the intelligentsia, and so on. The impact of the Marxist left on the labor movement was still limited, and organizational efforts by different left-wing organizations in shantytowns had been largely unsuccessful so far.

There is, finally, a third possibility: that the higher level of dissent among migrants was an effect of the context in which migration originated, i.e., Chaco. As was mentioned in Chapter 8, several traits of the social structure of this province could be conducive to the generation of agrarian radicalism: the existence of a class of small free peasants, the fact that most of these peasants are squatters, and the peculiarity that Chaco is an area of recent settlement and that its population is heterogeneous. Latent agrarian radicalism would have produced a propensity to dissent after migration. The hypothesis here is that intergroup differences might have resulted from the different political traditions in Tucumán and Chaco. A related proposition would link dissent to the integration of precapitalist peasants into industrial capitalism; the higher level of dissent among migrants would result from the fact that many of them had a precapitalist background. This latter proposition, however, would relate dissent to one of the structural properties rather than to the context as such, and will be examined in detail in the next chapter.

In principle, the level of organized political activity, especially among subordinate strata, was much higher in Tucumán than in Chaco. It is not impossible, however, that there was more latent dissent in Chaco and that, in spite of the rhetoric of dissent in Tucumán, the development of actual dissent would have been inhibited there by the more traditional social structure of this province. Tucumán is an area of old settlement, in which there was a powerful regional elite with a considerable degree of hegemony and in which the impact of European immigration was less than in Chaco. In the absence of specific evidence, however, any judgment on the validity of this hypothesis would be unwarranted.

It would seem, therefore, that hypotheses linking intergroup differences in the level of dissent with environmental variations, either temporal or spatial, should either be rejected or held in abeyance. The other possibility is, of course, that differences are determined by structural properties, and the remainder of this book shows that structural properties are associated with the forms of political action. As far as dissent is concerned, an inspection of the curvilinear pattern found in Table 9 and Figure 1 suggests the hypothesis that this dimension is positively associated with deprivation, and negatively with integration and centrality. The only samples whose size allows elaboration are the two working-class groups, and these are later studied in detail.

Table 10. *Forms of Political Action of the Different Samples*

Rural samples

	Transient Dissent				Permanent Dissent	
	Low	High			Low	High
Radicalism Low	72%	8%		Radicalism Low	75%	8%
High	13%	7%		High	14%	3%

$(N=60, Q=.62)$ $(N=36, Q=.29)$

Urban nonindustrial samples

	Unemployed Dissent				Services Dissent	
	Low	High			Low	High
Radicalism Low	52%	26%		Radicalism Low	.52%	27%
High	10%	13%		High	10%	10%

$(N=31, Q=.45)$ $(N=48, Q=.32)$

Industrial samples

	New Workers Dissent				Established Workers Dissent	
	Low	High			Low	High
Radicalism Low	61%	24%		Radicalism Low	66%	15%
High	8%	8%		High	10%	9%

$(N=144, Q=.44)$ $(N=147, Q=.59)$

NOTE: See Appendix for operationalization of variables and note on statistical significance.

Table 11. *Direction of Deviation from Acquiescence*

Sample		$D-$ $R+$ (Mobilization) %
Rural	Transient (N=17)	47
	Permanent (N=9)	55
Urban nonindustrial	Unemployed (N=15)	20
	Services (N=23)	22
Industrial	New workers (N=56)	20
	Established workers (N=50)	30

NOTE: See Appendix for operationalization of variables and note on statistical significance. Percentages for the permanent rural workers were computed on fewer than ten cases.

THE DEGREE OF CONSISTENCY BETWEEN IDEAS AND PROPENSITIES FOR BEHAVIOR

The typology of forms of political action discussed in Chapter 3 can be operationalized on the basis of the indicators presented in this chapter. The composition of the different groups is reported in Table 10. The table indicates, first, that the overall degree of consistency between anti–status quo beliefs and propensity for anti–status quo behavior is not very high. Yule's Q, not a very demanding coefficient, ranges from .20 to .62. Second, the degree of association varies substantially among the different subordinate strata. The distinction between dissent and radicalism, therefore, seems to be empirically useful. Further, the degree of consistency between ideas and propensities for behavior is higher for the two extreme strata: the most "traditional" group, the rural transient workers, and the most "modern" one, the established industrial workers. These are the only samples in which the value of Q exceeds .50. The implication is, of course, that one of the consequences of release and absorption processes occurring during modernization is the decrease in the degree of consistency between political ideas and propensities for behavior.

Groups differ in their composition. Even though acquiescence is the most frequent form of political action in all samples, the range of variability is wide: from half of the total in urban nonindustrial groups to three-quarters in the agrarian ones. As for the direction of

D+ R− (Reformism) %	D+ R+ (Revolutionary action) %
29	24
33	11
53	27
57	22
61	20
44	26

the deviation from acquiescence, the likelihood of the deviation toward alternative forms of political action varies for the different strata. The percentages of respondents deviating in different directions are shown in Table 11. This table indicates that, when subordinate strata deviate from acquiescence, agrarian groups are more likely to turn to mobilization, while urban and industrial groups tend toward reformism. When confronted with the problem of opposition to the status quo, rural strata are more prone to increase their radicalism than their dissent, while the opposite is true for urban and industrial strata. Finally, if rural permanent workers are excepted, the proportion of respondents with "revolutionary" propensities is fairly stable across the remaining five groups, for the probability of a simultaneous increase of dissent and radicalism is approximately the same.

10. The Effects of Integration and Centrality

INTEGRATION AND FORMS OF POLITICAL ACTION

Integration, as a structural property, refers to the incorporation of individuals into the working class. A difficulty in the study of integration arises from the fact that many times it is not possible to isolate this variable from centrality factors because integration in this sense is correlated with macrosociological processes associated with the development of capitalism: the increase in the productivity of labor and the corresponding changes in the division of labor. When the political consequences of the development of capitalism are studied, therefore, the differences between these micro and macro processes should be kept in mind. For instance, when the proposition that the development of capitalism leads to working-class acquiescence is advanced, the two independent variables are implied: the "macro" process of increase in the productivity of labor and the "micro" process of integration of individuals into the working class and the industrial world. The problem is compounded because, as will be seen, these two independent variables seem to have similar effects: both centrality and integration lead to acquiescence.

The opposite of integration is marginality, which is discussed in the literature on the political behavior of urban marginals, be they recent migrants or the "urban poor." (The effect of the incorporation into the working class will be considered later.) One of the reasons why the Bakunin-Marx debate is still alive is that hypotheses and data supporting both sides are in circulation. The proposition that marginality leads to discontent, radicalism, and deviance in general seems to be a common-sense generalization, but much of the contemporary research is inconsistent with that proposition.

Urban marginals are the stratum from which discontent-producing psychological states, such as relative deprivation, frustration, and anomie, have been most frequently predicated. A typical statement in this connection is the following one by Olson: "The man who has been tempted away from his village, . . . may well be a disaffected gainer from economic growth. He has been, albeit voluntarily, uprooted and is not apt soon to acquire comparable social connections in the city. He is, therefore, prone to join destabilizing social movements."[1] The underlying proposition is Durkheimian in nature: disintegration is expected to lead to deviant behavior, one of whose forms is political radicalism.

The opposite point of view holds that migrants, and the urban poor in general, tend to be politically passive or at least not especially prone to deviate from acquiescence. A persuasive argument in this regard has been articulated by Tilly and his colleagues: "On the face of it, we have no good reason to expect marginal and desperate populations to mount violence-producing collective actions. Unless breakdown and dissolution lead desperate and marginal populations to *re*organize themselves around new beliefs and claims, the observed sequence of actions leading to collective violence casts serious doubt on the classic breakdown-dissolution theory."[2] In their view, collective action flows from solidarity and organization rather than from dissolution and dislocation. For this reason, they expect recent migrants and new operatives to have a lower propensity than established workers to participate in mass political activity. In relation to industrial conflict, Shorter and Tilly argue thus against dislocation theory:

> To the extent that this line of argument foresees a connection between migration, dislocation and the appearance of organized conflict, we think it wrong. In our view, the motors of militancy are set in motion not by the marginal, the unintegrated and the recently arrived, but by workers who belong to firmly established networks of long standing at the core of urban industrial society. We would therefore expect the move to the city to *impede* worker capacities for collective action and to stifle militancy simply because recently arrived migrants, however hostile and sullen they may feel towards "bourgeois society," have great difficulty in forming effective organizations.[3]

Even though most empirical studies support Tilly's position, a significant amount of negative evidence exists. Tilly and his colleagues have found no direct positive correlations between the rates of urbanization and industrialization, on the one hand, and dependent variables such as strike activity (for France[4]) and collective protest (for France, Italy, and Germany[5]) on the other. Nelson, in an extensive review of cross-national research, has concluded that the level of discontent among the urban poor is low, the reason being that the amount of relative deprivation in these strata is lower than scholars think.[6] Most studies she examines are consistent with this generalization: data from India, Chile, the United States, and France show no relationship between mass migration into cities and support for the left or participation in violent activities.[7] Nelson reports, however, negative evidence for Italy, where she interprets a positive correlation between migration and support for the Communists and participation in demonstrations in terms of political socialization.[8] She also compares scores in a "radicalism scale" for different categories of urban lower classes in Argentina and Chile. The comparison reveals that low-level nonfactory workers—many of whom are likely to be recent migrants and/or urban marginals—have average scores that are similar to or slightly higher than those of the different categories of factory workers.[9]

Cornelius has conducted a comprehensive review of the evidence, this time with a focus on Latin America. After analyzing this literature, he concluded that urban migration "does not necessarily result in severe frustration of expectations for socioeconomic improvement or widespread personal and social disorganization; and that even where these conditions are present, they do not necessarily lead to political alienation. Nor does alienation necessarily lead to political radicalization or disruptive behavior. . . . With few exceptions these studies find that urban migrants fail in most respects to conform to the usual conception of a highly politicized, disposable mass."[10] Even though most of the studies he reviewed support these conclusions, Cornelius also reports a considerable amount of negative evidence in relation to some indicators. Thus, migration has been found to produce frustration in only two out of twenty-nine empirical studies, and political radicalization in only two studies out of twenty-two. On the other hand, migration appears associated with alienation and "non-supportive legitimacy orientation" in ten out of seventeen studies, and with increased politicization in five studies out of twenty-three.[11]

Instances supporting both the discontent and the passivity hypotheses, therefore, can be found. There are several reasons for this, besides the different types of political socialization. In the first place, migrants have diverse backgrounds. There are reasons to think that the political behavior of migrants released from capitalist agriculture will be different from that of migrants coming from the various types of precapitalist agriculture. In an analysis of the political behavior of marginals, therefore, the premigration background should be specified. Second, it is difficult to generalize on the intensity of postmigration relative deprivation, for the levels of expectations and rewards are empirically variable. Furthermore, relative deprivation is a short-term phenomenon; the theory predicts that, in the long run, there will be an adjustment of expectations to realistic levels.[12]

A first line of argument concerning the political behavior of new workers can be deduced from Marxist theory. Since organization and the development of class consciousness take time, there is no reason to expect new workers to have a high level of militancy. Shorter and Tilly, in the passage quoted above, reason along these lines.[13] The opposite viewpoint has been argued extensively. Most analyses of new working classes predict that massive discontent and protest will erupt in the early period of industrialization. This would be a consequence of the traumatic aftereffects of the incorporation of peasants and marginals into the working class and the industrial world. This trauma is caused not only by uprootedness as such, but also by the transition from precapitalist to capitalist social relations. This shift entails the separation from the means of production, the insertion in the labor market, the specialized division of labor of the manufacturing world, and the bureaucratic organization of the factory. Discontent arising from this transition is likely to convert itself into a propensity to support socialist ideologies in the case where the diffusion of these ideologies is made possible by the structural context, for socialism, and especially Marxism, appears as a theoretical statement of the trauma of incorporation. This point has been convincingly argued by Ulam:

> Without having read a word of Marx or Lenin, an illiterate peasant who is being squeezed economically or forced to give up his land and work in a factory experiences almost instinctively the feelings that Marxism formulates in a theoretical language: a sense of alienation springing from his loss of property and status, and an antagonism towards the people and authority personifying the mysterious forces that have made his previous social existence impossible or increasingly hazardous economically and that have destroyed the whole basis of his beliefs and values without giving him anything in return.[14]

Shorter and Tilly's hypothesis is supported by their study of France, where they found no positive relationship between the growth of the labor force and strike rates.[15] On the other hand, Kerr and his associates have concluded, after a review of the evolution of industrial conflict, that "worker protest in the course of industrialization tends to peak relatively early and to decline in intensity thereafter."[16] In a study of class consciousness among industrial workers in Detroit, Leggett found higher levels of class consciousness among uprooted workers and especially among those coming from traditional agrarian backgrounds.[17] Other types of evidence are also pertinent. It is well known that the large socialist and communist parties in industrial societies have acquired their mass base at relatively early points in the industrialization process and have thereafter preserved their support on the basis of the development of a political subculture, and Kautsky has found a curvilinear relationship between economic development and communist party strength.[18] There are indications that the political impact of incorporation into the working class is dependent upon the type of social relations in which individuals had previously participated. In a classic comparative analysis of Scandinavian labor movements, Galenson linked the lesser discontent among Danish workers, as compared to Norwegian and Swedish workers, to the fact that the Danish working class was formed on the basis of dependent laborers while in the other two cases workers had been independent farmers.[19]

Beyond the early stage of industrialization, the familiar debate reappears. For Marxists, the socialization of individuals into the working class and the industrial system is expected to lead to an increase in their revolutionary potential. The opposite argument is that working class alienation is reduced by the integration of individuals into the working class. It is also argued that what Kerr and his associates have called "the logic of industrialism"[20] will eventually lead to the institutionalization of conflict and the reduction of protest.

The results for the different samples presented in Table 9 suggest that integration has an adapting effect, thus lending apparent support to the propositions that discontent is higher among marginals than among integrated workers and higher among new workers than among established ones. The remainder of this chapter's discussion of integration analyzes the effect of several integration variables on both dissent and radicalism in the two working-class groups. Most of the analysis deals with the sample of less integrated workers, i.e., the new workers.

Industrial vs. Preindustrial Background

Ideally, in order to examine the possible relationships between the degree of modernity of fathers' occupations and their sons' levels of dissent and radicalism, it would be necessary to know whether the fathers were employed in agriculture or industry and, for those working in agriculture, whether they were wage laborers or precapitalist peasants. Unfortunately, the two studies differ in relation to the availability of this information. In the new workers sample, detailed data are available for both agrarian and urban occupations, but the proportion of fathers who were industrial workers is so small that no analysis of that group is possible. In the established workers sample, on the other hand, the occupation of fathers not working in the sugar industry—either as industrial or rural workers—has not been specified, except for nonsugar agriculture (eight cases). Therefore, the variable had to be broken down differently in the two samples.

Among new workers, fathers' occupations have been classified into three groups: independent agriculture, which in this case refers mostly to precapitalist minifundio operators, i.e., non–wage labor agriculture; dependent agriculture, i.e., wage labor; and urban. Among established workers, on the other hand, fathers' occupations were dichotomized into factory workers in the sugar industry and "other," the latter category probably being synonymous with nonindustrial occupations, given the characteristics of the economy and social structure of Tucumán.

A further difficulty is that the time reference of fathers' occupations is different in the two samples. In the case of new workers, there is information about fathers' occupations when the respondents entered the labor force—when they were twelve to sixteen years of age—while in the established workers study the question refers to the current occupation or to the last occupation (in the case where the father was unemployed, retired, or dead). Given the rigidity of the economy of Tucumán, however, it is reasonable to assume that those fathers who were industrial workers at or near the end of their careers had had the same occupation when their sons entered the labor force. The two samples are, therefore, comparable.

Table 12*a* indicates that, among new workers, the father's occupation does not affect dissent, but it does produce a weak effect on radicalism, for sons of precapitalist peasants are slightly more prone to high radicalism than sons of the other two categories of fathers. As I have detailed information on the type of agrarian background of the respondents of this sample, the effect of insertion into precapitalist versus capitalist agriculture is analyzed below when work careers are examined. Table 12*b* shows that, in the other sample, as in the case of new workers, occupation of the fathers is independent of dissent but that it also has a very small relationship with radicalism. Here also those respondents whose fathers belonged to the most

Table 12. *Dissent and Radicalism by Father's Occupation*

	Dissent		
a. Father's occupation (new workers)	Ind. Agr.	Dep. Agr.	Urban
	[31% (54)	29% (52)	30%] (20)
b. Father's occupation (established workers)	Factory	Other	
	[25% (77)	23%] (70)	
c. b by vulnerability to the crisis (% df)	Secure	Threatened	Closed
	+21%	−12%	[−9%]
d. b by size of plant	Small (390–572)	Medium (579–756)	Large (814+)
(% df)	−11%	[+2%]	+12%
e. b by efficiency	Low–Medium	High	
(% df)	[−4%]	[+5%]	

NOTE: *a* and *b* show percentages of "high" dissent and radicalism; *c–e* are elaborations of *b*: they show percentage differences between "factory" and "other." Differences of less than 10% are enclosed in brackets. See Appendix for operationalization of variables and note on statistical significance.

"traditional" category are somewhat more likely to exhibit high radicalism.

It is advisable to elaborate Table 12*b*: as will be remembered, the sample of established workers included mills whose degree of vulnerability to the crisis was very different. It might be argued that, when looking at the political action of established workers, it is important to discriminate the secure mills, for they represent the "pure" or typical working-class situation. Table 12*c* shows that, when exposure to the crisis is controlled, substantial differences emerge. Among secure workers, sons of factory workers are more adapted than sons of nonfactory workers, and the effect on dissent is much stronger than the effect on radicalism. It is when insecurity arises, on the other hand, that integration increases the level of dissent. Among workers in threatened mills, high integration into the working class produces a reformist effect. In this group, sons of industrial workers have more dissent and less radicalism than other

Radicalism

Ind. Agr.	Dep. Agr.	Urban
[20%	13%	15%]
(54)	(52)	(20)

Factory	Other	
[16%	23%]	
(77)	(70)	

Secure	Threatened	Closed
[+9%]	+13%	[−3%]

Small	Medium	Large
(390−572)	(579−756)	(814+)
[−7%]	+21%	+13%

ow−Medium	High	
[+4%]	+15%	

operatives. In the case of workers of closed mills, finally, the father's integration is also directly related to dissent, even though the effect is weak, and independent of radicalism. Therefore, in "normal" times, individuals born in the working class are more predisposed to acquiescence than their upwardly mobile counterparts, but their granting of legitimacy to capitalist institutions is contingent upon the performance of these institutions.

It is not possible to introduce skill as a test factor, due to the skewness of this variable: there are only six unskilled sons of industrial workers. The effect of size of plant is shown in Table 12*d*. This table indicates that the adaptive effect of the father's integration is concentrated among workers at the large mills. In medium-sized plants the father's integration reduces radicalism but has no effect on dissent; and in smaller mills integration is positively related to both components of the forms of political action—even though the effect on radicalism is weak. As for efficiency of mills, finally, Table

12*e* shows that the negative relationship between the father's integration and radicalism is strong in the highly efficient plants.

In summary, the elaboration of Table 12*b* indicates that, among secure workers and in large plants, sons of industrial workers are less likely to exhibit high dissent and high radicalism than sons of nonindustrial workers; and that in highly efficient mills the former are less prone to radicalism than the latter. On the other hand, sons of industrial workers are more likely than other workers to reject the social order in contexts of insecurity and in small plants, i.e., in less typical or central working-class situations.

I will now explore the consequences of the type of agrarian experience on the forms of political action. As this information is primarily available for the sample of new workers, the analysis focuses on them.

Table 13*a* indicates that, when workers with different degrees of exposure to agriculture in their premigration work careers are compared, the intensity of agricultural experience does not affect their level of radicalism, but rather their level of dissent. Migrants whose careers in the place of origin were in agriculture exclusively appear to be less predisposed to high dissent than those migrants who combined agriculture and other occupations.

Table 13*b*–*e*, however, show that the effect of agrarian experience is dependent upon the type of social relations in which individuals participated prior to their incorporation into the industrial world. In Table 13*b*, those respondents who belonged exclusively to precapitalist agriculture and those who belonged exclusively to capitalist agriculture throughout their agrarian careers are compared. It turns out that the two types of agriculture differ in their consequences for the forms of political action. Individuals who have been exclusively "independent" producers—in this context, precapitalist minifundio operators—are more likely to have both high dissent and high radicalism than migrants who have been rural wage laborers exclusively. The implication is that deviation from acquiescence among recent industrial workers results more from the clash between types of social relations than from the transition from agriculture as such to industry.

Table 13*c* and *d* offer further evidence. The first of these, Table 13*c*, shows that the higher the exposure to independent agriculture, the higher the level of both dissent and radicalism—even though there is a puzzling curvilinearity in the latter relationship, which cannot be analyzed further due to the small number of cases. And Table 13*d* indicates that participation in capitalist agriculture has the opposite effect: individuals who spent their entire rural careers as wage laborers are less predisposed to either high radicalism or high dissent than migrants who belonged to this type of agriculture only partially.

Table 13 *e*, which concerns the last occupation prior to migration, yields results that are consistent with previous findings. Migrants participating in precapitalist agriculture had higher dissent and higher radicalism than migrants who were wage laborers.

The conclusion is, therefore, that the extent of deviation from acquiescence among new workers of rural background probably depends on the type of social relations they participated in prior to their incorporation into the working class. Individuals who were independent precapitalist producers are more predisposed to high dissent and high radicalism than individuals who have already been socialized into capitalism. This finding suggests the hypothesis that the expansion of capitalist social relations in agriculture *prior* to industrialization could have stabilizing consequences for the social order. Furthermore, it offers a possible explanation for the cross-national differences in the political behavior of migrants and of recent members of the working class.

Insertion into the Industrial and Urban World

This section concludes with some references to the effect of integration into the current position on the forms of political action. We will look at the consequences of integration into the current job and, for the migrant sample, into the urban world. Information on length of employment in the current job is available for the two samples, but different levels of this variable are measured in each case. In the sample of new workers, the distribution of seniority permits a study of the initial exposure to the industrial world. Only 36 percent of the respondents in the sample had held their current jobs for more than two years. In the group of established workers, on the other hand, the distribution is so skewed that it is impossible to analyze the first impact of the industrial environment. There are only twenty-one cases, or 14 percent of the sample, of workers whose seniority was less than ten years. For the group of established workers I also have a measure of integration into the industry: the proportion of the work career spent in the sugar industry. There is, finally, information on the migrants' length of residence in Buenos Aires and Rosario. The effects of these variables have been summarized in Table 14.

In relation to the integration of established workers into the sugar industry, table 14 *a* shows that individuals who spent their entire work careers in this industry are less prone to high dissent and

Table 13. ***Dissent and Radicalism by Type of Agrarian Background (New Workers Sample)***

	Dissent			
a. Time spent in agriculture	<100%		100%	
	41% (63)		25% (77)	
b. Type of agrarian experience	Other	Indep. 100%	Dep. 100%	
	36% (89)	41% (17)	16% (38)	
c. Time spent in independent agriculture	0	1–49%	50–99%	100%
	33% (84)	25% (28)	27% (11)	41% (17)
d. Time spent in dependent agriculture	0	1–49%	50–99%	100%
	39% (54)	35% (17)	39% (31)	16% (38)
e. Last job prior to migration	Agr. Indep.	Agr. Dep.	Urban	
	36% (28)	24% (63)	30% (40)	

NOTE: Table shows percentages of "high" dissent and radicalism. See Appendix for operationalization of variables.

high radicalism than workers whose degree of integration is less, and that the effect on radicalism is stronger than that on dissent. Length of employment (Table 14*b*) seems to have similar consequences. Seniority reduces the proportion of workers with high dissent and high radicalism, and the latter effect is much stronger, even though the relationship is curvilinear. Unfortunately, it is not possible to disaggregate the effect of seniority from that of age, due to the high correlation between these variables. Given the skewness of the distribution of seniority among sugar workers and my focus on the initial exposure to the industrial world, it seems more interesting to go on to the new workers sample.

Table 14*c* indicates that the first impact of industrial experience on the forms of political action is partially different from the subse-

Radicalism

<100%	100%
[17% (63)	13%] (77)

Other	Indep. 100%	Dep. 100%
17% (89)	23% (17)	8% (38)

0	1–49%	50–99%	100%
11% (84)	29% (28)	— (11)	23% (17)

0	1–49%	50–99%	100%
15% (54)	18% (17)	23% (31)	8% (38)

Agr. Indep.	Agr. Dep.	Urban
25% (28)	13% (63)	12% (40)

quent one that we have seen among established workers. Among new workers, seniority is also negatively associated with dissent, but its effect on radicalism is very slight. Centrality variables specify the effect of seniority on the forms of political action of new workers. Table 14*d* shows that for individuals in construction, the only industry in the sample in which there is a proportion of skilled workers large enough to permit analysis, the original relationship holds—and is strengthened for radicalism—among the unskilled. For skilled workers, on the other hand, seniority produces a mobilizational effect. It reduces dissent—to a lesser extent than among the unskilled—but it also increases radicalism. This effect is the only instance in which there is a significant positive relationship between integration to the current position and one of the components

Table 14. *Dissent and Radicalism by Integration to Current Position*

	Dissent		
a. Time spent in the sugar industry (established workers)	<100%		100%
	30% (53)		20% (94)
b. Seniority (established workers)	0–9 yrs.	10–19 yrs.	20+ yrs.
	33% (21)	23% (53)	22% (73)
c. Seniority (new workers)	0–6 mos.	7–24 mos.	25+ mos.
	41% (46)	32% (44)	22% (50)
d. c by skill (constr. only) 0–6 mos./7+ mos. (% df)	Unskilled		Skilled
	−25%		[−7%]
e. c by size of plant (% df)	To 25		26+
	−3% −21%		−22% +5%
f. Time of residence in city (new workers)	To 2 yrs.	2–4 yrs.	4+ yrs.
	41% (46)	30% (57)	22% (41)

NOTE: *a–c* and *f* show percentages of "high" dissent and radicalism; *d–e* are elaborations of *c*: they show percentage differences among categories of seniority. A difference of less than 10 percent is between brackets. Seniority was dichotomized in *d* because there are only six construction workers in the highest level of seniority. See Appendix for operationalization of variables and note on statistical significance.

of the forms of political action. The very weak association between seniority and radicalism in Table 14*c*, therefore, hides diverging relationships.

On the other hand, Table 14*e* indicates that the impact of seniority on dissent occurs earlier in the larger plants, where a possible curvilinear effect is hinted at, and that the negative association with radicalism is concentrated in the larger plants; in the smaller ones, the relationship is small and curvilinear. Table 14*f*, finally, shows the effect of length of residence in Buenos Aires and Rosario. In this case integration also has an adaptive impact: the longer migrants

Radicalism

<100%	100%	
34% (53)	11% (94)	
0–9 yrs.	10–19 yrs.	20+ yrs.
48% (21)	8% (53)	19% (73)
0–6 mos.	7–24 mos.	25+ mos.
[20% (46)	14% (44)	14%] (50)
Unskilled	Skilled	
−20%	+12%	
To 25	26+	
−8% +6%	−7% −7%	
To 2 yrs.	2–4 yrs.	4+ yrs.
26% (46)	10% (57)	10% (41)

live in the city, the less prone they are to have high levels of both dissent and radicalism.

These findings confirm much of the theory and research on the effect of the amount of industrial experience on working-class political action. Except for skilled construction workers in relation to radicalism, the longer the individuals are exposed to the industrial and urban world, the less likely they are to deviate from acquiescence. Centrality variables affect this relationship, even though the consequences of skill and of size are different. The adaptive impact of integration occurs among the less central individuals—the unskilled—and, as far as dissent is concerned, more quickly in the more central settings, i.e., the larger plants.

The preceding analysis indicates that the differences between the two groups of industrial workers in relation to dissent and radicalism that we have seen in Table 9 are specified by integration factors. Tables 12–14 show that the relatively higher level of dissent among new workers is partially due to their lower level of integration and that the apparent similarity between the two groups in relation to the level of radicalism disappears when integration variables are considered.

The different dimensions of integration have, in most contexts, adaptive consequences, i.e., they are associated with reductions in the levels of dissent, of radicalism, or of both. These findings are consistent with the proposition that there is a curvilinear relationship between structural modernization and the legitimacy of capitalism. Ceteris paribus, of course, Table 12c suggests one of the possible factors that can reverse this relationship. In contexts of insecurity, i.e., when capitalism "fails to deliver," integration is positively related to dissent (this issue will be discussed in Chapter 11).

Even though the evidence reported here is not directly relevant to the proposition that marginals without industrial experience are more likely to deviate from acquiescence than established workers, these findings support the proposition that, after individuals are incorporated into the working class, their opposition to the social order is likely to decline. We have seen the adaptive effect of different variables: among new workers, seniority—especially among the unskilled and those employed in large plants—and time of residence in the city; and among established workers, father's occupation—in secure contexts and in large plants—time spent in the sugar industry, and seniority.

The association that was found, finally, between the type of workers' social relations in agriculture before their incorporation into the working class and their forms of political action suggests one of the microsociological linkages that could explain the covariation that exists between types of precapitalist society and types of industrial polity. Participation in capitalist agriculture prior to the entry into the working class tends to socialize individuals into capitalism and thus facilitate a smooth integration into the industrial world. On the other hand, the transformation of peasants, in the strict sense, into factory workers is likely to produce discontent. Instability during the process of modernization, then, is more likely to be caused by the transition between modes of production than by industrialization per se.

CENTRALITY AND FORMS OF POLITICAL ACTION

Four indicators of centrality are available. Three of them are characteristics of productive units: sector of industry—construction versus manufacturing—in the new workers sample; efficiency, in the established workers sample; and size of plant, in the two studies. The fourth variable, skill, is an indicator of centrality at the individual level and is also available in both groups. These four indicators cover the different dimensions of centrality. Sector of industry and efficiency are related to differences in the level of productivity of labor and to variations in the division of labor; size is an indicator of the degree of bureaucratization; and skill refers to the hierarchical differentiation of individuals within productive units.

Characteristics of Productive Units

Let us begin with sector of industry. The political action of the working class varies both among industries and among productive units within industries. Differences in the division of labor is one of the dimensions presumably underlying these variations.

The development of industry determines changes in the division of labor within productive units. Both technological progress and the increase in the productivity of labor—Marx's "development of productive forces"—cause the division of labor to change along two dimensions: the nature of the activities to be performed by the workers—the transition from the direct to the indirect execution of tasks—and the degree of centralization of the productive process. The nature of tasks changes due to mechanization and automation, and the degree of coordination of activities increases as a consequence of both technological and market imperatives.[21] In craft industries, such as construction or printing, productive units are the locus of coexistence of workers who perform their activities independently of each other; the introduction of machinery and the assembly line produces a higher level of coordination; and automation, finally, eliminates the direct execution of tasks.

The transition from craft industries to machine industry and then to automation—from phase A to phase B, and from phase B to phase C, to use Touraine's terminology—is associated with changes in the political action of the working class. Thus, the high propensity for dissent and radicalism of workers in some phase A industries (such as mining, docking, and shipbuilding) in many countries has been noted by several authors.[22] On the other hand, there is evidence pointing to a curvilinear relationship between the development of the division of labor and variables that indicate discontent, alienation, or class consciousness. Both Blauner's comparative study of industries in the United States and Touraine's analogous work in France suggest the proposition that deviation from acquiescence is higher in phase B industries.[23] As for phase C, most available evidence points to the decline of dissent and radicalism among workers in automated industries, the "new working class" theory notwithstanding.[24] In assessing these findings, it is not clear how much causal weight should be attributed to changes in productivity or in the division of labor as such. Revolutionary propensities among miners and other phase A workers, for instance, have been related to characteristics such as ecological isolation,[25] and the adaptation of phase C workers might be due mainly to their low deprivation and high job security, as well as to global characteristics of advanced industrial societies.

The data permit us to examine the effects both of interindustry differences and variations in the level of technological modernization within an industry. In the sample of new workers, it is possible to compare construction, a phase A industry, with manufacturing, which in the case of metal, meat packing, and other industries in Buenos Aires and Rosario, is most likely phase B. Finally, in the sample of established workers—a phase B setting—the index of efficiency that was mentioned in Chapter 8 is an indicator of the degree of technological modernization within the sugar industry. Tables 15 and 16 show the effects of sector of industry and efficiency on the forms of political action.

Let us begin with sector of industry. Table 15 a indicates that sector does not affect radicalism, but workers in manufacturing are less prone to high dissent than workers in construction. This difference is probably not caused by differences in the level of satisfaction. The proportion of construction workers earning less than 30,000 pesos was much lower than that of manufacturing workers— 11 percent versus 27 percent—and the proportion of construction workers who were satisfied with their jobs was higher than that of manufacturing workers. (The percentage of those considering their job to be "very good" or "good" was 81 percent among the former and 67 percent among the latter.)

Construction and manufacturing differ not only in terms of the type of division of labor—i.e., in terms of centralization of the productive process—but also in relation to the degree of bureaucratization, which is indicated by size. In Table 15 b size of plant has been introduced as a test factor. The original relationship is specified. In the larger plants, the effect of the transition to manufacture is adaptive. In the smaller shops, on the other hand, the level of dissent is independent of sector, but radicalism is higher in manufacture. This table indicates that dissent is not reduced by the shift from construction to manufacture as such, but by the changes in centralization and bureaucratization that are associated with size variations in manufacturing settings. These changes are much less noticeable in the construction industry. Furthermore, the apparent absence of association between sector of industry and radicalism actually results from two opposite relationships that cancel each other out.

The effects of size will be examined in greater detail later. We may turn now to the type of agrarian background of the workers in each sector. There are no selective recruitment patterns associated with sector, either in terms of percentage of the premigration career spent in agriculture or the type of agrarian experience. As for the effect of these variables on the original relationship, Table 15c and d indicates that the association between sector and dissent is specified also by the type of agrarian background. Table 15c shows that the greater difference in the level of dissent occurs among migrants who spent their entire work careers prior to migration in agriculture. And Table 15d suggests, in spite of the small number of cases, that the effect of the transition to manufacture is greater among workers with a more traditional background, i.e., independent agriculture.

Finally, Table 15e shows the impact of seniority. The differences between construction and manufacturing in relation to the level of dissent obtain during the first two years of experience in the job and cease thereafter. Dissent is reduced by experience in industry, whatever the sector, but this table suggests that the lower the level of development of the division of labor, the slower the effect of industrial experience on dissent. Differences between construction and manufacturing workers in relation to the level of dissent are, therefore, a short-term phenomenon. In conclusion, Table 15 shows that the transition from construction to manufacturing reduces dissent, chiefly among the workers less integrated into the industrial world. In large plants, radicalism drops as well. In this latter setting, therefore, the shift from phase A to phase B is adaptive. Thus, these findings do not support the proposition that deviation from acquiescence peaks at phase B.

The effect of efficiency of mills in the sample of established workers is presented in Table 16. Table 16a indicates that efficiency reduces dissent but is independent of radicalism. The relationship may be affected by the vulnerability to the crisis, but this variable cannot, however, be introduced as a test factor, due to its negative correlation with efficiency. The original relationship is shown, hence, for workers in "secure" mills only. Table 16b indicates that,

Table 15. *Dissent and Radicalism by Industry (New Workers)*

	Dissent		
a. Industry	Construction	Manufacturing	
	38% (69)	25% (75)	
b. a by size of plant	To 25	26+	
	[−2%]	−10%	
c. a by time spent in agiculture (% df)	<100%	100%	
	[−8%]	−17%	
d. a by type of agrarian experience	Other	Indep. 100%	Dep. 100%
(% df)	[—]	−64%*	−16%
e. a by seniority	0–6 mos.	7–24 mos.	25+ mos.
(% df)	−15%	−15%	[+2%]

*Percentages based on fewer than ten cases. There are eight construction workers and nine manufacturing workers who were independent farmers for 100 percent of their work careers in Chaco.

NOTE: *a* shows percentages of "high" dissent and radicalism; *b–e* are elaborations of *a*: they show percentage differences between "construction" and "manufacturing." Differences of less than 10 percent are between brackets. See Appendix for operationalization of variables.

Table 16. *Dissent and Radicalism by Efficiency of Mill (Established Workers)*

	Dissent		Radicalism	
a. Efficiency of mill	Low-Medium	High	Low-Medium	High
	30% (107)	7% (40)	[20% (107)	17%] (40)
b. a in secure mills only	23% (22)	6% (35)	[27% (22)	20%] (35)

NOTE: Table shows percentages of "high" dissent and radicalism. See Appendix for operationalization of efficiency and note on statistical significance.

Radicalism

Construction	Manufacturing	
[16% (69)	15%] (75)	
To 25	26+	
+12%	−15%	
<100%	100%	
[−3%]	[+3%]	
Other	Indep. 100%	Dep. 100%
[−2%]	[−3%[*	[+3%]
0–6 mos.	7–24 mos.	25+ mos.
[−1%]	[+1%]	[−3%]

for workers in this "pure" working-class position, technological efficiency exerts an adaptive effect on the forms of political action. The original relationship with dissent holds, and a small negative association with radicalism appears as well. This suggests that workers' rejection of capitalism is reduced by participation in efficient capitalist enterprises. It is in the inefficient plants that anticapitalist orientations are likely to develop. In this sample, even the elementary norms of the capitalist work contract, such as the regular payment of wages, were not regularly observed by the management in these plants. This is consistent with the expectation that the higher the levels of productivity and efficiency of industrial organization, the lower the level of discontent among industrial workers.

As regards the effects of size of plant, most available evidence suggests that the relationship between size and deviation from acquiescence is positive, even though no conclusion can be reached about the direction of that deviation. Many studies have found that workers in larger plants are more likely to strike, to support working-class parties, to select the communists over the socialists, and to express attitudes that indicate a revolutionary ideology. The relationship is, however, very weak in some cases, and there are studies that report a negative correlation.

Data from several industrial countries support the proposition linking size of plant and radical propensities. Lipset reports positive associations between size and variables such as leftism, among New York printers; support for the communists, in Weimar Germany; socialist and communist vote, in postwar Germany; and vote for communist-led unions, in Italy.[26] Likewise, Linz found a positive relationship among German workers between size of plant and support for the Social Democratic Party, as well as agreement with assertions indicating a left-wing ideology.[27]

Some evidence, on the other hand, suggests the opposite relationship. In principle, it is known that workers in small shops were more likely to support anarchism than workers in larger plants. In some surveys, a negative association between plant size and leftist orientations was established. In his study of French workers, Hamilton found that even though the association between plant size and the prevalence of pro-Soviet attitudes is positive, the relationship is weak and not linear, and the highest proportion of pro-Soviet workers corresponds to one of the "small" categories. And he reports a curvilinear association between size and expectation of change through revolution.[28] Also in France, Shorter and Tilly found that large plants have a higher propensity to strike, but strikes in these settings are worse organized and less successful than the ones in smaller enterprises. Large plants, as they put it, "enervate worker solidarity and organizational capacity."[29] Zeitlin's findings in Cuba do not yield a consistent pattern; his data show that plants belonging to the largest category had the lowest proportion of workers supporting the Communists before the revolution and the second lowest one of respondents currently supporting the revolution.[30]

Therefore, the research is not conclusive. This is possibly due to the fact that most hypotheses interpreting the relationship between plant size and working-class political action refer to variables that may have a different effect in different contexts. One of these variables, bureaucratization, for instance, may cut both ways. Discontent might plausibly be lower in small plants, as a consequence of the direct contact between owners and workers, than in large bureaucratized factories.[31] But conflict could also be heightened by direct contact and reduced by the bureaucratic management of labor relations. Another variable is differential recruitment. Linz found in Germany that children of farmers were more likely to be employed in the small shops and in the largest factories than in the medium-sized ones.[32] As the political orientations of peasants vary, selective recruitment might lead to different relationships between size and politics, according to the type of agrarian background.

In the data, the effect of plant size on the forms of political action can be analyzed in the two studies. Results are not comparable, however, because a different level of size is measured in each case. Most new workers were employed at small shops and factories (47 percent of them worked at plants having fewer than 25 employees) while all established workers belonged to large bureaucratic organizations (the smallest mill had 390 workers). It is possible, however, to distinguish different levels of size in each group. The basic relationships are summarized in Table 17.

Table 17a shows that, in a detailed breakdown of the new workers sample in terms of plant size, it appears that the larger the workplace, the lower the level of dissent, the threshold for the reduction of dissent being 100 workers. As far as radicalism is concerned, on the other hand, the relationship is very weak.

Table 15 above showed that the effect of sector of industry on the forms of political action was specified by size. Table 17b and c indicates that among construction workers size does not affect dissent, but it is positively associated with radicalism. It is in manufacturing, on the other hand, that the adaptive effect of size appears—even though the relationship between size and radicalism is curvilinear.

Even though the effect of size on dissent seems to vary according to sector of industry, Table 17b and c suggests the hypothesis of a consistent negative relationship. It should be remembered that construction establishments are smaller than manufacturing plants; two-thirds of the construction workers are employed in settings having twenty-five workers or less. The effect of size on radicalism, on the other hand, is different in the two sectors. The hypothesis that the positive relationship between size and radicalism among construction workers might be due to the association between size and composition of the work force in terms of skill was examined. As will be seen later, skill is negatively related to radicalism among construction workers, and small construction firms have a higher proportion of skilled workers than larger firms. When controlling for skill, however, the positive association between size and radicalism among construction workers still holds.

All of the established workers in the sample were employed at large plants. Table 17d indicates that, at the level of size found in the sugar industry, this variable has a curvilinear relationship with dissent and also a positive association with radicalism. If the two samples are juxtaposed, it is possible to suggest hypotheses about the effect of size on the forms of political action. As far as dissent is concerned, the negative association found in Table 17c seems to hold. Levels of dissent in plants having up to 100 workers are similar, re-

Table 17. *Dissent and Radicalism by Size of Plant*

	Dissent			
a. Size (new workers)	To 25	26–100	101–500	501+
	37% (60)	37% (24)	21% (19)	19% (26)
b. Size (construction only) (% df)	To 25		26+	
		[37% (43)	33%] (21)	
c. Size (manufacturing only)	To 25	26–100	101–500	501+
	35% (17)	40% (10)	17% (12)	19% (26)
d. Size (established workers)	Small (390–572)	Medium (579–756)		Large (814+)
	29% (51)	17% (52)		25% (44)
e. *d* by vulnerability to crisis (small–medium/large) (% df)	Secure		Closed	
	[−3%]		+33%	

NOTE: *a–d* show percentages of "high" dissent and radicalism; *e* is an elaboration of *d*: it shows percentage differences between "small–medium" and "large." Differences of less than 10 percent are between brackets. See Appendix for operationalization of variables and note on statistical significance.

gardless of sector of industry, and when plants having more than 100 workers in Buenos Aires and Rosario and secure mills in Tucumán are compared, differences are not very significant. In secure mills, the percentages of high dissent are 14 percent in the small and medium-sized plants and 11 percent in the large ones. In relation to radicalism, on the other hand, a sequential interpretation of Table 17c and *d* suggests the hypothesis of a curvilinear relationship among factory workers. The overall effect of size would, therefore, be mobilizational. These hypotheses are consistent with Shorter and Tilly's analysis of the effect of size on strikes. They found that workers in large plants are, on the one hand, more prone to strike, i.e., to display oppositional behavior, and on the other, less cohesive and less effective in their collective action.

Radicalism

To 25	26–100	101–500	501+
[15%	21%	16%	15%]
(60)	(24)	(19)	(26)

To 25	26+
12%	29%
(43)	(21)

To 25	26–100	101–500	501+
23%	10%	8%	15%
(17)	(10)	(12)	(26)

Small (390–572)	Medium (579–756)	Large (814+)
16%	13%	29%
(51)	(52)	(44)

Secure	Closed
[−3%]	+37%

In order to clarify further these relationships, vulnerability to the crisis was introduced in the sample of established workers. There were no large threatened mills, so only the secure and closed ones are included in Table 17e. This table shows that, among secure workers, size does not affect the forms of political action in a significant manner. On the other hand, when insecurity is very high and workers face unemployment, strong positive associations with both dissent and radicalism are activated in the largest category of size. This suggests that the level of insecurity is one of the factors that might explain cross-national differences regarding the effects of plant size on working-class political action. Workers in the largest establishments would have contradictory propensities. In "normal" times, they would not differ from their counterparts in the smaller plants, but their predisposition to "revolutionary action," i.e., to high dissent and high radicalism, would be much higher than that of other workers in situations of high insecurity. This finding is, thus, consistent with most research evidence: there would be a latent positive relationship between size and deviation from acquiescence.

Finally, it should be noted that the effect of size cannot be attributed to job satisfaction. The degree of dissatisfaction was measured on the basis of questions already mentioned in Chapter 8. It turns out that, among new workers, plant size and dissatisfaction are positively associated and that, among established workers, there is a small curvilinear relationship, the percentage of dissatisfaction being slightly higher in medium-sized mills.[33]

The Effect of Skill

Research on the effects of skill on working-class political action has also yielded contradictory results. While in some countries skill is negatively associated with leftist voting or with the support for leftist ideologies or organizations, the relationship is positive in other countries, and cases of independence between skill and politics have been reported. Lipset reports that in Australia, Britain, the United States, France, and Italy, skilled workers are less predisposed than the unskilled to support working-class parties.[34] Along the same lines, Hamilton found that unskilled workers in France are more likely to be pro-Soviet and to expect change through revolution.[35] This relationship is reversed in other countries such as postwar Germany and Sweden. And Lipset also shows that, in several countries, skilled workers are more likely than the unskilled to support small radical parties competing with larger moderate working-class parties.[36] Similarly, Zeitlin found that skilled Cuban workers were more likely to have supported the Communists prior to the revolution than the unskilled.[37] Other evidence, finally, suggests that skill does not affect political orientations and behavior. Hamilton has found that in the U.S., skill is independent of Republican vote among non-South white workers,[38] and Zeitlin reports that in Cuba there is no relationship between skill and support for the revolution.[39]

Different interpretations have been suggested for these findings. The negative association between skill and deviation from acquiescence is usually explained on the basis of deprivation and work satisfaction, and sometimes of *embourgeoisement*.[40] Hamilton has found, however, that in France the relationship holds, when controlling for income and work satisfaction.[41] And Lipset's hypotheses about international differences being due to the degree of rigidity of the status system in each society and to the complexity of the political outlook of different left-wing parties are well known.[42] Hamilton, finally, has interpreted the effects of skill in terms of the association between this variable and recruitment patterns.[43]

The relationship between skill and forms of political action can be examined in the two studies. Among migrants, however, 67 percent of the skilled workers in the sample were employed in construction. There were only fourteen skilled manufacturing workers, too small a number to permit analysis. And the meaning of skill differs so between a phase A setting (such as construction) and manufacturing, that the merging of the two groups of skilled workers did not seem advisable. For this reason, the effects of skill are examined in that sample among construction workers only. Results are summarized in Table 18.

Table 18a and b indicates that, in the two groups, skill has adaptive effects, even though the association with dissent among established workers is weak. It is possible that the consequences of skill among construction workers are related to job satisfaction, for there is a strong negative relationship between skill and dissatisfaction in this group. As far as established workers are concerned, however, it is the skilled who are slightly more dissatisfied than the unskilled.[44] And 18c shows that the original relationships hold for workers in the "pure" working-class situation, i.e., in secure mills. On the other hand, the threat of unemployment intensifies the impact of skill on dissent and maintains its impact on radicalism, even though the size of these relationships may be affected by the number of cases. Among workers in closed mills, finally, skill exerts a "reformist" effect: it increases dissent and decreases radicalism. This is the only instance in which a relatively strong positive relationship between skill and one of the components of the forms of political action was found. This deviant association can be interpreted in terms of relative deprivation. While in normal times skilled workers are better off than unskilled workers, the dissatisfaction of the former escalates when their exposure to marginalization is high, for the gap between current expectations and potential rewards would be greater among them than among the unskilled. This is particularly so in an activity such as the sugar industry, in which many workers' skills are hardly transferable to other industries.

In Table 18d–h, different test factors have been introduced in order to specify the original relationships. The first one is size of plant. Among construction workers, the examination of the effect of skill is only possible in small plants, due to the number of cases. Table 18d shows that, in these establishments, the original relationship holds. As for established workers, Table 18e indicates that the

Table 18. *Dissent and Radicalism by Skill*

	Dissent		
a. Skill (new workers: construction)	Unskilled		Skilled
	42% (40)		31% (29)
b. Skill (established workers)	Unskilled		Skilled
	[30% (30)		22%] (117)
c. *b* by vulnerability to the crisis (% df)	Secure	Threatened	Closed
	[−7%]	−35%*	+14%
d. *a* in small firms (up to 25)	Unskilled		Skilled
	43% (21)		32% (22)
e. *b* by size of mill	Small (390–572)	Medium (579–756)	Large (814+)
(% df)	[−4%]*	[−8%]	−15%*
f. *a* by time spent in agriculture	<100%		100%
(% df)	−25%		[−2%]
g. *a* by seniority	0–6 mos.		7+ mos.
(% df)	−21%		[−3%]
h. *b* by seniority	<20 yrs.		20+ yrs.
(% df)	−13%		[−4%]

*Percentages based on fewer than ten cases: there were eight unskilled workers employed at threatened mills, nine at small mills, and eight at large mills.

NOTE: *a−b* and *d* show percentages of "high" dissent and radicalism; *f−g* are elaborations of *a*; and *c, e,* and *h* are elaborations of *b*. Elaborations show percentage differences between "unskilled" and "skilled." Differences of less than 10 percent are between brackets. See Appendix for operationalization of variables and note on statistical significance.

Radicalism

Unskilled		Skilled
22% (40)		7% (29)

Unskilled		Skilled
30% (30)		16% (117)

Secure	Threatened	Closed
−16%	−14%*	[−9%]

Unskilled		Skilled
19% (21)		4% (22)

Small (390–572)	Medium (579–756)	Large (814+)
[+6%]*	−23%	−25%*

<100%		100%
−33%		[+3%]

0–6 mos.		7+ mos.
−36%		[−4%]

< 20 yrs.		20+ yrs.
−12%		−15%

adaptive effect of skill is specified by size. While in the small factories the relationships are very weak—this in spite of the small number of cases—in the medium and large mills the adaptive impact
holds, especially as far as radicalism is concerned. The significance
of this effect in the large category, however, could also be affected by
the number of cases.

The remaining test factors are integration variables. The role of
intergenerational mobility cannot be assessed, due to the skewness
of the distributions, so that my analysis focuses on work careers.
Table 18*f*, pertaining to construction workers only, indicates that
the adaptive effects of skill are only significant among the more
"modern" migrants, i.e. the ones whose integration into agriculture
had been less. The impact of the amount of industrial experience as
indicated by seniority, however, counteracts the effect of the preindustrial background. Table 18*g* shows that, among migrants working in construction, the adaptive consequences of skill are concentrated among the workers with less seniority, i.e., the ones with less
integration into the industrial world.

Finally, Table 18*h* indicates that, at the very high level of industrial experience of the established workers, the negative association
between skill and dissent is also concentrated among the less integrated individuals. With respect to radicalism, on the other hand,
its negative relationship with skill holds, regardless of the level of
seniority.

In conclusion, in a series of settings, skill has adaptive consequences. We have seen that this adaptive impact is affected by bureaucratization and integration to the working class. The evidence
from the established workers study suggests that in manufacturing,
the relationship holds in large plants only. The adaptive consequences of skill, finally, are only effective among the more "modern"
new workers—those with some nonagricultural experience—and
mostly during the first stage of manufacturing careers. However,
among established workers, the unskilled are more radical, regardless of seniority. On the other hand, there is a context, closed mills,
in which the effect of skill is reformist.

In this section, the relationship between different centrality variables—characteristics of the division of labor, technological efficiency, size, and skill—and the forms of political action has been examined. The overall conclusion is that the predominant effect of
this cluster of factors tends to be adaptive. The transition from construction to manufacturing produces in larger plants and among recently incorporated workers a decrease in the level of dissent; and
technological efficiency reduces, among "secure" workers, both dis-

sent and radicalism. Skill also has an adaptive effect in most situations. While the impact of sector of industry and efficiency is stronger on—or limited to—dissent, the effects of skill on radicalism are as strong as or stronger than—as is the case among established workers—the effects of dissent. As for size of plant, the evidence in Table 17c and d has suggested the possibility that this variable produces a reduction of dissent and an increase of radicalism, i.e., a "mobilizational" effect, even though it seems to have "revolutionary" consequences in contexts of high insecurity. Size of plant, however, interacts with other aspects of centrality—sector of industry and skill—and intensifies their adaptive effects. Finally, the impact of centrality variables is in most cases concentrated or stronger among the least integrated members of the working class. Thus, the consequences of integration and of centrality tend to be similar. The next chapter examines the effects of the two remaining structural properties, deprivation and marginalization.

11. The Effects of Deprivation and Marginalization

DEPRIVATION AND FORMS OF POLITICAL ACTION

Deprivation is always relative in the sense that the individuals' awareness of it necessarily derives from a comparison, either with an ideal standard or with other real-life individuals who might be either those same people in the past or other people in the present. These relative estimates are grounded on a "material base" in two ways. First, comparisons are based on actual rewards, even though these rewards are assessed by individuals according to their own expectations. Second, comparisons do not occur at random in the social structure. People are likely to contrast themselves with other people with whom they share one or more central characteristics—social class, social origins, and the like—and these comparisons are either facilitated or inhibited by the social structure. In the absence of conditions facilitating comparisons, objective deprivation is not likely to engender discontent: "steady poverty," Runciman has written, "is the best guarantee of conservatism."[1]

This section concerns the effects of the position in the sphere of consumption on working-class forms of political action. More specifically I am interested in examining the political consequences of variations in the level of "objective" deprivation within the working class. This analysis presupposes the existence of a setting that is conducive to the formulation of comparisons, for workers having different positions in the sphere of consumption work together and are fully aware of differences in standards of living.

It could be expected that in industrial society, in which the opportunities for interclass and intraclass comparisons are maximized, there would be an explosion of discontent among the most deprived. As far as the working class in particular is concerned, a common-sense expectation would be that, within its ranks, the degree of objective deprivation would be positively associated with the propensity to deviate from acquiescence. The evidence in this regard is far from conclusive, however. Even though the existence of a negative correlation between income and support for the left in national elections is a fairly well established fact, the relationship does not always hold for the lowest strata in the society or within classes such as the industrial working class. The same inconsistencies that were mentioned in connection with skill are also found in relation to objective deprivation.

Among industrial workers and other subordinate strata, the correlation between income, and other deprivation indicators, and attitudes or behavior indicating discontent is positive in some countries and negative in others. In some nations, the poor are the segment of the society most likely to deviate from acquiescence while in others the poor are a reservoir of apathy and conservatism. Both Bakunin's and Marx's propositions are consistent with some of the evidence.

Conditions which either block or facilitate the awareness of deprivation and its conversion into political discontent vary across countries. But when contexts whose social and political characteristics are conducive to these processes are compared, differences persist. Contemporary European industrial democracies are a good example, and France and Germany provide an interesting parallel. In France, Tilly et al. found no relationship between hardship indicators and collective violence, while Shorter and Tilly have concluded that there can be a short-run relationship between deprivation and collective action only when there is a high level of organization.[2] Hamilton found a negative correlation, within the working class, between income and procommunist attitudes.[3] Linz reports for Germany a positive relationship between income and support for the Social Democratic Party that holds when controlling for skill.[4] Research on the behavior of the better-paid segment of the working class also yields inconsistent results. While in several countries these workers are known to be less prone to support leftist parties, Goldthorpe and his associates have found in England that affluence does not reduce workers' support for the Labor Party.[5] These contrasts are probably the result of the different expectations that the poor have in different contexts as well as the variable conduciveness of social structures for intergroup comparisons.

We will now turn to the relationship between objective deprivation and the forms of political action in the two studies. We have already seen that the migrants were actually better off after migrating and that their overall level of satisfaction was very high, in spite of the fact that most of them were unskilled workers and were living in shantytowns. This high level of satisfaction did not prevent these migrants from having a high propensity for dissent. Established workers, on the other hand, were mostly skilled and likely to compare themselves favorably with any other social group with whom they were likely to interact. Now we will be concerned with the consequences of internal differences in the standard of living on their forms of political action. Since in the two cases the poorer individuals were exposed to higher standards of living, it makes sense to investigate the relationship between deprivation and deviations from acquiescence.

Different indicators of objective deprivation are available in the two studies. Only one of these indicators, quality of housing, was included in the two groups, and for this reason it will be emphasized. Information on income, on the other hand, exists only for the sample of new workers, as was pointed out above. Two other variables, which enhance the effect of deprivation, will also be considered: family size (or more precisely, number of persons living with the respondent) in the sample of new workers and number of children under the age of fourteen (i.e., dependent children) in the sample of established workers. The basic relationships are summarized in Table 19.

This table indicates that, while all the indicators of deprivation are positively related to dissent—even though the effect of quality of housing among established workers is curvilinear—no consistent pattern in relation to radicalism emerges.

As for quality of housing, table 19a and b indicates that, in the two samples, quality of housing is negatively associated with dissent, and its effects on radicalism are too weak to be taken into consideration. When the degree of exposure to the crisis is introduced as a test factor, however, a different picture for established workers appears. As Table 19c shows, among secure workers the effect of deprivation is a "revolutionizing" one, while among workers in threatened or closed mills, quality of housing produces "reformist" consequences. In these contexts, deprivation increases dissent, but it also reduces radicalism. The impact of size of the family is shown in Table 19d–e. The effect of this variable is similar in the two samples, and also "reformist": the larger the family in the migrants sample, the higher the level of dissent and the lower the level of radicalism. The equivalent indicator among established workers, number of dependent children, produces the same consequences. As for income, Table 19f shows that, among new workers, the lower the level of income, the higher the level of both dissent and radicalism, the effect on radicalism being twice as strong as the effect on dissent.

As quality of housing is the only variable that is available in the

two samples, its relationship with dissent and radicalism was elaborated. Results are presented in Table 20.

The impact of skill on the original relationship can only be ascertained in the sample of established workers, due to the high association between skill and quality of housing among construction
workers. Table 20a shows that, while deprivation is independent of
both dissent and radicalism among the unskilled, among skilled
workers the reformist effect appears again: deprivation increases dissent and reduces radicalism. This is a most interesting effect and
suggests that considerations of distributive justice involving the balance of statuses in production and in consumption are at work only
among the skilled. Within the unskilled stratum—whose higher levels of dissent and radicalism should be remembered—variations in
the standard of living are apparently not the source of resentment or
of relative satisfaction.

Table 20b–e shows the impact of integration variables. The
first of these tables indicates that, among established workers,
quality of housing also has a "reformist" effect among the most integrated individuals, i.e., the sons of factory workers. In this group, the
higher the level of deprivation, the higher the level of dissent and the
lower the level of radicalism. Among the workers who are less integrated, on the other hand, deprivation also increases dissent, but it
does not affect radicalism. In the sample of new workers, the positive relationship that was found between deprivation and dissent is
much stronger among the migrants whose integration into the working class is less, i.e., those who had spent their entire premigration
careers in agriculture.

Finally, let us look at the effect of length of employment. Table
20d indicates that, in the new workers sample, deprivation increases
both dissent and radicalism among the recently employed, but this
effect vanishes after two years of seniority. In the case of established
workers, and at their very high level of seniority, the positive association between deprivation and dissent holds irrespective of length
of employment, but the relationship with radicalism is negative at
first—the overall effect of deprivation is then "reformist"—but also
disappears later.

In summary, among new workers the effect of deprivation takes
place among those recently incorporated into the working class and,
in general, among the less integrated. In this sample, deprivation has
a positive impact on dissent and, in some instances, on radicalism as
well—such is the effect of income and quality of housing among in-

Table 19. *Dissent and Radicalism by Deprivation Indicators*

Dissent

a. Quality of housing (new workers)	High		Low	
	24% (50)		35% (83)	

b. Quality of housing (established workers)	High	Medium	Low
	23% (77)	12% (32)	33% (36)

c. b by vulnerability to the crisis (high–medium/low) (% df)	Secure	Threatened	Closed
	+14%	[+9%]	+15%

d. Family size (new workers)	To 3		4+	
	23% (65)		39% (77)	

e. Children under 14 (established workers)	Other	1–2	3+
	21% (53)	19% (43)	31% (51)

f. Income (new workers) (pesos)	To 30,000	30,000–39,999	40,000+
	37% (35)	31% (61)	27% (48)

NOTE: *a–b* and *d–f* show percentages of "high" dissent and radicalism; *c* is an elaboration of *b*: it shows percentage differences between "high–medium" and "low" quality of housing. Differences of less than 10 percent are between brackets. See Appendix for operationalization of variables and note on statistical significance.

dividuals with less than two years of seniority. Family size, on the other hand, has reformist consequences. In the case of established workers, deprivation, as measured by quality of housing, only affects the skilled. In "secure" contexts, it increases both dissent and radicalism, and the impact is reformist in a series of settings: among the insecure, the skilled, the sons of factory workers, individuals with large families, and the workers with less than the highest level of seniority (at the highest level, deprivation only increases dissent).

Radicalism

High	Low	
[12% (50)	17%] (83)	

High	Medium	Low
[22% (77)	16% (32)	17%] (36)

Secure	Threatened	Closed
+19%	−17%	−18%

To 3	4+
23% (65)	9% (77)

Other	1–2	3+
[25% (53)	16% (43)	16%] (51)

o 30,000	30,000–39,999	40,000+
26% (35)	16% (61)	6% (48)

MARGINALIZATION AND FORMS
OF POLITICAL ACTION

Even though the evidence related to the relationship between marginalization and the forms of political action of the working class is not completely consistent, disagreement in this regard is limited. Most studies suggest that employed workers whose level of insecurity is high tend to deviate from acquiescence, while unemployed workers are acquiescent. Much of the evidence has been summarized in two propositions by Lipset: "First, the unemployed are much more likely than those regularly employed to be uninformed and apathetic about politics. . . . Second, employed individu-

Table 20. *Dissent and Radicalism by Quality of Housing and Intervening Variables*

Dissent

a. Skill (established workers)	Unskilled		Skilled
(% df)	[+2%]		+16%
b. Father's occupation (established workers)	Factory		Other
(% df)	+16%		+11%
c. Time spent in agriculture (new workers)	<100%		100%
(% df)	[+7%]		+20%

d. Seniority (new workers)	0–6 mos.	7–24 mos.	25+ mos
(% df)	+25%	[−1%]	[−4%]

e. Seniority (Established workers)	<20 yrs.		20+ yrs.
(% df)	+12%		+15%

NOTE: Table is an elaboration of 19*a*–*b*. It shows percentage differences between categories of quality of housing. In the established workers sample, quality of housing has been dichotomized into high–medium/low. Percentage differences of less than 10 percent are between brackets. See Appendix for operationalization of variables and note on statistical significance.

als who report a past experience of unemployment, or areas which were once centers of high rates of unemployment, are much more likely to exhibit leftist voting propensities than those with more fortunate economic histories."[6]

The second of these propositions is supported by most studies of insecurity among employed workers. Lipset presents data from Britain, Finland, Weimar Germany, and France that indicate a relationship between experience of unemployment and vote or support for the left.[7] And Hamilton found that experience of unemployment is associated with leftist attitudes among French workers.[8] A similar correlation is reported by Zeitlin in the case of Cuba.[9] Current job insecurity is also a powerful determinant of workers' militancy. In their study of strikes in France, Shorter and Tilly found that ". . . it was the craftworkers threatened by industrialization whose animosity against their employers was most intense."[10] Sigal, in her analysis of responses to the crisis in the established workers study,

Radicalism

Unskilled		Skilled	
[+2%]		−14%	
Factory		Other	
−12%		[+2%]	
<100%		100%	
[+5%]		[+4%]	
0–6 mos.	7–24 mos.	25+ mos.	
[+5%]	+14%	[−1%]	
<20 yrs.		20+ yrs.	
[−9%]		[+2%]	

found a strong relationship between threat of unemployment and an index of questioning of management.[11] The only negative evidence comes from Germany, where Linz found that workers who had fear of unemployment were less likely than other workers to support the Social Democratic Party. This divergence may be due to the fact that, in the particular case of Germany at that period, the insecure workers tended to belong to the categories of the working class that were less likely to support the SPD.[12]

The proposition presented above concerning the effects of actual unemployment is supported by the well-known studies conducted during the depression by Lazarsfeld-Jahoda and Zeisel in Austria, Zawadski and Lazarsfeld in Poland, and Bakke in the United States and Britain.[13] And in Tucumán Sigal found that workers in closed mills were slightly less prone to "confrontation behavior" than their counterparts in secure mills; they were less likely to select strikes or factory seizures and more likely to prefer "talk with the govern-

Table 21. *Dissent and Radicalism by Indicators of Marginalization*

	Dissent		
a. Current dismissals (new workers)	Other	Yes	
	[30% (99)	33%] (43)	
b. Future dismissals expected (new workers)	Other	Yes	
	[33% (83)	29%] (59)	
c. Vulnerability to the crisis (established workers)	Secure	Threatened	Closed
	12% (57)	33% (45)	29% (45)
d. Time unemployed (unemployed migrants)	To 1 mo.	1.01–4 mos.	4+ mos.
	23% (13)	67%* (9)	29%* (7)

*Percentages based on fewer than ten cases.

NOTE: Table shows percentages of "high" dissent and radicalism. Percentage differences of less than 10 percent are between brackets. See Appendix for operationalization of variables and note on statistical significance.

ment" as a course of action for the union.[14] Negative evidence, however, also exists. In his study of postwar Germany, Linz found that the unemployed were more likely than the employed to support the SPD and equally likely to attend political meetings,[15] and Leggett reports that among workers in Detroit "in most cases the unemployed are more class conscious than the employed."[16]

We may turn now to the data under analysis. In the sample of new workers, the indicators to be utilized are the questions as to whether workers were being laid off at the firms where respondents were employed and whether the respondents expected layoffs to occur in the future. In the sample of established workers, on the other hand, mills were classified according to their exposure to the crisis as secure, threatened, and closed.

We have seen that established workers, whose level of insecurity was much higher than that of new workers, were less predisposed to high levels of dissent. This would seem to contradict the second proposition presented above. On the other hand, in the study of migrants, a small sample of unemployed workers is available, and the proportion of respondents with high dissent in this sample was greater than that of samples of employed workers, as was reported in

Radicalism

Other		Yes	
[16% (99)		14%] (43)	

Other		Yes	
[16% (83)		15%] (59)	

Secure	Threatened	Closed
23% (57)	13% (45)	20% (45)

To 1 mo.	1.01–4 mos.	4+ mos.
15% (13)	44%* (9)	14%* (7)

Chapter 9. These data, therefore, seem to be inconsistent with the first proposition as well.

The sample of unemployed workers cannot be elaborated, due to the small number of cases. In the group of new workers, on the other hand, the level of insecurity seems to be low, as reported in Chapter 8. For this reason, my analysis focuses on established workers. Here different levels of exposure to marginalization can be distinguished, even though the situation of individuals in closed mills is not totally comparable to that of the unemployed who were studied by the authors mentioned above: these workers were still living in company housing, receiving wages, and hoping their mills would reopen. Their exposure to marginalization was very high, however, due to the existence of monoculture in Tucumán. Workers in secure, threatened, and closed mills were placed in three different levels of vulnerability to the crisis. The effect of marginalization, therefore, can be examined in detail.

Table 21 presents the effects of these different indicators on dissent and radicalism in the two working-class samples, as well as the effects of the amount of time the migrants in the sample were unemployed.

Table 21*a* and *b* indicates that, among new workers, forms of political action are not affected either by the awareness or the expectation of unemployment. This finding is interesting in view of the fact that most of these migrants had experienced marginalization in the past and that research points to the existence of a strong relationship between past insecurity and political behavior among established industrial workers. This discrepancy suggests that a higher level of integration into the working class is a precondition for either the experience or the threat of marginalization to become an effective determinant of changes in the forms of political action.

Table 21*c* shows the effect of the different degrees of vulnerability to the crisis on the forms of political action among established workers. In analyzing a sample that included both permanent and transient factory workers, Sigal found, as mentioned above, that "the threat of unemployment leads simultaneously to a greater questioning of management and to a drop in the 'propensity for direct action.'"[17] In terms of her typology of responses to the crisis, this signaled a shift from negotiation through violence to latency.[18] With threat, the proportion of individuals with high "questioning"—this index included, in different versions, one or both of my indicators of dissent[19]—increased by 19 percent while the proportion of workers who wanted to seize factories—my indicator of radicalism—dropped 3 percent. With closure, the first proportion grew further by 11 percent, and the second one went down by 5 percent.[20] My results, as shown in Table 21*c*, are different, because the sample I am examining consists of the permanent workers—the ones in the "typical" working class position—and my index of dissent, which focuses exclusively on the property of the means of production, has a different distribution.[21] In these data, the impact of threat is reformist, but closure produces a small radicalizing effect. The consequences of threat are, then, similar to those found by Sigal in the combined sample, but the effect of closure is different. Dissent does not increase further, and radicalism grows again, almost to the level that existed in secure mills.

Finally, a glance at the sample of unemployed workers. The question of the consequences of protracted unemployment among established workers cannot be answered with data from the Tucumán study, but this information is available in the sample of unemployed. Table 21*d* shows the relationship between the amount of time spent unemployed and their forms of political action. In spite of the small number of cases, this table suggests the possibility that the apparent inconsistency between the level of dissent in this sample and what could have been expected on the basis of most of the research evidence is due to the effect of time. Over time, unemployment would have a curvilinear relationship with both dissent and radicalism. The two components of the forms of political action would rise initially and then drop, probably to levels lower than the ones employed workers have. If this inference is valid, then the fact that individuals in this sample have the highest levels of dissent should be attributed to the recent impact of unemployment among most of its members. Unfortunately, the size of this sample does not allow further analysis.

The conclusion that can be drawn from Table 21 is that, as expected, the threat of marginalization is associated with deviation from acquiescence among established workers. This structural property, on the other hand, does not seem to affect the forms of political action of migrants recently incorporated into the working class. The long-term consequence of unemployment seems to be, also as expected, acquiescence.

Let us return to the effect of exposure to marginalization in the sample of established workers. In Table 22, the original relationships between vulnerability to the crisis and dissent and radicalism have been elaborated by introducing integration, centrality, and deprivation indicators.

The consequences of integration will be explored first. Table 22*a* indicates that the effects of marginalization are mostly confined to the children of factory workers. It is among this group that the reformist impact of threat of unemployment takes place and a mobilizational effect of closure of the mills appears. Among individuals whose background was non–working class, marginalization does not produce significant changes on either component of the forms of political action.

Length of employment is the second integration variable. Due to the skewness of its distribution, it had to be dichotomized. Table 22*b* shows that the effect of threat of unemployment is specified by seniority: the higher the level of seniority, the higher the increase in the level of dissent, but radicalism drops only among individuals with less than twenty years of industrial experience. Among these workers, then, the impact of threat is reformist. As for closure of the mills, its effect in this category of seniority is "revolutionary," even though the increase in the level of dissent is very weak. On the other hand, in the highest category of seniority, vulnerability to the crisis is related only to dissent, which rises with threat and drops with closure.

Table 22. *Dissent and Radicalism by Vulnerability to the Crisis and Intervening Variables (Established Workers)*

Dissent

a. Father's occupation	Factory		Other
(% df)	+38% −6%		[+5% −3%]
b. Seniority	<20 yrs.		20+ yrs.
(% df)	+16% +6%		+25% −14%
c. Skill	Unskilled		Skilled
(% df)	+44% −44%*		+16% +5%
d. Size of plant (Secure−closed)	Small (390−572)	Medium (579−756)	Large (814+)
(% df)	+18%	−12%	+39%
e. Quality of housing	High−Medium		Low
(% df)	+22% −8%		+17% −2%

*Percentages based on fewer than ten cases. There were eight unskilled workers in threatened mills.

NOTE: Table is an elaboration of 21*c*: it shows percentage differences between categories of vulnerability to the crisis. Differences of less than 10 percent are between brackets. See Appendix for operationalization of variables and note on statistical significance.

The effect of integration on the original relationship is, therefore, complex. On the one hand, the reformist effect of threat is confined to respondents with a working-class background rather than among mobile individuals. This finding suggests an explanation for the absence of association between insecurity and forms of political action among new workers. On the other hand, this effect is not found among workers with very high levels of industrial experience, even though the impact of threat of unemployment on dissent is greater among them.

The role of centrality variables is explored in Table 22*c*−*d*. In spite of the small number of cases in the unskilled category, the first of these tables suggests that the positive relationship between threat of unemployment and dissent is stronger among the unskilled workers than among the skilled ones. Closure, on the other hand, seems also to reduce dissent among the unskilled. With respect to radical-

Radicalism

Factory	Other	
−9% +13%	[−5% −3%]	
<20 yrs.	20+ yrs.	
−15% +14%	[−3% −1%]	
Unskilled	Skilled	
−11% +2%*	−9% +7%	
Small (390–572)	Medium (579–756)	Large (814+)
−17%	−20%	+23%
High–Medium	Low	
−2% +9%	−38% +8%	

ism, finally, the small positive association between this variable and closure in the original relationship holds for skilled workers only. They are the ones who have more to lose as a consequence of the crisis, especially those workers whose skills are specific to the industry that is in crisis. This is also why, even though the threat of unemployment seems to have a greater impact on the unskilled workers, it is the skilled who retain their higher level of dissent once the mills have been closed.

The next test factor is size of plant. As there are no threatened mills in the large category, only workers in secure and in closed mills are compared in Table 22 *d*. This table shows that the increase in the level of dissent is higher in the large mills—even though dissent drops with closure in the medium-sized plants. And the overall association between marginalization and radicalism, which was small and curvilinear in the original relationship, is specified by

size. Marginalization increases radicalism in the large mills and reduces it in the other two size categories. The comparison between
workers in secure and closed mills suggests, therefore, the existence
of a reformist effect of marginalization in small plants, an adaptive
effect in medium-sized mills, and a "revolutionary" effect in the
large plants. We have already seen in the last chapter that insecurity
activates strong positive relationships between size and dissent and
radicalism. This table shows how size intensifies the deviation from
acquiescence produced by marginalization.

Finally, the role of deprivation. The impact of quality of housing
on the original relationship is summarized in Table 22e. This table
shows that deprivation also specifies the association between marginalization and forms of political action. The overall effect of marginalization among the most deprived workers seems to be a reformist one. Among the less deprived, dissent increases as a consequence
of marginalization, but radicalism does not decline. It even shows a
net increase as a consequence of closure, for closure exerts a small
mobilizational effect in this group.

We have seen that marginalization is an effective determinant of
dissent and radicalism among established workers and that it produces no effect among migrants recently incorporated into the working class. The proposition that insecurity generates a deviation from
acquiescence has been specified: the threat of unemployment exerts
a strong reformist effect, and actual unemployment tends to re-
establish the level of radicalism that existed prior to the threat of
marginalization. We have also seen that, among unemployed workers, the long-term consequence of unemployment is likely to be a
return to acquiescence.

The relationship between marginalization and the forms of political action was, finally, specified on the basis of integration, centrality, and deprivation variables. I conclude that the effects described
above take place only among individuals who were presumably born
in the working class, and that the reformist impact of threat of unemployment is confined to workers with fewer than twenty years of
industrial experience, and those whose level of deprivation is high.
This effect, finally, seems to be stronger among the unskilled than
among the skilled. And the first impact of unemployment is "revolutionary" among workers in large mills, reformist in small mills,
and adaptive in the medium-sized ones. Small "revolutionary" effects of closure are hinted at among workers with "low" seniority
and among the skilled, and small mobilizational effects among sons
of industrial workers and among the less deprived individuals.

The consequences of marginalization are, therefore, very complex. In general, these findings are consistent with most of the evidence that was mentioned at the beginning of this section, but my analysis has permitted me to specify the different directions that the deviation from acquiescence produced by marginalization might take at different points in time. The apparent incongruity that arises from the fact that new workers had a slightly higher level of dissent than established ones, even though the latter were more exposed to marginalization, disappears when the sample of established workers is broken down according to the degree of vulnerability to the crisis. Thus, workers in closed mills have a propensity to high dissent similar to that among new workers. Dissent is, however, the result of different structural properties in each case: marginalization in the former group and lack of integration in the latter. A second contradiction with other findings, the fact that the unemployed had a higher level of dissent than employed workers, vanishes when time is taken into consideration: the high level of dissent in that group results from the fact that most of its members had been unemployed for a short time.

CONCLUSION

12. The Working Class and the Legitimacy of Capitalism

We have already discussed the relationships between integration, centrality, deprivation, and marginalization indicators and dissent and radicalism. We will now examine the changes in the forms of political action—i.e., in the joint distribution of dissent and radicalism—that are associated with variations in selected indicators of the different structural properties. These variations are condensed in Table 23. This table permits the visualization of the consequences of the different indicators in relation to the deviation from acquiescence as well as the direction of that deviation. These are, of course, single relationships. The usual caveat about the interpretation of isolated propositions is more necessary than ever when dealing with generalizations as abstract as these, in which a single structural property is related with diffuse orientations and dispositions for action. These propositions can be affected by factors of different types. On the side of the independent variable, I have already discussed some of the interactions with other structural properties. In relation to the forms of political action, it is necessary to be aware of the contextually specific role of intervening variables that can influence these relationships: working-class organization and ideology, elite strategies, and what I have called environmental factors.

Table 23a is a good summary of the effect of the integration variables. Prior experience in capitalist agriculture, the amount of industrial experience, and the length of time migrants have resided in the city have adaptive consequences. The most intense of these effects is the one produced by the amount of industrial experience among established workers. In the sample of new workers, on the other hand, even though the amount of industrial experience is also strongly associated with adaptation, time of residence in the city seems to exert a slightly more intense impact. In this latter group, a prior background in precapitalist agriculture generates a deviation from acquiescence. The direction of that deviation is toward forms of political action having high radicalism: mobilization and "revolutionary action." These mobilizational and "revolutionary" effects are small, however, due to the fact that the overall impact is bifurcated.

Table 23*b* indicates that the general consequence of centrality variables is adaptation. The effect of skill is strongly adaptive in the two samples, and the transition from construction to manufacturing produces similar results. As for size of plant, however, its consequences are also strong and adaptive among new workers incorporated into manufacturing, but the impact is mobilizational among established workers (and also among new workers in construction, as shown by data not presented here). Chapter 10 interpreted these relationships sequentially and suggested that the overall effect of size is mobilizational.

Deprivation produces deviation from acquiescence, as Table 23*c* suggests. As far as quality of housing is concerned, the direction of the deviation varies in the two samples. Among established workers, this deviation is toward a strong reformist effect. Among new workers, on the other hand, the impact is diluted into small reformist and "revolutionary" effects. Family size seems to exert reformist effects in the two groups, but the deviation from acquiescence associated with this variable is stronger among established workers. Income produces, among new workers, the strongest impacts associated with deprivation: moderate but not very intense mobilizational and "revolutionary" effects. This table suggests that the consequence of an increase in the wage level is stronger than that of an improvement in other aspects of the position in the system of consumption, such as quality of housing.

Marginalization, finally, is only associated with changes in the forms of political action of established workers. As Table 23*d* indicates, the impact of the threat of unemployment is stronger than that of actual unemployment, and it is likely to result in a reformist effect.

The weak association between dissent and radicalism is a mechanism that contributes toward stabilizing the social order. The two components of the forms of political action are determined by different configurations of factors, and Table 23 suggests that structural properties, when they produce a deviation from acquiescence, are more likely to determine "reformist" or mobilizational effects than "revolutionary" ones. If we focus on nonadaptive consequences in-

'volving percentage differences of at least 10 percent, Table 23 shows two instances of mobilization $(D-R+)$ and three reformist effects $(D+R-)$. Mobilization is produced by size, among established workers, and by deprivation, in terms of income, among new workers. The reformist effects are generated by deprivation—in terms of quality of housing, among established workers, and of family size in the two samples—and by marginalization, as measured by threat of unemployment, among established workers. There are no "revolutionary" effects $(D+R+)$ of 10 percent and over.

Table 23 suggests that the impact of centrality and integration on the forms of political action is stronger than that of deprivation and marginalization. Since centrality and integration variables tend to produce adaptive consequences—with the exception of size of plant—and since nonadaptive effects, reformist ones in most cases, are mostly produced by deprivation and marginalization, this analysis suggests that, even at early stages of the process of industrialization, the pull toward acquiescence derived from the position occupied by workers in the economic system is likely to be stronger than the pull toward deviation from acquiescence. However, we have seen in Chapters 10 and 11 that the interaction among structural properties produces relatively strong nonadaptive consequences in specific settings. In addition to single relationships, I have examined effects produced by pairs of structural properties. The stronger complex relationships of this type leading toward deviation from acquiescence were found among established workers, and the effects were reformist and revolutionary. If we restrict our attention to contexts determined by the introduction of a second structural property in an original relationship in which the consequences of an increase of a structural property are examined, the following is the list of the effects involving percentage differences of at least 10 percent on *both* dissent and radicalism:[1]

Reformist effect $(D+R-)$. As with the simple relationships we have seen in Table 23c and 23d, these take place in relation to deprivation and marginalization. Thus, deprivation, as measured by quality of housing, increases dissent and reduces radicalism in contexts of high integration (among sons of factory workers, Table 20b), high centrality (among the skilled, Table 20a), and vulnerability to the crisis (among workers in closed mills, Table 19c). As for marginalization, threat of unemployment exerts a reformist effect in situations of low integration (in the "lower" category of seniority, i.e., among workers who have been in their jobs less than twenty years, Table 22b), low centrality (as indicated by size: in small mills, Table 22d), and high deprivation (among workers with the worst housing,

Table 23. Forms of Political Action by Structural Properties (Selected Indicators)

	Forms of Political Action			
	Acquiescence	Mobilization	Reformism	Revolutionary Action
Structural Property	D−R−	D−R+	D+R−	D+R+
a. Integration				
Time spent in independent agriculture (new workers) 0/100% (% df)	−14%	+6%	—	+7%
Time spent in dependent agriculture (new workers) 0/100% (% df)	+20%	+2%	−14%	−9%
Seniority (new workers) 0–6 mos./25+ mos. (% df)	+18%	+2%	−12%	−7%
Seniority (established workers) 0–9 yrs./20+ yrs. (% df)	+37%	−25%	−8%	−3%
Time of residence in city (new workers) To 2 yrs./4+ yrs. (% df)	+25%	−6%	−9%	−10%
b. Centrality				
Sector of industry (new workers) Construction/manufacturing (% df)	+12%	+1%	−10%	−2%
Size (new workers, manufacturing) To 25/501+ (% df)	+38%	−4%	−30%	−4%
Size (established workers) Small/large (% df) (390–527/814+)	−6%	+10%	−9%	+4%
Skill (new workers, construction) Unskilled/skilled (% df)	+36%	−7%	−20%	−9%
Skill (established workers) Unskilled/skilled (% df)	+20%	−12%	−6%	−1%

c. Deprivation

Quality of housing (new workers)				
High/low (% df)	−10%	−1%	+5%	+6%
Quality of housing (established workers)				
High/low (% df)	−10%	+1%	+16%	−6%
Family size (new workers)				
To 3/4+ (% df)	−5%	−11%	+18%	−3%
Children under 14 (established workers)				
1–2/3+ (% df)	−13%	+1%	+14%	−1%
Income (new workers)				
To 30,000 pesos/40,000+ pesos (% df)	+20%	−10%	−1%	−9%

d. Marginalization

Current and expected dismissals (new workers)				
Neither current nor expected/expected in the future (% df)	+4%	—	−6%	+3%
Vulnerability to the crisis (established workers)				
Secure/threatened (% df)	−8%	−13%	+17%	+4%
Threatened/closed (% df)	+2%	+3%	−8%	+4%

NOTE: Table shows percentage changes between categories of each independent variable. When indicated, differences have been computed between extreme categories. Differences do not always cancel out, due to rounding. Percentage changes of 10 percent and over have been underlined. See Appendix for operationalization of variables and note on statistical significance.

Table 22 *e*). Finally, integration (intergenerational) produces an effect of this type in contexts of high marginalization (sons of factory workers, in threatened mills, are more prone to high dissent and less prone to high radicalism than other workers, Table 12 *c*).

Revolutionary effect $(D+R+)$. We have found three settings in which the joint impact of two structural properties is positive on both dissent and radicalism. The independent variables are indicators of three of the structural properties, but the intervening factors are always size of plant and vulnerability to the crisis. The centrality indicator is size, which produces a revolutionary effect among workers in closed mills (Table 17 *e*). Deprivation, as measured by quality of housing, exerts a "revolutionary" impact in secure mills (Table 19 *c*), and the threat of unemployment increases both dissent and radicalism in large mills (Table 22 *d*).

Deprivation and marginalization are found in all these contexts. Furthermore, structural properties have a different probability of interacting with each other in order to produce nonadaptive effects: out of ten combinations, seven include high levels of marginalization, while deprivation participates in five, centrality in four, and integration in three. Since these complex effects are produced by pairs of structural properties, it is difficult to assess the probable distribution of the specific contexts as industrialization proceeds. Five of these settings, however, include objective deprivation, and since the weight of this structural property is likely to decline as capitalism develops—at least as far as the working class is concerned—we can speculate that these contexts will be less frequent over time. But the five remaining combinations involve marginalization, and the incidence of this structural property does not diminish necessarily with industrialization, due to economic fluctuations and to technical progress. I have speculated, however, that the nonadaptive effects associated with marginalization processes are likely to be short-term. The role of size, finally, is of some interest. Its effect as a single independent variable is mobilizational, but it interacts with marginalization, and generates "revolutionary" effects.

In the preceding pages, I have surveyed some of the relationships between aspects of the working-class position in the economy and forms of political action. These are only propensities, diffuse orientations and dispositions for action, the most elementary of the three levels of complexity of political action we have seen in Chapter 3; but they provide opportunities and constraints for the development of ideologically oriented action and political organizations. I can now comment on the implications of the findings discussed above for the theories of revolution I have examined and for the larger issue of the legitimation of capitalism.

IMPLICATIONS FOR CLASSICAL THEORIES OF REVOLUTION

As was noted at the end of Chapter 7, even though the evidence from the preceding analysis is pertinent in relation to the validity of propositions derived from classical theories of revolution, in no sense is this analysis a "test" of these propositions. The data I have discussed are certainly relevant in order to assess the effects of structural properties on forms of political action, but they do not permit an examination of the consequences of high levels of the structural properties, especially as far as the two "static" ones, centrality and deprivation, are concerned. Propositions about the revolutionary consequences of high centrality, ranging from Marx's statements to the "new working class" thesis, are predicated upon a much higher level of development of the division of labor—"workers-scientists" in automated industry—than the one found in the relatively traditional manufacturing sectors to which the workers in these samples belonged. And the level of objective deprivation experienced by the poorer segments of the working class in a middle-developed country with a relatively high standard of living is probably much lower than the one that would be necessary in order to test deprivation theories. Within the range that structural properties have in the studies I have analyzed, however, some limited conclusions can be drawn.

Supporters of the Bakunin-Marcuse argument could argue that the foregoing discussion is consistent with the deprivation/lack-of-integration theory, for it has shown that these factors produce a deviation from acquiescence, and that centrality variables such as skill and sector of industry—the transition from phase A, construction, to phase B, manufacturing—have adaptive consequences. And Bakunin would have been delighted with most relationships we have found between indicators of integration and forms of political action. However, deprivation tends to generate "reformist" effects rather than mobilizational or "revolutionary" ones, and integration processes reduce new workers' dissent and radicalism rather quickly. But there are instances in which deprivation and integration variables generate consequences that are consistent with anarchist and neoanarchist expectations. Thus, low-income workers are more likely to have high dissent and high radicalism than other workers;

deprivation, as measured by quality of housing, exerts a "revolutionary" effect among workers in secure mills; and a prior background in independent (precapitalist) agriculture among individuals recently incorporated into the working class leads to small mobilizational and "revolutionary" effects.

As far as Marxist theory is concerned, centrality has a stronger relationship with the forms of political action than deprivation does, and marginalization is associated with a deviation from acquiescence. Centrality variables, however, produce strong adaptive consequences, size of plant being an important exception. As for marginalization, its direct effect among established workers is not mobilizational or revolutionary, but reformist. And there are reasons to think that the nonadaptive impact of this structural property is operative mainly in the short term. Marginalization, however, interacts with other structural properties, and is the most powerful determinant of deviation from acquiescence. Some of these complex effects are congruent with Marxist hypotheses. Thus, a "revolutionary" effect is produced by the interaction between size of plant and vulnerability to the crisis. However, reformist effects are the most frequent nonadaptive result of the combination of structural properties. But, even if consequences of this type involve a decrease in the level of radicalism, they also entail a withdrawal of legitimacy from the social order. And, since the incidence of marginalization does not necessarily decline as capitalism develops, these findings support the proposition that marginalization processes are likely to be a recurrent source of strain, even in advanced capitalist societies.

Neither the Bakunin-Marcuse thesis nor the Marxist argument are catastrophic theories of revolution. If the two political traditions agree in something, this is the voluntaristic component. Far from predicting that capitalism will break down, they expect that, at a certain point in the process of social development, the working class will become a revolutionary force. In terms of the temporal configuration of structural properties, the deprivation/lack-of-integration argument fits the initial phase of industrialization, while the Marxist emphasis on centrality and marginalization corresponds to later stages—as far as centrality is concerned, to a very advanced level of development. In fact, if the interpretation of Marxist theory of revolution I have presented in Chapter 7 is correct, no society has attained yet the level of development of the division of labor presupposed by the complex argument about the conjunction of possibility and necessity in the transition to socialism.

My findings indicate that it is at the beginning of working-class formation that diffuse propensities toward deviation from acquiescence are likely to be most frequent and that, as capitalism develops, these propensities will persist and/or recur in specific settings or conjunctural situations. The crucial factor in determining the outcome of the crisis of incorporation, then, is whether, in this initial stage of class formation, the conduciveness of the forms of political action is matched by the presence of the other elements that determine the conversion of diffuse orientations and predispositions into ideologically oriented action.

IMPLICATIONS FOR THE LEGITIMACY OF CAPITALISM

The analysis of the relationship between structural properties and forms of political action suggests some of the reasons other than elite strategies and environmental factors for the existence of a curvilinear relationship between modernization and the legitimacy of capitalist institutions. When industrialization begins, the impact of most variables associated with deviation from acquiescence is likely to be maximum and, as capitalism develops, the incidence or efficacy of most of these variables is likely to decline. The effects of vulnerability to the crisis and size of plant among established workers are, of course, the exception.

The distribution of structural properties in the initial phase of industrialization varies in the different societies, according to characteristics of the preindustrial social structure and to peculiarities of the process of economic development. As far as the "static" properties, centrality and deprivation, are concerned, their distribution is associated with factors such as the size of the labor supply and the technological and market imperatives of the sectors that "lead" the industrialization process. It is clear that income levels and other aspects of deprivation will vary with the relative availability of labor. This in turn depends not only on population size, but also, in the beginning of industrialization, on the existence of a precapitalist agricultural sector and its rate of disintegration. For example, in the nineteenth century, deprivation was initially greater in societies such as Russia, where a large precapitalist peasantry generated a labor surplus, than in the United States, where labor was scarce and had to be imported. And the distribution of centrality is affected by the characteristics of the manufacturing sectors that lead the process of industrialization in different societies. The complexity of technology, the type of division of labor, the size of productive units, and the composition of the working class in terms of skill are associated with the technological and market imperatives of different industries.

The distribution of the "dynamic" properties, integration and marginalization, is associated with the social origin of the working class in the initial period of class formation, with quantitative aspects of the process of modernization, and with the strength of the industrialization impulse. Forms of political action of new workers are affected by the type of agrarian social structure in which they participated prior to their move to manufacturing: former independent peasants are prone to high levels of dissent and radicalism, while individuals with experience in capitalist agriculture tend toward acquiescence. This, incidentally, suggests strategies for reform and revolution in modernizing societies. Cunning established elites would gain by developing capitalism sequentially, first in agriculture and later in industry (presumably, the induction of peasants into capitalist agriculture would produce disturbances, but rural unrest is easier to handle in a society of that type than urban and industrial revolt). Learned revolutionaries, on the other hand, would profit by focusing their organizational activities on working classes, or fractions thereof, recently formed on the basis of a precapitalist peasantry. I have also referred to the importance of quantitative aspects of the process of modernization. The speed of the industrialization process, differences between rates of release of labor by the agrarian sector and of absorption by the industrial one, et cetera determine the size of the segment of the working class that, at a specific point in time, is undergoing the process of integration. The strength of the industrialization impulse, finally, affects the intensity of the exposure to processes of marginalization.

Beyond these international differences in the distribution of structural properties, there are regularities. It is in the initial phase of large-scale manufacturing that a large proportion of the working class is likely to have a low level of integration into the industrial world, to work in large plants, and to experience deprivation. In the contemporary world, countries in this stage of development are also latecomers to industrialization. In them, the capitalist impulse tends to be weak, discontinuous, and exogenous. For this reason, significant segments of the working class in these societies belong to relatively backward manufacturing sectors or productive units, and are therefore vulnerable to marginalization. It is in this phase, which corresponds to middle levels of development, that chances for the conversion of nonacquiescent forms of political action into ideologically oriented action are maximum.

However, as was pointed out in the discussion of levels of complexity of collective action, in Chapter 3 and above in this chapter, the institutionalization of dissent is a social process that involves other components besides the conduciveness of forms of political action: the availability of a codified ideology, the generation within the intelligentsia of a group of carriers of that ideology, and the development of an organizational infrastructure. In all societies having mass communist or other revolutionary parties with a working-class base, these organizations or their predecessors attained their support in the early phases of large-scale manufacturing. There are no instances of parties of this type acquiring their base in a mature capitalist society. When engines of dissent are established, rejection of the foundations of the capitalist order is institutionalized into a subculture and is thus reproduced from generation to generation by socialization mechanisms. Once nonacquiescent forms of political action crystallize into ideologically oriented action, the solution to the crisis of incorporation will be one of the two low-legitimacy outcomes discussed in Chapter 2, polarization or exclusion, and the resulting regime either unstable liberal democracy or authoritarianism.

I can now offer a conclusion about some of the links that mediate the curvilinear relationship between the degree of modernization and the legitimacy of capitalism. As far as the working class is concerned, the configuration of structural properties facilitates a deviation from acquiescence in the beginning of large-scale industrialization. Whenever such a deviation takes place, elite strategies are constrained. As I have suggested in Chapters 3 and 4, established elites are likely to pursue exclusionary strategies if working classes have high-dissent forms of political action, and mobilization can be coupled with inclusion only if a surplus is available for redistribution. Furthermore, we have seen in Chapter 5 that, in latecomers to industrialization, nonaccommodation outcomes are also facilitated by factors other than working-class forms of political action. Latecomers are more likely than early industrializers to have heterogeneous social structures and dependent economies; as a consequence, their preindustrial elites tend to preserve a significant amount of power once large-scale manufacturing is established, their bourgeoisies are not likely to be hegemonic, and their state apparatuses are prone to high levels of relative autonomy. The result is a conduciveness to noninclusionary elite strategies, either exclusion or co-optation. In latecomers, then, forces pulling the polity away from accommodation operate both on the side of the working class and on the side of established elites.

As for the stability of co-optation, we have seen that, even when a strategy of this type is facilitated by low levels of dissent and radicalism in the working class, corporatism is an intrinsically fragile solution to the crisis of incorporation. And it may even be counterproductive in the long run, from the point of view of the elite. For corporatism, in the specific sense in which the term is used here, presupposes the organization of the working class under elite control, and the availability of a surplus for redistribution. And whenever this second factor is absent—a likely occurrence in the economically unstable latecomers—the transformation of a highly organized and unified labor movement into an independent power contender is a strong possibility. Thus, the apparently high level of legitimacy in many of today's latecomers—among which the combination of acquiescence and co-optation is rather frequent—conceals a potential for polarization and exclusion.

The previous discussion has shown that the configuration of structural properties in advanced capitalist societies is conducive to the adaptation of the working class: besides the effects of size of plant, these societies are vulnerable to only one structural property associated with deviation from acquiescence, marginalization, whose impact is likely to be short-term. Furthermore, the size of the surplus in advanced capitalist societies provides a cushion for potential working-class discontent: the political consequences of marginalization can be controlled by the welfare state. It is the middle-developed countries, which in the contemporary world are the less advanced countries of the second wave of industrialization and especially those belonging to the third wave, that are modern enough to have a large working class yet also backward enough to have a dissatisfied one.[2]

Appendix

THE SURVEY SAMPLES

Established Workers

The established workers survey was conducted by Miguel Murmis, Silvia Sigal, and myself for a government planning agency in 1966–1967. The questionnaires were administered in October and November of 1966. In the twenty-seven mills that existed in Tucumán, random stratified samples of four categories of workers were selected: factory permanent (N=147), factory transient (N=163), rural permanent (N=36), and rural transient (N=60). Samples were drawn from lists of industrial and rural employees, the latter working on farms owned by the mills. Sampling ratios were: permanent factory workers, 1/40, transient factory workers, 1/70, permanent rural workers, 1/80, and transient rural laborers, 1/160.

New Workers

The new workers survey was a part of the Marginality Project, whose director was José Nun. The project was housed at the Di Tella Institute in Buenos Aires and supported by the Ford Foundation. In addition to this study of recent migrants in Buenos Aires and Rosario, surveys of other rural and urban marginal strata were carried out. The project is described in a report by Nun.[1] Interviews took place in Buenos Aires in 1968–1969 and in Rosario in 1969–1970. The sample was purposive. Criteria for inclusion were as follows. Individuals were to be male migrants from Chaco, over the age of twenty-one, who had arrived in Buenos Aires and Rosario after January 1, 1962, and who were or had been employed, or were unemployed and seeking a job. No more than one person per household was interviewed. The sample size was 223, of which 144 were in construction and manufacturing, 48 in services, and 31 unemployed.

Table 24. *The Dissent Index*

	Rural Transient (N=60)	Rural Permanent (N=36)	Unemployed (N=31)
% supporting expropriation of farms	62%	47%	90%
% supporting expropriation of mills	15%	11%	45%
Dissent index: high	15%	11%	39%

VARIABLES

Only the questions and categories used in the analysis of data, in Chapters 9–11, are included here. I do not refer to seniority, time of residence in the city, and time unemployed, for their meaning is obvious. Variables used only in the description of the samples, in Chapter 8, are presented in the footnotes of that chapter. I indicate only the first table in which each variable appears.

1. Dissent and Radicalism

a. *Dissent* (Table 9). Two questions, referring to the desirability of the expropriation of large farms and of factories, were combined in a summatory index. The two items were dichotomized into "yes/other," and the "high" value in the index means agreement with both. The texts of the questions are as follows.

Established workers: 1. "Do you approve of mill owners owning farms as well?" ("¿A Vd. le parece bien que los dueños de ingenios tengan fincas?") 2. "And how about the existence of individually-owned, very large farms?" ("¿Y que haya fincas muy grandes de un solo dueño?") [If the answer to any of these two questions was negative,] 3. "Do you think that land should be taken away [from its current owners] and given to other people?" ("¿Le parece que habría que sacarles las tierras y dárselas a otros?") 4. "Do you think that factories should be taken away from mill owners?" ("¿A Vd. le parece que deben quitarse las fábricas a los dueños de los ingenios?")

New workers: 1. "Do you approve of the existence of individually-owned very large farms?" ("¿Le parece bien que haya campos muy grandes de un solo dueño?") [If the answer was negative,] 2. [The same as question 3 above (established workers study)]. 3. "Do you think that factories should be taken away from the bosses?" ("¿A Vd. le parece que habría que sacarle las fábricas a los patrones?")

Services (N=48)	"New" Industrial Workers (N=144)	"Established" Industrial Workers (N=147)
75%	81%	50%
37% ·	33%	24%
37%	31%	24%

In all groups, the percentage agreeing with the expropriation of large farms is much higher than the percentage agreeing with the expropriation of factories, and the distribution of the index is highly correlated with the distribution of the latter variable. The index was retained because the correlation is not perfect in the migrant samples. The distributions are shown in Table 24.

b. *Radicalism* (Table 9).

Established workers: The text of the question was as follows: "What do you think the union should do when the management does not comply with the [collective] agreement?" ("¿Qué piensa Vd. que debe hacer el sindicato cuando los patrones no cumplen el convenio?") 1. "Talk to the government so that it intervenes?" ("¿Ir a hablar con el gobierno para que intervenga?") 2. "Strike?" ("¿Ir a la huelga?") 3. "Besides [1 or 2], seize the factory as a sign of protest?" ("¿Además [de 1 o 2], tomar la fábrica en señal de protesta?") 4. "To put pressure on the management, without striking or seizing the factory?" ("¿Presionar a los patrones, pero sin llegar a la huelga ni a la toma de fábrica?") 5. Other. Value 3 was considered the indicator of "high" radicalism.

New workers: The text of the question was: "Assume that a group of workers has been hurt in relation to their wages and working conditions, as a consequence of measures taken by the management. We are going to show you pictures that illustrate three different types of workers' response to these measures. Could you order the pictures according to the degree of effectiveness that you attribute nowadays to each type of reaction, i.e., placing the least effective one first?" ("Suponga Vd. que una cantidad de obreros se ven perjudicados en sus salarios y en sus condiciones de trabajo por medidas que adoptan los patrones. Vamos a mostrarle dibujos que muestran tres tipos distintos de reacción de los obreros ante esas medidas. ¿Podría ordenar los dibujos según el grado de eficacia que atribuye Vd. hoy en día a cada tipo de reacción, es decir poniendo primero a la menos eficaz?") The respondents were shown three cards, which had no titles. Each card consisted of two pictures. The first card was considered the indicator of individual demand. *Cell 1*: this picture shows a worker in a waiting room. He is being let into a manager's office. *Cell 2*: the same individual appears, standing in front of the manager, who is sitting at his desk. They talk about a letter the worker has in his hand. The second card was the indicator of collective demand. *Cell 1*: the same worker is seen standing and surrounded by his workmates. He has the letter in his hand and is clearly arguing with the other individuals about its contents. *Cell 2*: the scene is again the manager's office, but this time the protagonist is discussing the letter in the presence of the other workers. The third card was the indicator of collective mobilization. *Cell 1*: the central character is again shown surrounded by his workmates. This time he is not simply talking about the letter, but making a speech about it. *Cell 2*: the group of workers, apparently stirred up by the speech, stage a demonstration. The protagonist is brandishing the letter, and the other people are waving their arms and shouting. The selection of this alternative as the most effective one was considered an indicator of high radicalism.[2]

2. Structural Properties

a. *Integration.*

Father's occupation (Table 12). *Established workers*: dichotomized into "factory/other." "Factory" refers to industrial workers in the sugar industry; and "other" includes rural laborers in sugar farms, nonsugar agriculture, and other occupations. *New workers*: trichotomized into independent agriculture (operators of farms of twenty-five hectares or less), dependent agriculture (wage laborers), and urban. Ten cases were excluded because information on farm size was not available.

Time spent in agriculture (Table 13). The four categories (0, 1–49, 50–99, 100) refer to percentages of the work career in Chaco.

Type of agrarian experience (Table 13). Trichotomized into independent 100 percent of the time, dependent 100 percent of the time, and other. The latter category includes those respondents who have not worked in agriculture, and those who have done so but did not spend their entire work career in Chaco as either independent peasants or rural wage laborers.

Time spent in independent agriculture (Table 13). The four categories (0, 1–49, 50–99, 100) refer to percentages of the work career in Chaco spent as independent peasant exclusively. Unpaid family labor was included.

Time spent in dependent agriculture (Table 13). The four categories (0, 1–49, 50–99, 100) refer to percentages of the work career in Chaco spent as rural wage laborer exclusively. "Semiproletarians" were excluded.

Last job prior to migration (Table 13). Trichotomized into independent agriculture, dependent agriculture, and urban. Nine "semiproletarians" were excluded.

Time spent in the sugar industry (Table 14). Dichotomized into less than 100 percent and 100 percent of the total work career.

b. *Centrality.*

Sector of industry (Table 15). Dichotomized into construction (N=69) and manufacturing (N=75). The latter includes twenty-five cases in the meat packing industry, eighteen in the metal industry, and thirty-two in other industries.

Efficiency of mill (Table 16). This index consists of the averaging of two indicators: percentage of saccharose extracted from cane, reduced to 12.5 percent fiber; and ratio of retained saccharose to retainable saccharose. The index was elaborated by two experts, O. Calvelo and J. C. Bargo, who were working at the National Development Council in Buenos Aires. The twenty-seven mills existing in Tucumán were ranked on the basis of data for 1963–1965. The distribution is as follows: *high*: San Pablo, La Providencia, Concepción, La Corona, La Fronterita, and Santa Rosa; *medium*: Ñuñorco, La Trinidad, La Florida, Santa Bárbara, Aguilares, Leales, Cruz Alta, Santa Lucía, San Ramón, and Bella Vista; *low*: Nueva Baviera, Amalia, Lastenia, Mercedes, San Antonio, San José, Esperanza, Los Ralos, San Juan, Marapa, and Santa Ana.

Size of plant (Table 17). The meaning of the categories is obvious. In the established workers study, figures refer to the number of factory workers, both permanent and transient. The twenty-seven sugar mills were classified as follows: *small* (390–572): Esperanza, Los Ralos, Santa Bárbara, La Corona, La Providencia, Nueva Baviera, San Ramón, Santa Ana, San José, Aguilares, Lastenia, Ñuñorco, and Santa Rosa; *medium* (579–756): Amalia, Mercedes, San Antonio, San Juan, Cruz Alta, La Fronterita, Santa Lucía, La Florida, and Marapa; *large* (814 and over): La Trinidad, San Pablo, Leales, Bella Vista, and Concepción.

Skill (Table 18). Dichotomized as "skilled/unskilled."

c. *Deprivation.*

Quality of housing (Table 19). *Established workers*: The index consists of the averaging of the following scores for walls, roof, and stove. Masonry, brick, or concrete walls; tile, brick, or cement roof; and an electric, gas, or kerosene stove were given a score of 1. Adobe walls, fibrocement roof, and a coal or wood stove were given a score of 2. Inferior materials for walls and roof, such as boards, tin, mud, cardboard, et cetera, and inferior types of stoves were given a score of 3. The correspondence between scores and categories is as follows:

Score	Category
1	high
1.01–1.99	medium
2 or more	low

New workers: The following scores for walls, roof, and floors were averaged in the index, which was designed by the staff of the Marginality Project. Masonry, brick, or concrete walls; cement roof; and tile or parquet floors were given a score of 3. Zinc, fibrocement, wood, and thatched roofs and cement floors were given a score of 2 (walls were not given this score). Adobe, wood, and fibrocement walls; cardboard sheet roofs, and brick or board floors were given a score of 1. Pieces of cardboard, tin, refuse, or other inferior materials for walls and roofs along with dirt floors were given a score of 0. The distribution was dichotomized, and the cutoff point was 1.5.

Family size (Table 19). The number of family members living with the respondent were dichotomized into "1–3" and "4 or more."

Children under 14 (Table 19). Trichotomized into "other," "1–2," and "3 or more." This variable refers to children under fourteen years of age rather than to the total number of children. "Other," therefore, includes childless workers as well as workers who only have children over fourteen.

d. *Marginalization*.

Vulnerability to the crisis (Table 21). The twenty-seven mills have been classified as follows: *secure*: Concepción, Cruz Alta, La Corona, La Fronterita, La Providencia, Leales, San Juan, San Pablo, San Ramón, and Santa Bárbara; *threatened*: Aguilares, Amalia, Los Ralos, Marapa, Mercedes, Ñuñorco, San José, Santa Lucía, and Santa Rosa; *closed*: Bella Vista, Esperanza, La Florida, La Trinidad, Lastenia, Nueva Baviera, San Antonio, and Santa Ana.

Current dismissals/future dismissals expected (Table 21). Based on two questions: "Are people being laid off at your job?" ("¿En su empresa se están produciendo despidos?") and "Do you think that it is likely that there will be layoffs in the future?" ("¿Le parece que es fácil que se produzcan despidos en el futuro?") The alternatives were, in the two cases, 1. Yes; 2. More or less; 3. No; 4. Does not know.

A NOTE ON STATISTICAL SIGNIFICANCE

Since this is a substantive study, focused on the analysis of relationships among variables rather than on the description of a specific population, I am not reporting results of significance tests. Such tests could be computed for the tables which include data from the established workers study, for this is a random sample. I agree with the arguments against using significance tests—which, as Galtung contends, should be called generalizability tests[3]—in research of the type presented here, and I also think that, in relation to generalization hypotheses, replications on independent samples are an alternative more satisfactory than tests of statistical significance. The classical formulation of this position was made by Coleman.[4] Galtung has presented an excellent discussion of the statistical and epistemological assumptions and consequences of significance tests.[5] As far as survey analysis is concerned, the standard policy of the Columbia school was to reject them. Finally, these tests have not been used in the large majority of the books dealing with working-class surveys that I cite.

Notes

1. The Problem

1. For different approaches and models, see L. Binder et al., *Crises and Sequences in Political Development* (Princeton: Princeton University Press, 1971); S. N. Eisenstadt, *Modernization: Protest and Change* (Englewood Cliffs: Prentice-Hall, 1966); S. M. Lipset and S. Rokkan, "Cleavage Structures, Party Systems, and Voter Alignments: An Introduction," in *Party Systems and Voter Alignments*, edited by S. M. Lipset and S. Rokkan (New York: Free Press, 1967); B. Moore, *Social Origins of Dictatorship and Democracy* (Boston: Beacon Press, 1966); A. F. K. Organski, *The Stages of Political Development* (New York: Knopf, 1968); D. A. Rustow, *A World of Nations* (Washington, D.C.: The Brookings Institution, 1967).
2. G. Germani, "Social Change and Intergroup Conflicts," in *The New Sociology*, edited by I. L. Horowitz (New York: Oxford University Press, 1964).
3. S. P. Huntington, *Political Order in Changing Societies* (New Haven: Yale University Press, 1968).
4. S. M. Lipset, *Political Man* (Garden City: Doubleday, 1963), p. 71. See also Lipset and Rokkan, "Cleavage Structures."
5. R. Bendix, *Nation-Building and Citizenship* (Garden City: Doubleday, 1969), Chapter 3.
6. T. H. Marshall, *Class, Citizenship and Social Development* (Garden City: Doubleday, 1965).
7. S. Rokkan, "Mass Suffrage, Secret Voting, and Political Participation," *Archives Européennes de Sociologie* 2, no. 1: 132–152.
8. Huntington, *Political Order*, Chapter 6.
9. S. M. Lipset, *The First New Nation* (Garden City: Doubleday, 1967), Chapter 6.
10. Moore, *Social Origins*, especially Chapter 8.
11. T. Parsons, "Comparative Studies and Evolutionary Change," in *Comparative Methods in Sociology*, edited by I. Vallier (Berkeley: University of California Press, 1971).
12. In Bendix's terms: "In Europe the rising awareness of the working class

expresses above all an experience of *political alienation*, that is, a sense of not having a recognized position in the civic community or of not having a civic community in which to participate. . . . If this is a correct assessment of the impulses and half-articulated longings characteristic of much popular agitation among lower classes in Western Europe, then we have a clue to the decline of socialism" (*Nation-Building and Citizenship*, pp. 88–89). See also S. M. Lipset, *Revolution and Counterrevolution* (Garden City: Doubleday, 1970), Chapter 8; Marshall, *Class, Citizenship and Social Development*.

13. This classification of models of strain in a social system differs from those discussed by Shorter and Tilly, who distinguish among deprivation, breakdown, and interest theories (E. Shorter and C. Tilly, *Strikes in France, 1830–1968* [New York: Cambridge University Press, 1974], pp. 4–11), and by Tilly et al., who contrast breakdown and solidarity theories (C. Tilly, L. Tilly, and R. Tilly, *The Rebellious Century: 1830–1930* [Cambridge: Harvard University Press, 1975], pp. 4–11, 271–274). Breakdown and deprivation would correspond to the second model, but the "interest" or "solidarity" type is much narrower than the first model and in fact could fit both. The reason is that the "solidarity" paradigm is defined in terms of processes of mobilization and organization rather than at the level of the structural sources of action.

14. See the discussion in K. Marx, *Grundrisse* (New York: Vintage, 1973), pp. 471–514.

15. M. Dobb, *Studies in the Development of Capitalism* (London: Routledge and Kegan Paul, 1967), Chapter 2.

16. G. Germani, "Social Change and Intergroup Conflicts." See also Germani, "Fascism and Class," in *The Nature of Fascism*, edited by S. J. Woolf (New York: Vintage, 1969).

17. S. Rokkan, "Mass Suffrage, Secret Voting, and Political Participation"; R. Bendix, *Nation-Building and Citizenship*, p. 117.

2. Outcomes of the Process of Incorporation

1. An earlier version of this chapter was included in C. H. Waisman, "The Integration of the Working Class into the Political System" (Paper presented at the annual meeting of the American Sociological Association, Chicago, September 5–9, 1977).

2. Lipset, *Political Man*, p. 73.

3. J. Blondel, *Comparing Political Systems* (New York: Praeger, 1972), Chapter 4.

4. Ibid., p. 50.

5. Huntington, *Political Order*, p. 196.

6. W. J. Goode, "Presidential Address: The Place of Force in Human Society," *American Sociological Review* 37, no. 5: 507–519.

7. See J. Linz, "An Authoritarian Regime: Spain," in *Cleavages, Ideologies, and Party Systems*, edited by E. Allardt and Y. Littunen (Helsinki: West-

ermarck Society, 1964); and "Opposition to and under an Authoritarian Regime: The Case of Spain," in *Regimes and Oppositions*, edited by R. Dahl (New Haven: Yale University Press, 1973).

8. G. A. O'Donnell, *Modernization and Bureaucratic-Authoritarianism: Studies in South American Politics* (Berkeley: Institute of International Studies, University of California, 1973).

9. M. Fainsod, *How Russia is Ruled* (Cambridge: Harvard University Press, 1963), Chapter 1.

10. See the discussion in I. K. Feierabend and R. L. Feierabend, "The Relationship of Systemic Frustration, Political Coercion, and Political Instability: A Cross-National Analysis," in *Macro-Quantitative Analysis*, edited by J. V. Gillespie and B. A. Nesvold (Beverly Hills: Sage, 1971), pp. 420–421.

11. B. Bettelheim, "Individual and Mass Behavior in Extreme Situations," in *Readings in Social Psychology*, edited by E. Maccoby et al. (New York: Holt, Rinehart and Winston, 1958).

12. After having asked "whether it is better to be loved than feared, or the contrary," Machiavelli argued that "a person would like to be the one and the other; but since it is difficult to mix them together, it is much safer to be feared than loved, if one of the two must be lacking . . . men are less concerned with hurting someone who makes himself loved than one who makes himself feared, because love is held by a link of obligation, which, since men are wretched creatures, is broken every time their own interests are involved; but fear is held by a dread of punishment which will never leave you" N. Machiavelli, *The Prince* (New York: St. Martin's Press, 1964), pp. 137–139.

13. P. C. Schmitter, "Still the Century of Corporatism?" in *The New Corporatism*, edited by F. B. Pike and T. Stritch (Notre Dame: University of Notre Dame Press, 1974), pp. 93–94.

14. See Pike and Stritch, eds., *The New Corporatism*; also H. J. Wiarda, ed., *Politics and Social Change in Latin America* (Amherst: University of Massachusetts Press, 1974).

15. See G. A. O'Donnell, "Corporatism and the Question of the State," D. Collier and R. B. Collier, "Who Does What, to Whom, and How: Toward a Comparative Analysis of Latin American Corporatism," and J. M. Malloy, "Authoritarianism and Corporatism in Latin America: The Modal Pattern," in *Authoritarianism and Corporatism in Latin America*, edited by J. M. Malloy (Pittsburgh: University of Pittsburgh Press, 1977).

16. H. Seton-Watson, *The Decline of Imperial Russia: 1855–1914* (New York: Praeger, 1969), p. 120. Gapon's activities on the eve of the 1905 revolution are well known.

17. See Schmitter, "Still the Century of Corporatism?" and also his *Interest Conflict and Political Change in Brazil* (Stanford: Stanford University Press, 1971).

3. A Conceptual Framework for the Analysis of Collective Political Action

1. A previous draft of this chapter formed part of Waisman, "The Integration of the Working Class into the Political System."
2. J. R. Gusfield, *Symbolic Crusade: Status Politics and the American Temperance Movement* (Urbana: University of Illinois Press, 1966), pp. 20–23.
3. C. Tilly, L. Tilly, and R. Tilly, *The Rebellious Century*, pp. 48–55, 248–252. See also E. Shorter and C. Tilly, *Strikes in France*.
4. L. Trotsky, *The Russian Revolution*, translated by M. Eastman (Garden City: Doubleday, 1959), p. ix.
5. R. Mousnier, *Peasant Uprisings in Seventeenth Century France, Russia, and China* (New York: Harper, 1973), pp. 341–342, 343–344.
6. The distinction between the two dimensions and the typology were developed in connection with my work in the established workers study (see Chapter 9).
7. See W. A. Gamson, *The Strategy of Social Protest* (Homewood, Ill.: Dorsey Press, 1975); J. D. McCarthy and M. N. Zald, "Resource Mobilization and Social Movements: A Partial Theory," *American Journal of Sociology* 82, no. 6 (1977): 1212–1241; A. Oberschall, *Social Conflict and Social Movements* (Englewood Cliffs, N.J.: Prentice-Hall, 1973). Cf. C. Tilly, *From Mobilization to Revolution* (Reading, Mass.: Addison-Wesley, 1978).
8. McCarthy and Zald, "Resource Mobilization and Social Movements," pp. 1214–1215, are willing to assume that there is always enough discontent in any society to supply support for an effectively organized movement.
9. K. W. Deutsch, "Imperialism and Neocolonialism," *Papers of the Peace Science Society (International)* 23 (1974): 1–25.

4. Three Cases: Disraelian Britain, Bismarckian Germany, and Peronist Argentina

1. The classical description of this process is found in T. H. Marshall, *Class, Citizenship and Social Development*, Chapter 4.
2. A. Briggs, *The Making of Modern England—1783–1867: The Age of Improvement* (New York: Harper, 1965), p. 504. See also R. Harrison, *Before the Socialists* (London: Routledge and Kegan Paul, 1965), p. 85.
3. Harrison, *Before the Socialists*, p. 86.
4. Ibid., p. 108.
5. R. Blake, *The Conservative Party from Peel to Churchill* (London: Eyre and Spottiswoode, 1970), p. 98.
6. P. Smith, *Disraelian Conservatism and Social Reform* (London: Routledge and Kegan Paul, 1967), p. 5.
7. Quoted in F. J. C. Hearnshaw, *Conservatism in England* (New York: Howard Fertig, 1967), p. 215.

8. Briggs, *The Making of Modern England*, p. 518.
9. Harrison, *Before the Socialists*, p. 113.
10. Smith, *Disraelian Conservatism*, p. 14.
11. Quoted by Smith, ibid., p. 15.
12. Briggs, *The Making of Modern England*, pp. 507–508.
13. See ibid., pp. 508–514, and Smith, *Disraelian Conservatism*, Chapter 4.
14. Harrison, *Before the Socialists*, Chapter 3.
15. Ibid.
16. Ibid., pp. 92–93.
17. Ibid., p. 94.
18. Briggs, *The Making of Modern England*, p. 505.
19. M. Cowling, *1867, Disraeli, Gladstone and Revolution* (London: Cambridge University Press, 1967).
20. Quoted by Harrison, *Before the Socialists*, pp. 113–114.
21. On Tory Democracy, see R. Blake, *Disraeli* (London: Eyre and Spottiswoode, 1966), p. 476; and Blake, *The Conservative Party*, p. 100. Smith, in analyzing the debates, has shown that "Disraeli had no clear plan, that he thought in terms of the old stereotypes (country = Conservative; borough = Liberal), that he was only 'educating his party' in retrospect, (and) that the final version of the Act though it owed little to Gladstone was in no sense what Derby or Disraeli intended" (F. B. Smith, *The Making of the Second Reform Bill*, summarized by Blake, *The Conservative Party*, p. 101).
22. H. Perkin, *The Origins of Modern English Society, 1780–1880* (London: Routledge and Kegan Paul, 1969), p. 134.
23. E. J. Hobsbawn, *Industry and Empire* (Hardmondsworth: Penguin, 1968), p. 160.
24. Ibid., pp. 159–164.
25. See A. Gerschenkron, *Bread and Democracy in Germany* (New York: Howard Fertig, 1966); and A. Rosenberg, *Imperial Germany: The Birth of the German Republic, 1871–1918* (Boston: Beacon Press, 1968), Chapter 1.
26. V. L. Lidtke, *The Outlawed Party: Social Democracy in Germany, 1878–1890* (Princeton: Princeton University Press, 1966), p. 13.
27. Ibid, p. 14.
28. Quoted by G. Roth, *The Social Democrats in Imperial Germany* (Totowa, N.J.: Bedminster Press, 1963), p. 87.
29. ". . . It was at the moment when Deputy Bebel or Deputy Liebknecht . . . held up the French Commune as the model of political institutions, and openly vowed the creed professed by the Parisian assassins and incendiaries. Thenceforth I clearly perceived the extent of the danger threatening us . . . the invocation of the Commune opened my eyes to what we had to expect, and I instantly recognized the fact that Social Democracy is an enemy against whom the state and society are bound to defend themselves." Quoted by M. Busch, *Our Chancellor (Bismarck)* (Freeport, New York: Books for Libraries Press, 1970), Vol. 2, p. 198.

30. Ibid., p. 206.
31. Roth, *The Social Democrats*, p. 69.
32. Rosenberg, *Imperial Germany*, p. 7.
33. A. J. P. Taylor, *The Course of German History* (New York: Capricorn, 1962), p. 120.
34. As Rosenberg writes, ". . . Bismarck knew very well that the German Empire could neither be established nor maintained against the will of the middle classes to whom, however, no constitutional rights were to be accorded at the expense of the crown" (*Imperial Germany*, p. 6).
35. Taylor, *The Course of German History*, p. 120.
36. Rosenberg, *Imperial Germany*, p. 2.
37. Lidtke, *The Outlawed Party*, p. 71.
38. Ibid., p. 72. See E. Eyck, *Bismarck and the German Empire* (New York: Norton, 1968), p. 240.
39. See the text of the law in Lidtke, *The Outlawed Party*, pp. 338–345.
40. H. Grebing, *The History of the German Labor Movement* (London: Oswald Wolff, 1969), p. 59.
41. Lidtke, *The Outlawed Party*, p. 80.
42. Quoted in J. Ziekursch, "The Campaign Against Socialism," in *Otto von Bismarck: A Historical Assessment*, edited by T. S. Hamerow (Lexington, Mass.: Heath, 1972), pp. 119–120.
43. Lidtke, *The Outlawed Party*, p. 80.
44. Ibid., p. 83.
45. Ibid., p. 80.
46. H. Holborn, *A History of Modern Germany, 1840–1945* (New York: Knopf, 1969), p. 292.
47. Taylor, *The Course of German History*, p. 130.
48. A. J. P. Taylor, *Bismarck: The Man and the Statesman* (New York: Vintage, 1955), p. 203.
49. Busch, *Our Chancellor*, p. 218.
50. Taylor, *Bismarck*, p. 204.
51. Holborn, *A History of Modern Germany*, p. 292.
52. Grebing, *The History of the German Labor Movement*, p. 60.
53. Taylor, *Bismarck*, p. 206.
54. Holborn, *A History of Modern Germany*, p. 289.
55. Roth, *The Social Democrats*, p. 159.
56. Lidtke, *The Outlawed Party*, pp. 89–97.
57. Roth, *The Social Democrats*, p. 159.
58. Ibid., p. 179.
59. Ibid., pp. 170–171.
60. Quoted by Roth, ibid., p. 201.
61. Lidtke, *The Outlawed Party*, p. 178.
62. For a sociological analysis of the evolution of Argentina, see J. E. Corradi, "Argentina," in *Latin America: The Struggle With Dependency and Beyond*, edited by R. H. Chilcote and Joel C. Edelstein (Cambridge: Schenkman, 1974), pp. 305–407.

63. G. Germani, *Política y sociedad en una época de transición* (Buenos Aires: Paidós, 1962), pp. 197–198.

64. In 1914, 66 percent of the owners and 50 percent of the personnel of industrial establishments, 74 percent of the owners and 53 percent of the personnel of commercial establishments, and 45 percent of the members of the liberal professions were foreign born (ibid., p. 195).

65. G. Germani, "El surgimiento del peronismo: el rol de los obreros y de los migrantes internos," *Desarrollo económico* 13, no. 51: 435–488, 452.

66. J. D. Perón, *Doctrina revolucionaria* (Buenos Aires: Freeland, 1973), p. 28.

67. Ibid., p. 189.

68. Ibid., p. 108.

69. See R. J. Alexander, *The Perón Era* (New York: Columbia University Press, 1951), pp. 15–19; G. I. Blanksten, *Perón's Argentina* (Chicago: University of Chicago Press, 1953), pp. 55–56; Germani, "El surgimiento del peronismo," pp. 468–470; and S. L. Baily, *Labor, Nationalism, and Politics in Argentina* (New Brunswick: Rutgers University Press, 1967), Chapter 4.

70. Blanksten, *Perón's Argentina*, pp. 175–176.

71. In one case—the railroad strike of 1951—strikers were drafted into the army, several hundreds of them were arrested and tried for sedition, and two thousand were laid off. For an account of labor opposition, see Baily, *Labor, Nationalism, and Politics*, Chapter 6.

72. C. F. Diaz-Alejandro, *Essays on the Economic History of the Argentine Republic* (New Haven: Yale University Press, 1970), p. 538.

73. See M. Murmis and J. C. Portantiero, *Estudios sobre los orígenes del peronismo* (Buenos Aires: Siglo XXI, 1971), pp. 59–126; Germani, "El surgimiento del peronismo"; W. Little, "The Popular Origins of Peronism," in *Argentina in the Twentieth Century*, edited by D. Rock (Pittsburgh: University of Pittsburgh Press, 1975), pp. 162–178.

74. Murmis and Portantiero, *Estudios sobre los orígenes del peronismo*, pp. 77–82.

75. R. J. Alexander, *Labor Relations in Argentina, Brazil, and Chile* (New York: McGraw-Hill, 1962), pp. 177–181.

76. Germani, "El surgimiento del peronismo," p. 469.

77. See Baily, *Labor, Nationalism, and Politics*.

5. Structural Correlates of Outcomes

1. A previous version of this chapter was C. H. Waisman, "Industrialization, the Incorporation of the Working Class, and Liberal Democracy" (Paper presented at the Ninth World Congress of Sociology, Uppsala, Sweden, August 1978). It was published as "Modelos teóricos de industrialización tardía," *Papers* 11 (1979): 269–299.

2. Moore, *Social Origins of Dictatorship and Democracy*.

3. P. C. Schmitter, "Paths to Political Development in Latin America," in *Changing Latin America*, edited by D. A. Chalmers (New York: Academy of Political Science, Columbia University, 1972); Schmitter, "Still the Century of Corporatism?" and Schmitter, *Interest Conflict and Political Change in Brazil.*

4. O'Donnell, *Modernization and Bureaucratic-Authoritarianism.*

5. A. Gerschenkron, *Economic Backwardness in Historical Perspective* (Cambridge: Harvard University Press, 1962).

6. A. O. Hirschman, "The Political Economy of Import-Substituting Industrialization in Latin America," *Quarterly Journal of Economics* 82, no. 1 (1968): 2–32.

7. G. Germani, *Sociología de la modernización* (Buenos Aires: Paidós, 1969), Chapter 2.

8. K. Marx, *Karl Marx on Colonialism and Modernization*, edited by S. Avineri (Garden City: Doubleday, 1969), pp. 88–95.

9. Trotsky, *The Russian Revolution*, Chapter 1.

10. Organski, *The Stages of Political Development*, Chapter 5.

11. Typical examples are the works of Furtado and Frank. See, for instance, C. Furtado, "Development and Stagnation in Latin America," in *Masses in Latin America*, edited by I. L. Horowitz (New York: Oxford University Press, 1970); and A. G. Frank, *Capitalism and Underdevelopment in Latin America* (New York: Modern Reader Paperbacks, 1969).

12. Moore, *Social Origins of Dictatorship and Democracy.*

13. See F. Engels, prefaces to *The Peasant War in Germany*, translated by M. J. Olguin, and *Germany: Revolution and Counter-revolution*, Chapters 1 and 2 and passim, in *The German Revolutions* (Chicago: University of Chicago Press, 1967); and F. Engels, *The Role of Force in History* (New York: International Publishers, 1968), Chapter 7.

14. See Moore, *Social Origins of Dictatorship and Democracy*, Chapter 7.

15. See K. Marx, *The Eighteenth Brumaire of Louis Bonaparte*, in K. Marx and F. Engels, *Selected Works* (New York: International Publishers, 1974).

16. See the prefaces to Engels, *The Peasant War in Germany*; and F. Engels, *The Housing Question* (New York: International Publishers, 1935), pp. 71–72.

17. C. W. Anderson, "Toward a Theory of Latin American Politics," in *Politics and Social Change*, edited by Wiarda, p. 257.

7. Structural Properties in Classical Revolutionary Theories

1. M. Bakunin, *Bakunin on Anarchy*, edited and translated by S. Dolgoff (New York: Vintage, 1971), p. 294.

2. Ibid., p. 185.

3. M. Bakunin, *The Political Philosophy of Bakunin*, edited by G. P. Maximoff (New York: Free Press, 1953), p. 315.

4. K. Marx and F. Engels, *Manifesto of the Communist Party*, in Marx and Engels, *Selected Works*, p. 44.
5. M. Bakunin, *Statism and Anarchy*, quoted in Dolgoff, ed., *Bakunin on Anarchy*, p. 14.
6. Bakunin, *Bakunin on Anarchy*, p. 294.
7. Ibid., p. 14.
8. H. Marcuse, *An Essay on Liberation* (Boston: Beacon Press, 1969), p. 16.
9. Ibid., p. 80.
10. H. Marcuse, *One-Dimensional Man* (Boston: Beacon Press, 1964), p. 256.
11. J. A. Schumpeter, *Capitalism, Socialism and Democracy* (New York: Harper and Row, 1962), p. 42.
12. For references, see the discussion in E. Varga, *Essais sur l'économie politique du capitalisme* (Moscow: Ed. du Progrès, 1967), pp. 123–137. Varga himself disagreed with this line of interpretation.
13. Marx and Engels, *Selected Works*, p. 44.
14. K. Marx and F. Engels, *The Holy Family, or Critique of Critical Criticism*, translated by R. Dixon and C. Dutt (Moscow: Progress Publishers, 1975), p. 44.
15. K. Marx, Preface to *A Contribution to the Critique of Political Economy*, in Marx and Engels, *Selected Works*, p. 183.
16. Ibid., p. 182.
17. See the operationalization of this concept in J. Robinson, *An Essay on Marxian Economics* (London: Macmillan, 1971), Chapter 2.
18. N. Bukharin, *Historical Materialism* (Ann Arbor: University of Michigan Press, 1969), p. 289.
19. See the classic passages in the *Manifesto*, in Marx and Engels, *Selected Works*, p. 43.
20. K. Marx, *Grundrisse* (New York: Vintage, 1973), p. 705.
21. Ibid., pp. 705–706. These passages are discussed by M. Nicolaus, "The Unknown Marx," *New Left Review* 48 (1968): 41–61.
22. Marx, *Grundrisse*, p. 708.
23. This issue will be briefly considered in Chapter 10. On this issue, see M. Mann, *Consciousness and Action Among the Western Working Class* (London: Macmillan, 1973).
24. "The greater the social wealth, . . . [and] also the absolute mass of the proletariat and the productiveness of its labour, the greater is the industrial reserve army. The same causes which develop the expansive power of capital, develop also the labour power at its disposal. The relative mass of the industrial reserve army increases therefore with the potential energy of wealth. But the greater this reserve army in proportion to the active labour army, the greater is the mass of a consolidated surplus-population, whose misery is in inverse ratio to its torment of labour" (K. Marx, *Capital: A Critique of Political Economy*, translated by S. Moore and E. Aveling, edited by F. Engels [New York: International Publishers, 1967], 1: 644).

25. Ibid., pp. 640–643.
26. "It follows therefore that in proportion as capital accumulates, the lot of the labourer, be his payment high or low, must grow worse. The law . . . that always equilibrates the relative surplus population, or industrial reserve army, to the extent and energy of accumulation, this law rivets the labourer to capital more firmly than the wedges of Vulcan did Prometheus to the rock. It establishes an accumulation of misery corresponding with accumulation of capital" (ibid., p. 645).
27. Ibid., p. 763.
28. Ibid.
29. This passage is quoted by Schumpeter in support of the thesis that Marx was a theoretician of deprivation. See Schumpeter, *Capitalism, Socialism and Democracy*, pp. 37–38.
30. Marx and Engels, *Manifesto*, in Marx and Engels, *Selected Works*, p. 44.
31. Engels, *The Peasant War in Germany*, p. 9.
32. In this regard, see Marx, *Wages, Price and Profit*, in Marx and Engels, *Selected Works*. In Chapter 14 of that work, Marx refers also to the role of cultural factors in the determination of wages.
33. Marx, *Grundrisse*, p. 408.
34. See K. Marx and F. Engels, *Karl Marx and Frederick Engels on Britain* (Moscow: Foreign Languages Publishing House, 1953), pp. 23–31.
35. See V. I. Lenin, *Imperialism: The Highest Stage of Capitalism* (New York: International Publishers, 1939), pp. 13–14.
36. See J. Linz, "The Social Bases of West German Politics" (Ph.D. dissertation, Columbia University, 1959), 1:299; and M. Zeitlin, *Revolutionary Politics and the Cuban Working Class* (New York: Harper and Row, 1970), pp. 89–90.
37. H. Pelling, *Popular Politics and Society in Late Victorian England* (London: Macmillan, 1968), p. 41.

8. Two Studies of the Argentine Working Class

1. Díaz-Alejandro, *Essays*, p. 1n.
2. Ibid., p. 428.
3. For analyses of the stalemate in contemporary Argentine politics, see O'Donnell, *Modernization and Bureaucratic-Authoritarianism*; and O'Donnell, "Estado y alianzas en la Argentina," *Desarrollo económico* 16, no. 64 (1977). See also T. S. Di Tella, "Stalemate or Coexistence in Argentina," in *Latin America: Reform or Revolution?* edited by J. Petras and M. Zeitlin (Greenwich, Conn.: Fawcett Publications, 1968).
4. Organski, *The Stages of Political Development*.
5. See M. Diamand, *Doctrinas económicas, desarrollo e independencia* (Buenos Aires: Paidós, 1973); R. Mallon and J. Sorrouille, *Economic Policymaking in a Conflict Society: The Case of Argentina* (Cambridge: Harvard University Press, 1974); O'Donnell, "Estado y alianzas en la Ar-

gentina"; and M. Brodersohn, "Conflictos entre los objetivos de política económica de corto plazo de la economía argentina," documento de trabajo 77 (Buenos Aires: Instituto Di Tella, 1977).

6. E. J. Hobsbawm, *Labouring Men* (New York: Basic Books, 1964), pp. 5–22.

7. Banco Central de la República Argentina, *Origen del producto y distribución del ingreso: Años 1950–69* (Buenos Aires, 1971).

8. Diaz-Alejandro, *Essays*, p. 351. Based on Central Bank data.

9. Ibid., p. 352. Based on Central Bank data.

10. Mallon and Sorrouille, *Economic Policymaking in a Conflict Society*, p. 138.

11. Linz, "An Authoritarian Regime: Spain."

12. The middle-class component of Peronism included, to be sure, groups ranging from the radical right to the radical left. But the latter were becoming much more significant in the sixties, especially in the youth organizations. This was due to two processes: the conversion to Marxism of formerly nonleftist Peronists—including many who had been radical rightists—and the massive inflow into the movement of middle class youths, many of them with a leftist background.

13. The CGT was controlled by the first group, whose leader was Vandor, the head of the metalworkers' union. The second faction eventually formed an alternative CGT, led by the printer Ongaro.

14. The sample to be described originated in a study of the sugar industry that was carried out between 1966 and 1967 by M. Murmis, S. Sigal, and myself. The sample is described in the Appendix. For general information about the sugar industry and its workers, see Centro Azucarero Regional del Norte Argentino, *El problema del azúcar en la Argentina* (Buenos Aires, 1964); and M. Murmis and C. H. Waisman, "Monoproducción agroindustrial, crisis y clase obrera: la industria azucarera tucumana," *Revista latinoamericana de Sociología* 69, no. 2 (1969): 344–383. (The latter work includes a preliminary presentation of some of the distributions to be analyzed in this section.) See also S. Sigal, "Crisis y conciencia obrera: la industria azucarera tucumana," *Revista latinoamericana de Sociología* 70, no. 1 (1970): 60–99; and Sigal, "Acción obrera en una situación de crisis: Tucumán 1966–1968," documento de trabajo 86 (Buenos Aires: Instituto Torcuato Di Tella, September 1973).

15. Only factory workers, both permanent and transient, are included in these figures.

16. Most independent farmers are minifundio operators. According to a reliable estimate, 51 percent of the sugar farms had fewer than 3 hectares, or 7.4 acres, in 1965 (data supplied by the government agency Dirección Nacional de Azúcar y Envases).

17. Argentine Republic, Instituto Nacional de Estadística y Censos, *Censo nacional económico (1964)* (Buenos Aires, n.d.).

18. See F. J. Delich, *Tierra y conciencia campesina en Tucumán* (Buenos

Aires: Signos, 1970), pp. 57–58, for some of these estimates. A reliable figure for 1965 is 18,602, according to Dirección Nacional de Azúcar y Envases.

19. In 1964, the last year for which comparative data on basic wages established in collective agreements were available, the average hourly basic wage was 63.4 pesos for skilled workers and 53.1 pesos for unskilled ones (CONADE-CEPAL, *Distribución del ingreso y cuentas nacionales en la Argentina* [Buenos Aires, 1965], 5: 198–199). Dollar equivalents were $0.45 and $0.38, according to the average free exchange rate for that year (see data from Banco Central de la República Argentina, *Boletín Estadístico*, in J. R. Scobie, *Argentina: A City and A Nation*, 2nd ed. [New York: Oxford University Press, 1971], p. 309). These figures were compared with average wages in a sample of ten industries, out of twenty-nine for which this information was available. The data are presented in Table 12. These industries were: tobacco, garment, rubber, metal, meat packing, paper, printing, tile, construction, and electricity (CONADE-CEPAL, *Distribución*). Sugar industry wages were found to be slightly higher than that average. The difference was only 3 percent for skilled workers, but for the unskilled it was 10 percent. As for the income differential associated with skill, it was lower in the sugar industry than in the ten-industry sample: 19 percent versus 23 percent.

20. Quality of housing is also associated with the size of the mills. While the percentage of workers living in "good" housing was 44 percent in the smaller mills—those having from 390 to 572 factory workers—it was 59 percent in medium-sized mills—those having from 579 to 756 workers—and 57 percent in the larger mills—with 814 to 1,953 workers.

21. Efficiency was not, however, uniformly low in Tucumán. According to an index of technological efficiency (see Appendix), six Tucumanian plants had a level of efficiency comparable to that of the northern mills.

22. See Centro Azucarero Regional del Norte Argentino, *El problema del azúcar en la Argentina*.

23. See the detailed account in Sigal, "Acción obrera en una situación de crisis," especially pp. 19–21, 27–29; and Murmis and Waisman, "Monoproducción agroindustrial, crisis y clase obrera," p. 359. For the text of Law 16926, see *La prensa*, August 23, 1966.

24. The percentage of permanent factory workers declined from 73 percent in 1943 to 53 percent in 1953, 33 percent in 1963, and 28 percent in 1966 (computed on the basis of provincial statistics and data furnished by Dirección Nacional de Azúcar y Envases).

25. The text of the open-ended question was: "What is it that you like least in your job here?" ("¿Qué es lo que menos le gusta de su trabajo aquí?"). The answers given by the respondent were coded on the basis of references to the work being hard or dangerous, the job unstable, and the wages low.

26. The text of the question was: "People are talking a lot about the problem of sugar. Which is, in your opinion, the problem?" ("Se habla mucho del problema del azúcar. ¿Cuál es, a su modo de ver, el problema?")

27. Murmis and Waisman report the distribution of an index of the orientation toward global or mediate factors that affect the work environment. In a series of open-ended questions, a distinction was made between answers that referred only to immediate aspects (such as existence of jobs, level or regularity of payment of wages, et cetera) and to global ones (such as the state of the sugar industry, the national economy, or the political system). These questions dealt with the relative situation of the worker's mill, the problem of sugar, and Perón's epoch. Permanent factory operatives were more likely to rank "high" in this index than the other category of worker. See Murmis and Waisman, "Monoproducción agroindustrial, crisis y clase obrera," p. 367.

28. "What should be done?" ("¿Qué debería hacerse?")

29. Murmis and Waisman, "Monoproducción agroindustrial, crisis y clase obrera," p. 369, reports data concerning workers' orientation toward modernization. An index was constructed combining a question about what should be done in relation to new machinery, and another, which asked what the union should do in relation to the sugar problem. The proportion of operatives scoring "high" on the index—people accepting machinery and proposing solutions that imply diversification or economic development—was again much higher among permanent factory workers than among rural laborers. Sigal, "Crisis y conciencia obrera," analyzes the relationship between answers to the question on the "problem of sugar" and vulnerability to the crisis, in a sample that included permanent and transient factory workers (the latter group is excluded from my discussion). She found that operatives in closed factories were more likely than their counterparts in secure or threatened mills to respond in terms of diversification (p. 72). The relationship between these variables was much stronger among workers who favored government intervention in the industry (p. 91).

30. These were closed questions: "And would you like to work in something other than the sugar industry?" ("¿Y a Vd. le gustaría trabajar en otra cosa que no fuera el azúcar?"); and (if the answer was yes) "Do you believe that the likelihood [of getting a nonsugar job] is high, low, or nonexistent?" ("¿Cree que las posibilidades de hacerlo son muchas, pocas, o ninguna?"); "Would you like to be self-employed, i.e., not working under a boss?" ("¿Le gustaría ponerse por su cuenta, trabajando sin un patrón?"); and (if the answer was yes) "Do you believe that the likelihood [of achieving this] is high, low, or nonexistent?" ("¿Cree que las posibilidades de conseguirlo son muchas, pocas, o ninguna?"). Sigal examined the relationship between desire to have a nonsugar job and vulnerability to the crisis, and found a positive relationship ("Crisis y conciencia obrera," p. 71). Control by trade union participation indicates that the relationship only holds for workers with high participation (p. 73). Results are for a sample that combines permanent and transient workers.

31. The question was: "Do you think that the son of a worker, if he is intelligent, can become a doctor or a lawyer?" ("¿A Vd. le parece que un hijo

de obrero, si es inteligente, puede llegar a ser médico o abogado?") The alternatives were: easily, difficult, very difficult, impossible.

32. For an excellent analysis of the organization and its strategy, see Sigal, "Acción obrera en una situación de crisis."

33. Practically all workers, both industrial and rural, permanent and transient, belonged to the organization. The intensity of participation was associated with the degree of stability. The permanent workers, both industrial and rural, were more likely than the transient ones to vote in elections, attend meetings, and become officials. High level union positions, however, were mostly held by permanent factory operatives. Participation in the union is discussed in Murmis and Waisman, "Monoproducción agroindustrial, crisis y clase obrera," pp. 373–374. The effects of participation on attitudes are examined in the same article (pp. 377–382). For a more extensive discussion of these effects, see Sigal, "Crisis y conciencia obrera" (especially tables on pp. 73, 80, and 81) and "Acción obrera en una situación de crisis."

34. For discussion of this strike, see Alexander, *The Perón Era*, pp. 96–97.

35. Sigal, "Acción obrera en una situación de crisis."

36. See ibid. for an analysis of global and local conflicts.

37. E. P. Thompson, "The Moral Economy of the English Crowd in the Eighteenth Century," *Past and Present* 50: 76–136.

38. Sigal, "Acción obrera en una situación de crisis"; and Murmis and Waisman, "Monoproducción agroindustrial, crisis y clase obrera."

39. See Sigal, "Acción obrera en una situación de crisis," for an analysis of the intensification of protest and its gradual decline toward the middle of 1968.

40. The Peronists, excluded from political participation, voted blank.

41. Provincial electoral statistics can be found in D. Canton, *Materiales para el estudio de la sociología política en la Argentina* (Buenos Aires: Editorial del Instituto, 1968).

42. The text of the question was: "[Do you have the impression that] in Perón's epoch [the workers' situation was different than it is now, or the same?] 1. The same; 2. Different . . . In what way?" (open-ended question) "[Tiene Vd. la impresión de que] en la época de Perón [la situación de los obreros era diferente o igual que ahora?] 1. Igual; 2. Diferente . . . ¿En qué?"

43. However, 18 percent referred to rights and benefits granted by the Peronist regime, and 14 percent asserted that workers were respected more, or treated better, under Peronism.

44. The question was: "Do you have the impression that the vote of people like you, 1. is effective; 2. is futile?" ("¿Tiene Vd. la impresión de que el voto de la gente como Vd., 1. Sirve para algo; 2. es inútil?")

45. The question was: "What do you think of justice in Argentina?: 1. That it is equal for everybody; 2. That it favors the upper classes; 3. Other." ("¿Vd. qué piensa de la justicia en la Argentina?: 1. que es igual para todo el mundo; 2. que favorece a las clases superiores; 3. otros.")

46. The other groups were: white collar employees, big farmers, religious

groups, owners of big mills, politicians, small farmers, and the military. The question was: "Which of these groups should have more power?" (than they had at that time). ("¿Cuál de esos grupos debería tener más poder?")

47. For descriptions of the economy and society of Chaco, see G. Miranda, *Tres ciclos chaqueños* (Resistencia: Norte Argentino, 1955); D. Piñeiro and M. Caracciolo de Basco, *Historia económica y social del Chaco,* Centro de Investigaciones en Ciencias Sociales, Serie estudios 11 (Buenos Aires, n.d.); Inter-American Committee for Agricultural Development, *Land Tenure Conditions and Socio-Economic Development of the Agricultural Sector: Argentina* (Washington, D.C.: Pan American Union, 1965), Chapter 5; and N. D'Alessio, "Chaco: Un caso de pequeña producción campesina en crisis," *Revista latinoamericana de sociología* 69, no. 2 (1969): 384–409.

48. Tannin extract was exported, and production was controlled by foreign corporations. Manpower was provided by Creole lumbermen. Forestry expanded up to the late 1930s, and it entered a deep crisis during the 1960s, when the market was captured by South Africa. Most processing plants in Chaco were closed, and entire villages which depended on this industry disappeared.

49. The extent of the concentration of land ownership can be seen in the following figures. In 1960, 78 percent of the cotton farms had fewer than twenty-six hectares, the threshold for minifundia; the percentage was 30 percent in 1937 (Piñeiro and Basco, *Historia económica y social del Chaco,* p. 49). Land tenure is associated with ethnic stratification. Almost all minifundio operators and rural laborers are Creole, while a high proportion of farmers with middle-sized farms are of European origin. In a study of peasants with small farms, it was found that only 3 percent were European immigrants (D'Alessio, "Chaco," p. 400). On the other hand, the percentage of Europeans in the Chaco population is significant. According to the 1960 census, 18 percent of the population fifty years of age or older was born in Europe (Argentine Republic, Dirección Nacional de Estadística y Censos, *Censo nacional de población 1960* [Buenos Aires, 1961?]).

50. That year, 41 percent of the active population was working in agriculture, and only 23 percent in manufacturing, construction, and mining (*Censo nacional de población 1960*).

51. Instituto Nacional de Tecnología Agropecuaria (INTA), *Programa de producción de algodón y su mejoramiento integral, 1968,* quoted by Piñeiro and Basco, *Historia económica y social del Chaco,* p. 62.

52. D'Alessio, "Chaco," p. 398.

53. Computed on the basis of data reported by ibid., p. 399.

54. Argentine Republic, Instituto Nacional de Estadística y Censos, *Censo nacional de población, familia y viviendas, 1970, resultados provisionales* (Buenos Aires, 1970).

55. D'Alessio, "Chaco," p. 398.

56. The breakdown of fathers who were in independent agriculture accord-

ing to size is as follows: 22 percent were minifundio operators (up to twenty-five hectares), and 16 percent were middle peasants (more than twenty-five hectares). Four percent did not report size. As for those who were dependent in agriculture: 22 percent of the fathers were permanent laborers and 13 percent were transient. Data correspond to the father's occupation when the respondents were twelve to sixteen years old.

57. Some migrants had been in agriculture only as wage laborers while in Chaco: 28 percent had been so as permanent laborers and 32 percent as transient ones. On the other hand, these two positions had been occupied at some point by 65 percent and 71 percent of the respondents respectively. As for independent farming—which includes family labor—this had also been the only agricultural occupation of some migrants in Chaco, 10 percent of them on a permanent basis and 14 percent intermittently. Finally, these two positions had been held at some point by 37 percent and 44 percent of the respondents respectively.

58. The distribution of occupations prior to migration is as follows: 21 percent had been independent farmers (13 percent as unpaid family laborers and 9 percent self-employed); 51 percent had been wage laborers in agriculture (43 percent transient ones); and 27 percent had had urban occupations, most of whom (15 percent of the total) were in manufacturing and construction.

59. The only city over 20,000 was Resistencia, the capital. Its population (84,000 in 1960) increased as a consequence of the crisis by 40 percent from 1960 to 1970.

60. *Censo nacional económico (1964)*.

61. This was an open-ended question: "Why did you leave Chaco?" ("¿Por qué se fue del Chaco?") On the basis of the answers, different alternatives were coded: 1. Lack of work, or of stable jobs; 2. Hard work, or low pay; 3. Lack of land, or of good land; 4. Lack of resources to cultivate the land; 5. Bad living conditions; 6. Orientation toward personal advancement; 7. Purely personal or family reasons; 8. Desire to know other places; 9. Other.

62. *Censo nacional de población, familia y viviendas, 1970*.

63. Ibid.

64. Ibid.

65. I.e., Buenos Aires or Rosario. Even though a substantial proportion of the migrants had had prior urban experience, the rural-urban opposition will be used as shorthand.

66. Unemployment rates in April, July, and October of 1968–1970 fluctuated between 4 percent and 5.4 percent in greater Buenos Aires, and between 4.7 percent and 5.9 percent in the city of Rosario (Argentine Republic, Instituto Nacional de Estadística y Censos, *Anuario estadístico de la República Argentina*, [Buenos Aires: 1973], p. 96).

67. According to one source, the cost of living increased by 37 percent from 1968 to 1970 while the average increase of real wages was 13 percent in the same period; cost-of-living data correspond to workers with an average-sized family (Economic Commission for Latin America, *Economic*

Survey of Latin America, 1970 [New York: United Nations, 1972],
p. 143].

68. Banco Central de la República Argentina, in Scobie, *Argentina*, p. 309.'

69. D'Alessio reports that a seasonal laborer, working with his family, could
earn 1,100 pesos per day in 1967–1968. This would probably amount to
no more than 30,000 pesos per month and would apply during the harvest season only. On the other hand, 76 percent of the industrial workers
in the sample were earning more than 30,000 pesos. As for peasants
with small farms, he estimates that minifundio farmers having up to
ten hectares were earning 7,600–13,000 pesos per month, and for farmers having up to twenty-five hectares, the amount was only 19,800 pesos
(D'Alessio, "Chaco," p. 406).

70. This excludes eleven respondents living in lower-class hotels, nine of
which were industrial workers.

71. While 49 percent of the skilled workers lived in the "better" houses, the
percentage among the unskilled was 29 percent. This variable is also related to sector of industry: the percentage living in "better" housing is
also 49 percent among manufacturing workers, and 25 percent among
construction workers.

72. The questions were: "Are you in general very happy, happy, more or less,
or unhappy for having come to Buenos Aires (or Rosario)?" ("¿Está en
general muy contento, contento, más o menos o nada contento de haber
venido a Buenos Aires [o Rosario]?"), and "If, on the basis of what you
know today, you would have to decide between remaining in Chaco and
leaving, which would you choose?" ("¿Si con lo que sabe y conoce ahora
tuviese que volver a decidir entre quedarse en el Chaco e irse, qué ele-
giría?") 1. To leave Chaco; 2. To remain; 3. Does not know.

73. The question was: "What do you think of your job?" ("¿Qué le parece su
trabajo?") The alternatives were: 1. Very good; 2. Good; 3. More or less;
4. Bad; 5. Very bad.

74. The first question was: "Which are the two aspects of your current job
that satisfy you the most? and which are the two that satisfy you the
least?" ("¿Cuáles son los dos aspectos que lo tienen más satisfecho en su
trabajo actual? y ¿cuáles los dos que lo tienen menos satisfecho?") The
alternatives were: 1. Everything; 2. Interest in the work; 3. Wages; 4. Social benefits; 5. Workmates; 6. Promotion possibilities; 7. Job stability;
8. The boss; 9. Distance from home; 10. Other. A second question was:
"Do you think you are currently earning what you deserve?" ("Actualmente, ¿considera Vd. que está ganando lo que merece?") Spontaneous
replies were latter codified as a "yes" and "no" dichotomy.

75. The question was: "Would you like to become self-employed?" ("¿Le
gustaría poder establecerse por su cuenta?") [If the answer is yes], "do
you think it would be possible for you to become self-employed?" ("¿Le
parece probable poder llegar a instalarse por su cuenta?") The alternatives were: 1. Very likely; 2. Likely; 3. Unlikely.

76. The question was: "Do you think that the son of a worker, if he is intelligent, can become a lawyer, doctor or engineer?" ("¿Cree Vd. que el hijo

de un trabajador, si es inteligente, podrá llegar a ser abogado, médico o ingeniero?") The alternatives were: 1. Easily; 2. Difficult; 3. Very difficult; 4. Impossible.

77. The question was: "Do you think that voting is important?" ("¿Cree que el voto es importante?") Answers were dichotomized into "yes" and "no."

78. The questions were: "In general terms, are you interested in politics a lot, a little or not at all?" ("En términos generales, ¿la política le interesa mucho, poco o nada?"); and "The issue of whether elections must be held again soon in the country is being discussed. Does it matter a lot to you personally that elections be held again, does it matter relatively, or is this an issue that does not matter to you at all?" ("Actualmente se está discutiendo si es que tiene que haber pronto otra vez elecciones en el país o no. Personalmente, le importa mucho que vuelva a haber elecciones, le importa relativamente, o es un asunto que no le importa para nada?")

79. This closed question, which referred to the Peronist administration of 1946–1955, was: "What opinion do you have of each of the following administrations?" ("¿Qué opinión le merece cada uno de estos gobiernos?") [Perón, Frondizi, Illía, Onganía.] Data shown correspond to the total sample. The alternatives were: 1. Very good; 2. Good; 3. More or less; 4. Bad; 5. Very bad; 6. Does not know.

80. The question was: "Are you, or have you been a sympathizer of any political party?" ("¿Simpatiza o simpatizó con algún partido político?") (If the answer was "yes"), "of which party?" ("¿Cuál?")

81. Canton, *Materiales*.

82. See E. R. Wolf, *Peasant Wars of the Twentieth Century* (New York: Harper and Row, 1969), pp. 276–302; R. F. Hamilton, *Affluence and the French Worker in the Fourth Republic* (Princeton: Princeton University Press, 1967), pp. 128–130.

83. Wolf, *Peasant Wars*, p. 271.

84. See R. Carri, *Isidro Velázquez: Formas prerrevolucionarias de la violencia* (Buenos Aires: Sudestada, 1968).

9. Structural Modernization and Forms of Political Action: A Diachronic View

1. The existence of seasonal factory workers is a specific trait of the sugar industry. Due to space constraints, I decided against discussing that sample in this chapter. And I did not merge transient and permanent factory workers, for in that case the "typical" or "pure" working class would be mixed with this atypical group.

2. Murmis and Waisman, "Monoproducción agroindustrial, crisis y clase obrera." I was responsible for the part of the article dealing with orientations and behavior.

3. Murmis and Waisman, "Monoproducción agroindustrial, crisis y clase obrera," pp. 377–378.

4. C. H. Waisman, "Availability and Populist Coalitions," typescript (Department of Social Relations, Harvard University, December 1969). These issues were discussed also in C. H. Waisman, "Dependency and Political Cleavages," mimeographed (Oslo: Peace Research Institute, August 1971).

5. She called the dimensions "questioning of capitalist management" and "propensity for confrontation behavior," and the types "conciliation," "negotiation through violence," "latency," and "explosive" (Sigal, "Crisis y conciencia obrera," p. 83; and Sigal, "Acción obrera en una situación de crisis," p. 35). "Questioning" was operationalized on the basis of an index, and "confrontation" with the item I use as the indicator of radicalism. Chapter 11 refers to those of her findings which are directly relevant for my discussion. Sigal examined the relationship between vulnerability to the crisis and these two dimensions, plus other attitudinal variables and union participation. In Table 21c our analyses overlap—her "questioning" and "confrontation" by vulnerability. My results are different, because I am using partially different indicators and a partially different sample (Sigal merged permanent and transient factory workers).

6. In the Tucumán study, the question on factories referred to sugar mills. In the Buenos Aires–Rosario study, that question was general.

7. The distributions of the items and of this index are presented in the Appendix. Sigal constructed an index of "questioning of capitalist management." Its first version consisted of the two indicators of dissent I have used, plus three other items: whether industrialists are mentioned among those responsible for the crisis, agreement with the cooperativization of mills, and a question about expropriating land from farmers who do not cultivate it (Sigal, "Crisis y conciencia obrera," p. 77). A second "questioning" index consisted of the questions on expropriating factories (which I have used), on responsibility for the crisis, and on cooperativization (Sigal, "Acción obrera en una situación de crisis," p. 31 and note 16).

8. Sixty-five percent of the permanent industrial workers in Tucumán supported, however, the conversion of the privately owned mills into cooperatives. See Murmis and Waisman, "Monoproducción agroindustrial, crisis y clase obrera," p. 370.

9. J. Kirkpatrick, *Leader and Vanguard in Mass Society: A Study of Peronist Argentina* (Cambridge: M.I.T. Press, 1971), p. 186. She found that the expropriation and redistribution of private lands was favored by 73 percent of the "laborer" and 68 percent of the "lower socioeconomic status" categories in her sample. On the other hand, the elimination of private property from key sectors was favored by 45 percent of the "laborers" and 42 percent of the "lower SES." Only the first of these items is strictly equivalent to the question I am using, for the wording of the sec-

ond one is more general and more moderate than the question about the expropriation of factories.

10. Cf. Table 24 (Appendix) and Kirkpatrick, *Leader and Vanguard*, p. 186.

10. The Effects of Integration and Centrality

1. M. Olson, "Rapid Growth as a Destabilizing Force," in *Political Development and Social Change*, edited by J. L. Finkle and R. W. Gable (New York: Wiley, 1971), p. 561.
2. Tilly et al., *The Rebellious Century*, p. 251.
3. Shorter and Tilly, *Strikes in France*, pp. 272–273.
4. Ibid., Chapters 8, 10.
5. Tilly et al., *The Rebellious Century*, pp. 83–84.
6. J. M. Nelson, *Migrants, Urban Poverty, and Instability in Developing Nations* (Cambridge: Center for International Affairs, Harvard University, 1969), pp. 66–67.
7. Ibid., p. 8–10.
8. Ibid., pp. 21–22, 25.
9. Ibid., p. 40.
10. W. A. Cornelius, "The Political Sociology of Cityward Migration in Latin America: Toward Empirical Theory," in *Latin American Urban Research*, edited by F. F. Rabinovitz and F. M. Trueblood (Beverly Hills: Sage, 1971), 1 : 103.
11. Ibid., pp. 104–105.
12. T. R. Gurr, *Why Men Rebel* (Princeton: Princeton University Press, 1970), Chapter 2.
13. Shorter and Tilly, *Strikes in France*, pp. 272–273.
14. A. B. Ulam, *The Unfinished Revolution* (New York: Vintage, 1960), p. 284.
15. Shorter and Tilly, *Strikes in France*, p. 234.
16. C. Kerr et al., *Industrialism and Industrial Man* (New York: Oxford University Press, 1964), p. 184.
17. J. C. Leggett, *Class, Race, and Labor* (New York: Oxford University Press, 1968), Chapter 4.
18. J. H. Kautsky, *Communism and the Politics of Development* (New York: Wiley, 1968), p. 185.
19. W. Galenson, "Scandinavia," in *Comparative Labor Movements*, edited by W. Galenson (New York: Russell and Russell, 1968).
20. Kerr et al., *Industrialism*.
21. R. Blauner, *Alienation and Freedom*. (Chicago: University of Chicago Press, 1964); G. Friedmann, *Le travail en miettes* (Paris: Gallimard, 1956); A. Touraine, "L'organisation professionnelle de l'entreprise," in *Traité de sociologie du travail*, edited by G. Friedmann and P. Naville (Paris: Colin, 1970), Vol. 1.
22. Lipset, *Political Man*, pp. 104–105; C. Kerr and A. Siegel, "The Interindustry Propensity to Strike: An International Comparison," in *Indus-*

trial Conflict, edited by A. Kornhauser, R. Dubin, and A. M. Ross (New York: McGraw-Hill, 1954); J. H. Goldthorpe et al., *The Affluent Worker: Political Attitudes and Behavior* (Cambridge: Cambridge University Press, 1968); and others.

23. Blauner, *Alienation and Freedom*; A. Touraine, *La conscience ouvrière* (Paris: Seuil, 1966). Some of the relationships reported by Touraine are very small, and for some indicators percentages are lower in phase B than in phase A industries (see pp. 58, 123, 173, 290).

24. Mann, *Consciousness and Action*, pp. 57–58.

25. Lipset, *Political Man*, pp. 104–105. For negative evidence concerning the Kerr-Siegel hypothesis on interindustry variations in the propensity to strike, see Shorter and Tilly, *Strikes in France*, Chapter 11.

26. Lipset, *Political Man*, pp. 249, 262–267.

27. J. Linz, *The Social Bases of West German Politics*, pp. 377–380.

28. Hamilton, *Affluence and the French Worker*, p. 207.

29. Shorter and Tilly, *Strikes in France*, p. 227.

30. Zeitlin, *Revolutionary Politics*, p. 171.

31. Hamilton, *Affluence and the French Worker*, pp. 205–206; Lipset, *Political Man*, pp. 248–249; Linz, *The Social Bases of West German Politics*, pp. 396–397.

32. Linz, *The Social Bases of West German Politics*, p. 389.

33. In the sample of new workers, migrants were asked, "What do you think of your job?" Those who gave answers other than "very good" or "good" were considered to be dissatisfied. In the Tucumán study, on the other hand, workers agreeing that their wages were low, their job was unstable, and work in the sugar industry was hard or dangerous, were classified as being highly dissatisfied. Among new workers, the percentages of dissatisfied were 17 percent in small plants and 30 percent in large plants; among established workers the percentages were 29 percent in the small and large mills and 36 percent in the medium category.

34. Lipset, *Political Man*, pp. 252–253.

35. Hamilton, *Affluence and the French Worker*, p. 122.

36. Lipset, *Political Man*, pp. 116–118, 252–253.

37. Zeitlin, *Revolutionary Politics*, p. 97.

38. R. F. Hamilton, "Skill Level and Politics," *Public Opinion Quarterly* 29, no. 3 (1965): 390–399.

39. Zeitlin, *Revolutionary Politics*.

40. See the discussion of the literature in Hamilton, *Affluence and the French Worker*, pp. 121–124; and Zeitlin, *Revolutionary Politics*, pp. 89–92.

41. Hamilton, *Affluence and the French Worker*, pp. 122–123.

42. Lipset, *Political Man*, pp. 252–254; and S. M. Lipset and R. Bendix, *Social Mobility in Industrial Society* (Berkeley: University of California Press, 1967), pp. 67–68.

43. Hamilton, *Affluence and the French Worker*, pp. 125–130.

44. In the indicators reported above, the percentages of dissatisfied are, among construction workers, 27 percent for the unskilled and only 7

percent for the skilled. Among established workers, 27 percent of the unskilled and 33 percent of the skilled are dissatisfied.

11. The Effects of Deprivation and Marginalization

1. W. G. Runciman, *Relative Deprivation and Social Justice* (Berkeley: University of California Press, 1966), p. 9.
2. Tilly et al., *The Rebellious Century*, pp. 81–85; Shorter and Tilly, *Strikes in France*, p. 8.
3. Hamilton, *Affluence and the French Worker*, p. 137; see also pp. 161, 174.
4. Linz, *The Social Bases of West German Politics*, pp. 326, 333.
5. Goldthorpe et al., *The Affluent Worker*. See also S. M. Lipset and J. Linz, *The Social Bases of Political Diversity in Western Democracies* (Stanford: Center for Advanced Research in the Behavioral Sciences, 1956), Chapter 6.
6. Lipset, *Revolution and Counterrevolution*, pp. 293–294.
7. Lipset, *Political Man*, pp. 247–248.
8. Hamilton, *Affluence and the French Worker*, p. 189.
9. Zeitlin, *Revolutionary Politics*, pp. 55–57.
10. Shorter and Tilly, *Strikes in France*, p. 226.
11. Sigal, "Crisis y conciencia obrera," p. 77. See also Sigal, "Acción obrera en una situación de crisis," p. 31.
12. Linz, *The Social Bases of West German Politics*, pp. 421, 431.
13. M. Lazarsfeld-Jahoda and H. Zeisel, *Die Arbeitlosen von Marienthal*, summarized by Lipset, *Political Man*, p. 192; B. Zawadski and P. F. Lazarsfeld, "The Psychological Consequences of Unemployment," *Journal of Social Psychology* 6 (1935): 224–251; E. W. Bakke, *Citizens Without Work: A Study of the Effect of Unemployment Upon the Workers' Social Relations and Practices* (New Haven: Yale University Press, 1940).
14. Sigal, "Crisis y conciencia obrera," p. 83. This is the item I am using as an indicator of radicalism in the established workers study.
15. Linz, *The Social Bases of West German Politics*, pp. 414, 416–417. See also Lipset, *Political Man*, p. 248.
16. Leggett, *Class, Race, and Labor*, p. 79.
17. Sigal, "Crisis y conciencia obrera," p. 77.
18. Ibid., p. 83–87. See the distribution of the typology on p. 85.
19. For the version that includes my two indicators of dissent, see ibid., p. 77. For the index that contains only the seizure of factories, see Sigal, "Acción obrera en una situación de crisis," p. 31.
20. See the tables in Sigal, "Crisis y conciencia obrera," pp. 77 and 83.
21. Ibid., p. 77.

12. The Working Class and the Legitimacy of Capitalism

1. Percentage differences computed on groups having fewer than ten cases are excluded.
2. In the last sentence I am paraphrasing Deutsch, who, in turn, is discussing Lenin's concept of "the weakest link" (Deutsch, "Imperialism and Neocolonialism," p. 8).

Appendix

1. J. Nun, "Informe general sobre el Proyecto Marginalidad," *Revista latinoamericana de sociología* 69, no. 2 (1969): 410–413.
2. The pictures will be shown in a forthcoming work by J. Nun.
3. J. Galtung, *Theory and Methods of Social Research* (Oslo: Universitetsforlaget; London: Allen S. Unwin; New York: Columbia University Press, 1967), p. 372.
4. S. M. Lipset, M. Trow, and J. S. Coleman, *Union Democracy* (Glencoe: The Free Press, 1956), pp. 427–432.
5. Galtung, *Theory and Methods of Social Research*, pp. 358–389.

Index